D1148498

Joseph O'Connor was born in Dublin in 1963, lived in London for many years and now divides his time between there and Dublin. The author of two acclaimed novels, **Cowboys and Indians** and **Desperadoes**, and a collection of short stories, **True Believers**, he writes a weekly column for *The Sunday Tribune*, a monthly column for *Esquire* Magazine and is a regular contributor to *The Late Show* on BBC 2.

He wrote the introduction and contributed to the anthology, **Ireland in Exile,** (New Island Books, 1993), and his interview about social class in Ireland is contained in **A Class of Our Own** (New Island Books, 1994).

for my brother,
John

The Secret World
of the Irish Male

JOSEPH O'CONNOR

First published in Ireland in 1994 by New Island, 2 Brookside,
Dundrum Road, Dublin 14
First published in the United Kingdom in 2008 by Little Books Ltd,
London W11 3QP

10 9 8 7 6 5 4 3 2 1

Text copyright © Joseph O'Connor, 1994
Cover design and layout copyright © New Island
Cover illustration ©Annie West

All rights reserved. No part of this work may be reproduced or utilized in
any form or by any means, electronic or mechanical, including photocopying,
recording or by any information storage and retrieval system, without the
prior written permission of the publisher.

A CIP catalogue record for this book is available from the British Library.

ISBN 978 1 906251 15 4

Every attempt has been made to trace any copyright holders.
The author and publisher will be grateful for any information that will assist
them in keeping future editions up to date. Although all reasonable care has
been taken in the preparation of this book, neither the publisher, editors nor
the author can accept any liability for any consequences arising from the use
thereof, or the information contained therein.

Printed and bound in Ireland by Colour Books, Ltd.

Contents

A good deal of this material has appeared previously in *The Sunday Tribune, Esquire magazine, The (London) Independent magazine, The Observer, The New York Times, New Woman* magazine and other quality publications. Many thanks to editors and commissioning editors for permission to reproduce. (Articles, that is.)

Thanks also to Tim Hulse, Moira Reilly, Marie O'Riordan, John O'Connor (The Brother), Colm Tóibín and Catriona Crowe for ideas.

Special thanks to Peter Murtagh, editor of *The Sunday Tribune*, to all the staff at the paper, to the former editor Vincent Browne, and to Dermot Bolger, for suggesting, editing and publishing this book.

Chapter One
My Difficult Childhood

I have never actually met anybody called Valentine, and I suspect there is a bloody good reason for this. Calling one's child after one of the more obscure saints — Boniface, say, or Begnet or Bede — I can actually understand. But calling one's child Valentine would bring back wistful memories to most people. What does Valentine's Day really mean? I'm thinking of the exuberant canter down to the letterbox on the morning of February 14th, the blood scuttling through the veins at top speed, the tongue flapping with anticipation, the nerves doing gymnastics, the exquisite agony of it all, only to be followed by disappointment, the bare doormat, the poignantly cardless climb back up to the scratcher, the placing of the head beneath the duvet, the agonized screeching of abusive epithets and the subsequent moistening of the pillowcase with tears so salty you could sprinkle them on chips. Calling one's child Valentine would be like calling it Disappointment. And Disappointment O'Connor would not be much of a name for a child, even though, no doubt, it would eventually get abbreviated to Dizzy O'Connor — and I've met one or two of those in my time, God only knows. Sappy O'Connor would be another possibility, I suppose.

Anyway, in the whole dismal cornucopia of abject anniversaries, foul festive frolics and rancid rejoicings is there anything really worse than Saint Valentine's Day? Fresh from prising the shekels out of us for Christmas, the greetings card hucksters need a little extra just to keep them in the style to which they are accustomed, and, let us face it, desire is the most marketable concept there is. The people who make greetings cards are bandits of the lowest order, if you ask me. They should be wearing tights over their faces.

When I was six I had a teacher called Miss Glennon. She was a very good teacher. She believed that there was more to early education than the repetitive chanting of ideologically suspect nursery rhymes and the digital manipulation of plasticine, and so, when Saint Valentine's Day came around one year, she made every boy and girl in the class write a Valentine card, complete with a poem. For those less creatively gifted students, Miss Glennon explained that it was acceptable to start off with the time-honoured couplet "roses are red, violets are blue." We got ten minutes. The completed cards were then placed in two piles at the top of the class, one for boys and one for girls. We each had to pick one at random, and read it aloud to the assembled unwashed.

At the time, I entertained an uneasy but quite fervent affection for Michele Killen, a tempestuous redhead who could play conkers like nobody's business, and whose pipe-cleaner men were the talk of Saint Joseph of Cluny School. Michele did not like me much. On one occasion she called me "a weird little fecker", I recall, but, hey, it was kind of a Burton and Taylor thing. The card I picked out, however, came from a girl called Sheena whose hand I always had to hold whenever Miss Glennon took us on nature walks, which was a little too often for my liking. All I remember about Sheena is that she had a perpetually runny nose. The contents of her incontinent nostrils ebbed and flowed like the proud majestic Shannon, and the hand which she used to wipe said nostrils was also, invariably, the hand which she then used to hold my own as tightly as she could. My own hand, that is. Not my own nostrils. But anyway. Me and Sheena were frequently stuck together by something more than just love.

Flushed with romantic excitement, I stood up at the top of the class that morning long ago and began to read out the words Sheena had written. They were, and here I quote in full, "Roses are red, Violets are blue, I think you're horrible [sic] and you are like a poo." I was shattered. Not only was the thought less than affectionate, but I mean, it didn't even bloody scan properly.

Every time I even think about it, I still blush to the colour of ribena. Saint Valentine has an awful lot to answer for, in my book. In the unlikely event of my ever making it into paradise, be assured, I will certainly have a thing or two to say to him.

Another person from my difficult childhood I would like to meet, either in this life or the hereafter, is the famous and talented Australian entertainer, Mr Rolf "Didgeridoo" Harris. You know, I actually used to like him a lot. When I was a nipper, the words of "Tie Me Kangaroo Down Sport" were as important to me as the words of the *Hail Holy Queen* were to other children.

I remember seeing his supreme Rolfness on the *Late Late Show* when I was a youngster. I think it was 1975. People had been on the show talking about Northern Ireland, about their lives and their sufferings, and about the deaths and maimings of their loved ones. It had been harrowing, to say the least. Rolf Harris had been listening to all of this in the wings, and he had been so moved that when he came on to perform he just broke down in tears in mid flow. It was an extraordinary sight, to a child. Rolf Harris simply stopped miming and took off his glasses and put his hands to his face and cried, while the tape of his disembodied voice singing "Two Little Boys" continued to echo through the *Late Late Show* studio. It was one of the most important moments of my difficult childhood.

Yes, I had a spot in my heart for Rolf Harris. But the little antipodean cur has burnt his boats with me now. Last year he released a cover version of Led Zeppelin's song "Stairway To Heaven." It got to number nine in the charts, which is eloquent argument, if such were needed, that young people today are only rabble and scum. Anyway, if I ever get my mitts on him, Rolf Harris will certainly be crying again.

You see, "Stairway to Heaven" is more than a song to me. The first girl who ever broke my heart did so while "Stairway to Heaven" was playing in the background. I was a mere boy, and I was in the Connemara Gaeltacht one summer. She was a little older than me, and she was popularly reputed to know how to kiss people. When she kissed me, I became a little over-enthusiastic and my tongue got stuck in the brace on her teeth. It was agonizingly painful. It took me ten whole minutes to free myself. My eyes still moisten, in fact, whenever I hear Irish spoken. Sometimes people misinterpret this as national pride.

She was from Baldoyle and I was from Glenageary, which delightful Dublin suburbs are separated by a distance of perhaps a dozen miles. But a dozen miles is a veritable ocean when you're only a dozen years old, and anyway, immediately following her return to Baldoyle the fickle and heartless little Jezebel seemed to suddenly remember that she had to play handball on a Wednesday after school — now *there's* a thought-provoking excuse — the very afternoon we had set aside for our secret and passionate trysts. She tried to let me down lightly but it was abundantly clear that the magic had just died. "Stairway to Heaven" came on, as she gave me the big E. When the almost Yeatsian observation *"woarghh-oh, coz you know sometimes words have two meanings, unghg"* rang out of the jukebox, I told her I would never get over her. (By the way, if she's reading this now, I was lying through my bloody teeth.)

But ah, that delicately descending A minor chord sequence with the bass part slithering down to F, then soaring with the grace of a young albatross back up to the final plaintive G, A minor. Every two-bit guitarist in the world can play it. It's banned in some guitar shops, because people play it so much.

It used to be the last song of the night at the Presentation College disco, Glasthule, where I first strutted my funky stuff. "Prez", as it was known, was a pretty rough joint. They searched you outside for strong drink and offensive weapons and if you didn't have any, they didn't let you in. But "Stairway to Heaven" reduced even the most hardened knackers, savage boot boys and nefarious ne'er-do-wells to wide-eyed blubbing wrecks. I can still see it now, a great head-banging mass of denim and cheesecloth and existential angst.

You know the bit with Robert Plant plangently wailing *"wooooh-ooooh, and it makes me wonder, woooh yeah"*? I mean, you can keep your Seamus Heaneys, *that's* deep. And what does Rolf Harris do? The heartless reprobate "sings" this line — *"wooooh-oooh, and it makes me wonder"* — and then he quips, presumably to his backing group, "and how does it affect you blokes?" It's blasphemy. It's sacrilege. It's like spitting in the face of the *Mona Lisa*. When the time of retribution comes, this backing group needn't bother whimpering to me that they were only obeying orders.

And the brilliant bit at the end? You know the bit that goes BLAM BLAM, *CHUNK*, BLAM BLAM, *CHUNK*, BLAM A BLAM A BLAM A BLAM A *CHUNK CHUNK*? *And as we wind on down the road*....Only the crowning glory, I mean the musical equivalent of the Sistine bloody Chapel ceiling, and Rolf leaves it shagging well out!!! God, it's like saying the Mass without bothering to have the consecration. It's pointless.

This is surely the worst period ever for popular music. When I was a teenager, people were embarrassed about liking Slade, The

Sweet, Mudd and Alvin Stardust. But these days, Alvin's "Won't You Be My Cooka-Choo" seems like a Bach prelude and Mudd's "Tiger Feet" has all the brooding sexual magnetism of the early Elvis. The charts are full of trite cover versions, and rich kiddies chanting about machine guns and the size of their penises over stupefyingly dull synthesizer beats. Me, I'm pining for Horslips. I'm missing Thin Lizzy. I wake up in the night, pondering the subtle nuances of Gary Glitter's proud ethical challenge, "D'ya Wanna Be in My Gang, My Gang, My Gang, D'ya Wanna Be In My Gang, oh yeah?" This is my past here, that Rolf Harris and his hell-spawned ilk are messing with. Hold me down, boys, till I strap on my air guitar. Rolf Harris, I'm coming after you, sucker. In my dreams, you are forever in the playground of Saint Joseph of Cluny School, Glenageary, and I am there too, giving you an eternal dead leg.

But dreams work strangely. One minute you are in Casablanca with Cindy Crawford, the next you are in Castlepollard with Michael Crawford. You never know what is going to happen in a dream. You never know what's going to happen in real life either, but some things you can be relatively confident about. The truth will always hurt, half your socks will always disappear in the washing machine and John Bruton in full flight will always be strangely reminiscent of Kermit the Frog in *The Muppet Show*.

One night recently I had a strange dream, one which I've had many times before. In this dream I am seventeen. My face is a sordid mess of oozing carbuncles and leaking pustules. I am about to do my leaving certificate maths exam. The *cigire*, a tall ungainly fellow with wings and a large yellow beak, is flapping up and down the aisle. Another teacher is sitting at the desk next to mine, laughing at me. I should explain that this dreamlike teacher is, or more accurately was, a real teacher, a kind-hearted priest who taught me once and has now passed on to what I hope will be a pleasant reward. If he's up there now I expect he's got the jacuzzi, because janey mack, does he deserve it.

This poor holy man had been on the missions in Africa, and had regrettably gotten a chunk chawed out of him by some malevolent and toothsome insect. To recuperate, he had been sent home to Ireland to teach teenage boys. Wonderful, huh? Rampant malaria must have seemed almost cuddly compared to the suffering we put him through. Truly, we made his life such a purgatory that he must have often wished he was back on the banks of the Zambezi taking his chances with whatever vicious and carnivorous beastie might next come cantering wild-eyed and peckish out of the jungle. He was a thick-haired avuncular cove when he began to instruct us in second year. By the time we got to the leaving cert he was a gibbering basket case, bald as a billiard ball. He was thus given the affectionate nickname "Penis Head." In the end, I think that's what drove him over the edge. I used to imagine him looking at himself in the mirror while shaving every morning and hoarsely whispering "I don't really look like that, do I? I don't. No, I don't. I *couldn't*."

Anyway, back to this dream. There I am in the hall, with poor old PH (RIP) munching his fingernails and mumbling incoherently about the Zulus, and I turn over the mathematics exam paper and begin to read. With cold horror, I realise that I cannot answer any of the questions. I have to sit and watch everyone else write. It is horrible. So horrible, indeed, that I always like having this dream, because it is so incredibly pleasant to wake up from.

My leaving certificate mathematics exam has haunted my nights for the last thirteen years. I was always desperate at maths. I could never understand it. Teenage life seemed so full of real problems that inventing artificial ones purely in order to solve them seemed utterly farcical. Why was it important to know how quickly a half-full train doing average speed would get to Limerick Junction via Portarlington when I could spend my days dreaming up witty things to murmur during the slowsets at Prez? ("Listen, Concepta, can I buy you a fizzy orange after 'Freebird' or would you rather just have the money?") Even now, I only remember one mathematical fact. The square on the hypotenuse equals the sum of the squares of the other two sides. The other two sides of *what*, I never knew. (Smoked salmon, is it?)

My schooldays were darkened by my hatred of examinations. In college, I confess, things improved, but I still had my recidivist moments. I recall a question on my second year history paper, "What are your views on red China?" I said it was really quite pretty if you used a plain white tablecloth.

Each and every June, Ireland is full of pressurised young people worrying about exams. They are important, of course, but one thing should be made clear. Exams examine your ability to do exams. They have nothing at all to do with education, and they're not worth going bananas over. If God must test us, Woody Allen quipped, I wish he'd give us a written. But God, if he exists, and if he is testing us at all, is doing so by continuous assessment. There will not be a *cigire* on the last day of judgement. No way. So what I want to know is this: if it's good enough for God, then, why, damn it all, *why* couldn't it have been bloody well good enough for the civil service?

Anyway, in time, my difficult childhood ended, I grew up and out, and I started going to pop concerts instead of just listening to Mudd records. It was a decision I was often to regret. What is this tragic madness that takes hold of the youth of Ireland? It is still beyond my understanding that every summer in our country young people trek off to Slane or some other sad little town to git on up, shake their booties, sink ankle deep into country muck and consume dubious hamburgers, some of which have prices as artificially pumped up as the cows from which they once came.

In the entire panoply of cultural tortures, is there anything really worse than the outdoor rock festival? I mean, yours truly is no party pooper. Be assured, yours truly has gotten down with the best of them, put my funk in numerous faces and agreed, quite fervently, that boogie nights are always the best in town. My own bootie has been shaken as thoroughly as James Bond's martini. But I draw the line at the rock festival. If there is a Hell being prepared for me somewhere — and I feel sure there is — it is an eternity of Lord Henry Mountcharles and his famous back garden.

I spent my teenage years going to rock festivals. I have seen the horror. I know what gives. You go down the country on a rattling coach, suffering from an appalling hangover. When you arrive in Slane/Thurles/Tramore, you realise that the locals have discovered the fine art of fleecing Van Morrison fans instead of sheep. You mortgage your as-yet-unborn first child to pay for a Coca Cola and begin the three mile trek over rough country to get to the venue. It is your luck to come across one of those festering assassins who masquerade as security staff. By the time you are granted admission,

Sting is on stage, saying that we all godda, y'know, do a liddle bit more for the environment and animal rights. You feel you would be quite happy not to buy shoes made of animal skin, if only you could buy shoes made of *Sting's* skin, and that you just want to go home and back to bed, but you can't, because you're *having a good time*.

As Prince says in one of his songs, "Dig, if you will, the picture." There are 70,000 punters all being whipped into a quite advanced and dangerous state of sexual excitement by the throbbing primitive beat. All of them are very much the worse for strong drink. 35,000 of them are sitting on the shoulders of the other 35,000, waving instamatic cameras and plastic bottles of hooch in the air. The place is crawling with lost and screeching infants, savage dogs, arguing couples, plain-clothes members of the drug squad, stoned ravers in psychedelic shirts, Fine Gael TD's and recently released political prisoners trying to get their photographs into the newspapers. And Neil Young is on the stage now, yowling and wailing and falling about and thrashing his tuneless guitar — "*I wanna live, I wanna give, I've been a miner for a heart of gold*" — and the hippies think it's deep and people are trying to dance to this, although in truth you couldn't even do your shopping to it. And all around the edges of this vast and restless crowd, people are queuing up to evacuate their bowels in the nettle bushes. And you can't face this, so you go back, and you try to find your friends, but it's impossible, and it's getting terrifically hot now, and The Saw Doctors come on and everyone jumps up and down and roars and someone tramples on your toes. And there are long lines of punk rockers all puking and fighting and interfering with each other and sticking safety pins in their faces, and there are sunstroke victims having visions of the Blessed Virgin Mary, and there are Chris De Burgh fans having terrible fits, insanely screaming the words of "Patricia The Stripper", and there are young fainting women being passed over the heads of the fevered crowd, and there are bottles of lager being passed through the crowd too, and parched punters down the back are gratefully swigging, only they don't realise the diehards up the front have finished their homebrew, and, not wanting to lose their places in the throng, have put those plastic bottles to a use that nature never intended, then turned and flung them into the sea of bodies. And your nose starts to bleed with tension, all over your shirt, and you look like the victim of a gang attack. And as one more fat once-relevant pop star in unwise trousers bounds out on stage and bellows "YEAH, WOAH, yeah, alRIGHT, SLANE you're BEAUTIFUL!! HOW YA DOIN'? I CAN'T HEAR YOU. Rock and ROLL, ALLRIGHT!!" you stop and realise that you may be young, but you're already pining for the time you can stay in of a Summer afternoon and lie on the couch with a large gin and tonic and watch the bloody television, instead of going to rock concerts.

Of course, you have to be careful about relaxing too. It can be a very dangerous activity. One afternoon recently, I actually tried to do this. Relax, I mean. I wandered casually over to my parents' house with the intention of spending a few pleasant quiet hours with my loving brothers and sisters. An hour later, to drown out the noise of the roaring, I turned on the radio. Who was on, talking about emigration and our young people, only the very lovely chrome-dome himself, Minister Ruairi Quinn?

Ruairi was in generous mood. He had no problem at all with the emigrants being given the vote, he said. I thought this was big of him, considering that the disastrous policies of the last Labour-Fine Gael government are what has most of them emigrants in the first place. Still, it was nice to hear old Ruairi again. Ah, the memories of my university days came flooding back.

Ruairi's socialist and progressive comrade Barry Desmond was Minister for health when I was in my second year in University. One of the really progressive things Bazza wanted to do was to take the medical card away from students. OK, so I know that's not exactly the bombing of Guernica, but, hey, we were upset about it at the time. We were young, I suppose.

We all met in Trinity College. There was going to be an occupation. Our student union leader told us to be inconspicuous. Fifty of us took our busfares, our banners and our bullhorns and we marched down to Bazza's office, looking about as inconspicuous as the massed Serbian irregulars on a day trip to a mosque.

Once we had penetrated Bazza's office, we all sat down on the shag pile and waited for something revolutionary to happen. I had taken along my cigarette lighter so that if anyone struck up a sudden chorus of "We Shall Not Be Moved" or "Blowing in the Wind" I could hold it up in the air and wave it meaningfully from side to side. I was very optimistic in those days.

After a while the police arrived. They were quite angry. They said they would "do whatever was necessary" to get us out. They repeated the phrase a few times. We scoffed, heroically. We'd be here, we said, until all of our demands had been met. They asked what these demands were. There seemed to be a bit of confusion at this point. Personally, in addition to having Ireland immediately declared a 32 county socialist republic, I wanted to have a regular girlfriend and "Brideshead Revisited" repeated on a Monday night. Anyway, while we argued, the coppers left, no doubt happily reflecting on the fact that their monthly PAYE payments were helping to subsidise our youthful exuberance.

Their sergeant came in then, a nice big fellow from Cork. He parked his ample behind on Bazza's desk. He told us that we were all very bright young people (which, incidentally, was questionable in a number of cases) and that we were very lucky to be getting an education (which, incidentally, was true). Then he asked us to leave. We told to shag away off to hell, him and his fascist free state, goose-stepping, imperialist paymasters. Well actually, I think we just said no. He shook his head, sadly. He took off his cap. It was a terrifying sight, for some reason, a policeman taking off his cap.

OK, he sighed, there was one thing he wanted to say, before giving the order for us to be forcibly removed. The phrases "give the order" and "forcibly removed" were quite effective actually, now that I think of it. You could almost hear the sound of fifty pairs of middle class buttocks being simultaneously clenched   with anxiety.

He pointed a finger. "If any of you are arrested today," he breathed, "you'll get a criminal record." We greeted this threat with jeers and coarse whistles. "And if you get a criminal record", he continued, "you will never get into America." There followed a silence which can only be adequately described as stunned. "Never," he said, "Never. Think it over." He told us he would give us ten minutes to consider our options. He slipped from the room like a graceful phantom.

Reader, no water cannon was ever so effective. There was a stampede out of that office. There was dust coming out of the carpet. It was like the back door of a brothel during a raid.

I hung on with the hard core. At the time, I was going through that stage of adolescence known as virulent anti-Americanism, so I didn't really care what would happen. What did happen was that two hefty guards carried me out and dumped me down on the steps so hard that I nearly shattered my spine. It was ten years ago. I've put on a bit of weight since. It would take the whole cast of "Hill Street Blues" to do the same job now.

Anyway, that sergeant understood something very important. He understood that our politicians are such embarrassing, dismal failures that emigration is an utterly ingrained part of the Irish psyche. Growing up in Dublin, you just expect emigration to happen to you, like puberty. In Chile the cops attach electrodes to your private parts. In Ireland they just tell you you'll never be able to emigrate. It works too. It's the biggest threat of them all.

Chapter Two
The Birds and the Bees: How to fall in love

Even before my difficult childhood had ended, I already knew that the most important thing I would learn in school was that almost everything I would learn in school would be utterly useless. When I was fifteen I knew the principle industries of the Ruhr Valley, the underlying causes of World War One and what Peig Sayers had for her dinner every day. Did even one minuscule titbit from this smorgasbord of knowledge ever come in handy in later life? Did it my buttocks. What I wanted to know when I was fifteen was the best way to chat up girls. That is what I still want to know.

It's something I have never been able to do. I have "friends" who know how to do it and I loathe them with an almost religious intensity. You know the type. Relaxed easy manner, cheekbones you could hang a sombrero on, normal, well-adjusted men who've had their teeth capped, read three of the novels on the *Booker Prize* short list and once been to an opera directed by Jonathan bloody Miller. Vile unspeakable pondscum, in other words, but boy do they know how to get on — and indeed off — with women.

Last summer I was in New York, reading a copy of the *Village Voice* one day, when my eyes fell upon an advertisement for flirting classes. "Huh," I thought, "I don't care if I can't chat anyone up, only a *really* sad pathetic person would ever do something as incredibly stupid as a flirting class."

On the first night I was ten minutes late. By the time I arrived there were six men and seven women, all of them fidgeting, blushing, biting their fingernails, gnawing their lips, and all of them hoping too that by the end of the evening the lips they would be gnawing would be firmly attached to the face of somebody else. It was a hot Manhattan night and the sexual tension in that classroom was positively sparking. The air seemed drenched with pheromones. If you had inhaled suddenly you would have got pregnant with quads.

The teacher breezed into the room like a pop star arriving backstage at Wembley. Her name was Lucy. She was a wonderful gal, a vision in stretch lycra and black 501s. She made us feel that it was

OK not to know how to flirt. It didn't necessarily mean that we weren't attractive, she confirmed, (I have to say, I wasn't too crazy about that "necessarily") but it was an important skill to acquire. Most relationships, after all, began with a flirtation. My own usually began with an act of emotional hara-kiri, I reflected, but that was another story.

Lucy kicked off with a bit of guff on feeling good about ourselves in social situations. Dinner parties, for example. I ignored this. Dinner parties, after all, are not there to make us feel good about ourselves. Dinner parties are there to remind us that God does exist and that he hates us. And anyway, if we were the kind of people who felt good about ourselves at dinner parties, then why the fuck weren't we at one, rather than forking out good hard-earned spondulix to sit in a stuffy classroom reeking of testosterone and sexual panic and trying to look like we were only here because we wanted to write an article.

Things improved when we got down to the specifics. Step one: Basic Flirtation. Lucy said you had to look the desired person in the eye. You had to smile and use the person's name. You had to pay compliments and, if at all humanly possible, touch the person. Not run your mitts all over them, of course, just "lightly brush" against them, preferably while "sharing a joke." A joke came thundering into my mind. What's the difference between a raw egg and a good ride? You can beat a raw egg. Perhaps that was not the kind of joke you would share with a total stranger. Above all, Lucy said, you had to ask questions. So far so good, I felt. I like asking people questions anyway; it is a very good way to stop people asking questions about you.

Next stage was Getting That Date. Lucy said she would give us her secret weapon. The hormonal activity in the room seemed suddenly to surge. She leaned forward. "Little pauses," Lucy whispered.

Basically, the gist was that we were not supposed to go blundering in, grinning "howarya petal? Fancy a tequila sunrise or what?" We were supposed to "insert a little pause."

Lucy showed us what she meant. I was selected as guinea pig. She came over, sat down and gazed into my face, touching my wrist with just the right degree of pressure. My God, if there was one thing this woman understood, it was gravitational pull. She smiled. She moved her hair gently out of her sparkling eyes. She was so close now that I could smell her musky perfume. The class inhaled, *en masse*. I felt my palms moisten.

"Listen Joe," she beamed, "Do you, uh, want to have a drink with me sometime?"

The class exhaled and almost burst into applause. "Are turkeys fucking nervous in November, Lucy?" I thought, silently. "I see what you mean," I said.

"Now you try it," she grinned.

We broke into pairs and I got Alison, a very nice legal secretary from The Bronx. I noticed that on the name badge she was wearing she had drawn a little smiley face where the dot over the "i" in her name should have been, but that apart, things were looking up. "Now," Lucy said, in the cool tone of voice used by brain-surgeons who are just about to go into someone's cranium with a revved-up black and decker, "Look into the eyes." I peered into Alison's pupils as though she were Dan Quayle and I was trying to find measurable evidence of human life.

"OK, people," Lucy urged, "now smile, speak, and *insert that pause.*"

I could feel the sweat trickling down my back. "Emmm," I grinned, maniacally, "you, uh, want to have a drink with me sometime?"

Alison laughed so hard that a ball of snot came shooting out of her nose with the force of an exocet missile. I wondered whether this was my opportunity to "brush lightly" against her by offering her a tissue, or, at the very least, the back of my sleeve.

"Use Alison's name, Joe," Lucy chuckled, throatily. "You've inserted, but you haven't used her name yet." I conceded that this had indeed been an error of some magnitude.

I tried again. "Urgh, Alison, you, um, want to have a drink some time, hrnmgh?" The entire class collapsed into a frenzy of tittering. It was dreadful. You could have eliminated the national debt of a small third world country with the amount of money these people had spent on psychotherapy. Yet here they were, control-freaks, social inadequates and tragic misfits all, weeping tears of laughter, slapping not only their own thighs but each other's also. It was very unfair, I felt.

I attempted it once more. "Urff, Alison, I dunno, you hmmmm, wanna go...?" People were practically on the floor now. Bill, a very pleasant chap from Queens, had to get up and leave the room, shaking uncontrollably, hankie clasped to his frantically guffawing gob. I just couldn't figure it out. Every time I asked Alison if she wanted to have a drink, I sounded like I was already pissed. It was a hopeless situation. My little pauses were yawning chasms of existential angst.

Outside, later, fourteen of us stood on the sidewalk. We all agreed, quite dishonestly in my view, that it had been "a lot of fun," but that some of us would have to work harder than others. We said our goodbyes and went to leave. I walked a block with Alison and Bill in nervous silence. Then, very suddenly, Bill stopped and slapped himself on the forehead, as though swatting some particularly virulent breed of mosquito.

"Urm, Alison?," he said, "Hey I just thought, I'm like, going uptown. You, er, wanna share a taxi?"

She turned, the pale pink haze of the streetlight caressing the side of her angelic face. She reached out and touched his wrist. "Uh, yeah, Bill," she smiled. "Yeah. That'd be really neat."

"Errmm?," I ejaculated, hopefully, "urrfmfgh?" But, tragically, too late. The taxi pulled up and in an instant they were gone.

And as I stood on the pavement alone, watching their yellow cab roar off into the sultry heat of the Manhattan night, I couldn't help but reflect that when dealing with women, it is a truly wonderful thing to have had an education.

This was a thought that had occurred to me many times before, of course, particularly in my student days. I should explain that in my home town of Dublin, in the grounds of Trinity College, a near-legendary event called The Trinity Ball is held every year. Although officially only open to students at that marvellously appointed Inner-City university, it is actually attended by large numbers of students from other establishments, including my own fair and glorious alma mater, University College Dublin.

Anyway, The Trinity Ball begins at midnight and ends with a huge outdoor disco at dawn the following morning. During this time, attending students are expected to get togged up in formal gear, get drunk, get stoned, and, perhaps most importantly, get off vigorously with the person they came with, or, failing that, whoever else they can lay their hands on. Well, hey, it didn't actually say that on the tickets, but that was certainly my understanding. For I went to The Trinity Ball some ten years ago. It was, without a doubt, the worst evening of my entire life.

The woman I went with was a lithe creature with blonde hair, a stunning smile and legs that seemed to go all the way up to her neatly coiffured armpits. When I tell you that she had something of the startled deer about her, I do not mean that she had antlers or anything. Rather, her eyes, when she turned suddenly to look at you, were just mesmerisingly cute. If bodaciousness was a commodity covered by the GATT talks, she would have been responsible for Ireland coming up with a very considerable surplus. She was a stunner. She was the princess of Babelonia. I would with equanimity have consumed a large portion of *pommes frites* out of her intimate undergarments.

I was highly surprised that she had agreed to go with me to the ball, because I knew that I was not at all her type. She tended to bestow her favours on aspiring rockstars, Keanu Reeves look-alikes, men with silky skin and broad shoulders and a total lack of musical talent. I don't know now why I asked her, but somehow I did, and to my astonishment she agreed.

However, at the pre-ball party which our mutual friends had thrown, I began to intuit that the evening was not going to end in the shattering banquet of mutual carnal fulfillment which I had had in mind. It was the small things really. The look of cold horror that came over her face when she saw my hired evening suit, its stained lapels flapping like the wings of a deranged angel. The way she vomited up her twiglets with the force of a broken-down fruit machine when I tried to hold her hand in the kitchen. I dealt with my teenage nervousness by drinking an entire bowl of rum punch, smoking several joints and trying to snog somebody else upstairs in the toilet.

I was very drunk by the time the fleet of taxis arrived to convey us all into town, and, for some reason, my date did not seem to want to sit beside me. In fact, it was only with considerable effort that I managed to dissuade her from strapping herself to the roof-rack, or following us in on the bus.

We stood in the queue outside Trinity for half an hour, during which time we did not exchange one single word. Well, I think I tried out my favourite joke. Once upon a time there were three bears. Now there's bloody millions of them. Astonishingly, she didn't even titter. Once in, I got even more drunk and I fell asleep on the floor of the Examination Hall, where, as I recall, The Pogues were playing; a difficult band to fall asleep to. When I woke up, my head was hammering, my left shoe *and* sock were missing and there was a large muddy footprint on the front of my tuxedo. For some reason I have never been able to figure out, my date was gone. I searched the room, elbowing my way through the perspiring swarm of diddley-eying Trinity students, but she was nowhere to be seen.

I sought her in the bar and the restaurant, on the rugby pitch and in the Arts Block. I got the security men to broadcast a message over the intercom. I lurched up and down the quad, trying to describe her to total strangers, most of whom laughed, jeered or pelted me with water-inflated condoms. One of them tried to piss on me. I spent the entire night hopping around Trinity College with one shoe on, cursing my parents for ever having had the cruelty to conceive me, swigging from a bottle of gin, puking copiously in the hydrangea bushes and trying to find her. I suppose it's just as well I didn't succeed because she probably would have shrieked and called the police. I do not think I will ever forget the full horror of that night. The map of Trinity College Dublin is burned into my soul, and bits of its gravel are probably still embedded in my right foot.

I finally caught up with her at the dawn disco, at seven thirty in the morning. It was very cold, a light rain was falling, and she was efficiently snogging the gob off my best friend's brother. She had her hand up the back of his shirt, I noticed. Had she been sucking his face any harder his skin would have simpy peeled away in her mouth. I turned around and hopped all the way home, where I collapsed on my bed, took off my tuxedo, lit my last cigarette and cried myself into oblivion.

Fun, I think it is called. I remember my kind and gentle stepmother consoling me at the time, saying that relationships become easier the older you get. Little did I know how spectacularly untrue that was. Love is never easy. Getting into it is almost impossible and getting out of it is even harder. I remember once having a relationship with this crazed woman who really didn't like me very much. Things were kind of tense between us. In fact, things got so tense that it often felt that our relationship was being directed by Alfred Hitchcock. I tried my best to sort things out. I tried to be honest and straightforward about our problems. For instance, I remember asking her on one occasion if she ever thought about anyone else when we were making love. She told me no, she only ever thought about herself. So nothing to worry about there. That was a week before she dumped me.

I had cause to reflect on all this recently, while having dinner with a close woman friend. It was one of those upmarket restaurants where there is a wafer-thin sliver of kumquat in the water jug and the waiter insists that you call him Serge, when, really, you would much rather call him waiter, or gell-haired oleaginous dickfeatures, actually, if you have to call him anything at all. And the subject turned, as for some reason it often does when you eat polenta, to love.

This woman is going out with a prize bozo, who possesses the brains of a piece of toast, the charm of Margaret Thatcher and the looks of Rod Steiger. He is an aspiring actor, actually, and his performances are not so much wooden as finest mahogany. "I haven't got the guts to finish with him," my friend said to me, "I'll break his heart." I sat there nodding sympathetically, hoovering up lengths of spaghetti into my gob as discreetly as possible, and reflecting that it wasn't dreamboat's heart that needed breaking, so much as his coccyx, when suddenly, a very simple solution occurred to me. "I'll do it," I said. "I'll finish it for you."

I am now prepared to extend this new service to the readers of this book. "A JOE O'CONNOR DUMP-THE-CHUMP PROMOTION!" Here's how it works. You send me your hard-earned shekels, and I do your dirty work for you. Simple or what? For ten pounds plus VAT you get the basic service. I ring up the mistreating brain-dead sap you used to be sad enough to snog and tell them they can shag away off and die because you are fed up wandering about with WELCOME on your back. You don't want them any more. Furthermore, actually, you never *did* really want them. If the survival of the entire human race depended on you having sex with them just one last time, for about thirty seconds, and for a billion pounds afterwards, you would say no, you scum-sucking sweaty-buttocked foul-breathed bandy-legged ballocks.

For thirty pounds, we can go a little up-market. I will turn up on their doorstep masquerading as an elder of the Mormon church, invite myself in for coffee, and say, "listen........(your name here) really does like you a lot, an *awful* lot, straight up, but he/she just doesn't like you *in that special way*". I will then dry their weeping eyes with a kleenex, wipe their nose on my newly-laundered sleeve and tell them not to worry about it, because while there may admittedly be not too many more fish in the sea, post-Sellafield, there are certainly plenty more poison-spitting snakes in the cesspit.

After that, it does start to get a bit pricey. But worth it. Spare yourself all the guilt, the recrimination, the tears and accusations, the ripped-up lovey-dovey photographs of you and your formerly better half sharing *pina coladas* on a balcony somewhere, returned to you in a re-useable envelope with the word "bastard" inserted between your first name and your second. Avoid the cute little fluffy toy rabbit wearing the "Gee, I weally wuv you cos you're such a cuddlesome funny bunny" T-shirt that you gave her/him last Valentine's Day being anonymously delivered back to your place of work in a shoebox with a stake through its heart, its eyes gouged out, its ears hacked off and inserted into its anal cleft and a rather unattractive heart-shaped scorch-mark where its leporid genitalia should be. It's simple. You just pay me, and I take the rap.

There are several optional extras of course. For twenty pounds, I am prepared to say you have some dreadfully infectious venereal disease that will surely rot the very fundament off anyone misfortunate enough to come within a donkey's bray of you. For thirty, I will tell them you are a Spurs supporter or a secret born-again Christian. For fifty, I will say you once owned a copy of "Shang A Lang" by The Bay City Rollers, and were secretly and erotically fixated on drummer Derek Longmuir.

I will, however, have to ask for danger money if you expect me to use corny lines. You're just not good enough for them? A tenner surtax. You're coming out of quite a long relationship in which you were deeply hurt and you're just, you know, not ready for that kind of serious commitment again yet? Twenty. You don't really know what's wrong but it's all down to your difficult childhood and the fact that you didn't get enough hugs from your parents — a particular favourite of my own, I must say — thirty five. And then there's the deluxe service.

For one hundred and ninety five pounds, I will take your partner out to supper in a fancy joint, ply them with veal's throats, pheasant's tongues and vintage champagne, flirt like Zza Zza Gabor, discourse at length on W H Auden (or any major twentieth century poet of your choice — January is a special Pablo Neruda Month), make them feel great about themselves, tell them how beautiful and intelligent they are (even — perhaps *especially* — if they are stupid and ugly enough to turn water sour, which, let's face it, they probably are, otherwise you wouldn't be in need of this service), cackle maniacally at their abysmal jokes, then slowly, inexorably bring the subject around to *you*. I will explain with tenderness and sensitivity that, hey, it's so *so* tragic, but the magic just slipped right away while you weren't looking. Still, I shall say, it was a beautiful thing while it lasted, and you feel that you're not so much closing a door on your love as sealing a perfectly wonderful memory in the emotional aspic of the past. The hankies with which I mop your now ex-beloved's tears will be of finest hand-spun Chinese silk. The shoulders of my jacket, into which the broken-hearted dumpee may plunge her or his wailing and hysterically snivelling chops, will be efficiently padded. The songs I gently croon as I take hold of your trashed darling-no-more's screeching face and slap, *slap*, slap again to calm them down will be purest Manilow. Go on. Christmas is coming. You know it makes sense. Dump that chump.

It's not that I want to be cynical. If you have met the right person, you should do the right thing, and marry them immediately. In fact, two good friends of mine who have been going out together — and, worse, God help us all, quite frequently staying in together and refusing to answer the telephone — told their families recently that they were going to get married soon. (Happily enough, to each other.) I was pleased to hear this news, because I am a great believer in the institution of marriage, and I can hardly wait to get married myself. In fact, I intend to do so as often as possible. Not that I am a romantic or anything. It is just that if I am going to get fat, disillusioned and sad anyway, I am bloody well taking somebody with me.

We talked for a while about their impending nuptials, my friends and myself. I am to be a witness on the happy occasion. I dislike the word witness, really, for its unpleasant legal overtones. I mean, you could just as easily be a witness at somebody's divorce as their marriage. And am I to be a witness for the prosecution or the defence? I think I should be told.

I am to make a speech on the glorious day, and I was instructed by the bride-to-be not to use the ideologically tainted words "wedding" or "marriage" in this speech. We finally settled on "the bonding," which phrase I am not particularly happy about, as I feel it conjures up agonizing and highly embarrassing scenes involving superglue, crowbars, teams of strong men and large tubs of axle grease. But who am I to disappoint a blushing bride? Bonding it is.

Marriage has not been very fashionable in ultra-liberal circles for some time. I lived in London for some years, and in certain parts of that right-on, politically correct city, if you happened to let slip at a dinner party that you were thinking of getting married, people tended to peer at you as though you had just piercingly farted during the funeral of a prominent member of the ANC. There then ensued a turgid lecture from some scrawny poloneck-wearing part-time poet about just how preposterously conventional and middle-class marriage was, immediately before the hostess brought in the desiccated kiwifruit for dessert, some bored ex-Stalinist architect lit up a joss-stick and everybody began twittering ruefully about how bad Mrs (now, of course, Lady) Thatcher had been for property prices.

I cannot figure out why marriage has such a bad press. It is a romantic and idealistic institution, but surely we need more romance in this lonely world. Yes, I know some marriages sadly do not work out. But governments do not work out either, from time to time, and we do not pooh-pooh the general idea of parliamentary democracy as a result. We do not demolish Dail Eireann, for instance, just because of the existence of Sean Haughey, formidable argument though he may be for direct rule from Mars. And yes, on paper, marriage makes very little sense. How in the name of God are you supposed to find the one person you can love for the rest of your life, and go on loving them and putting up with their weird antics, cranky opinions and off-putting personal habits? How are you supposed to perpetually cleave to this one special soulmate, even in the event that some balmy night, just after you have enjoyed frenzied connubial congress, she may sigh deeply, light up a fag, rest her head on your breast and languidly confide that she feels Daniel O'Donnell isn't actually *that* bad, y'know, if you really listen to the words of "Whatever Happened to Old Fashioned Love"?

The idea that marriage provides security is incorrect. But insecurity is the whole point of matrimony. You may think you are certain of your feelings, yet marriage at its most essential is the emotional equivalent of jumping out of an airplane not knowing whether the bundle so firmly strapped to your back contains a parachute or a grand piano. I've never been spliced myself, but I can understand how some folks find it more exciting to plummet through mid-air thinking "so far, so good" than to sit in the cockpit, fly the plane and admire the scenery below.

Not that I'm necessarily recommending marriage for everybody. Different strokes, as the conservative MP exclaimed in the massage parlour. I spoke to another pal about the subject recently. The unhappy chap is knocking about with a woman who wants to marry him, but he does not share her desire. (In conversation, he often refers to his unfortunately intense beloved by the pseudonym

Wanda, which, he says, stands for 'What? Another Neurotic Disaster? Absolutely!' "It's awful," he sighed, "Wanda's gone and bought herself a one year subscription to *Bride-To-Be Magazine*". His face took on the length of a fortnight's holiday in Termonfeckin. "Well, look," I suggested, "her birthday's coming up. You could always extend it to five years as a present." He looked at me blankly, then. And for one awful moment, I felt sure he thought I was serious.

Chapter Three
Getting to know the English

Part I: The Iceman Cometh

London: Summer, 1993. Keith "Ice Man" Bristol is a tall handsome black guy with fists the size of most people's heads. He wanders up and down the dressing room in his natty multicoloured tracksuit, swinging his arms and mumbling softly to himself. From time to time the other boxers wander in to use the toilet. Through the floorboards you can hear the loud bass throb of rock music. Keith cocks his head and listens for a moment. The song is "That's Entertainment," by The Jam. He looks calm, in control, cool as an eskimo's toes. The only sign of nervousness is that he keeps glancing at his expensive watch.

Keith begins to talk, at about one hundred words per minute and in a tone with which you feel you would be extremely well-advised not to disagree. "I'm the 'kin' best, man," he snaps. "That's the thing. They just wanna stop me. But they won't, they won't, no way, I'm telling you, man, and I'm telling you good, and I'm telling *them* that it just ain't on." He stops and points at my notebook. "And you better write that down in your notebook as it 'kin' 'appens, man, cos I'm serious here."

"They" are the British Boxing Board of Control, the men who currently run the professional fight game in England. They won't give Keith a licence, he says they are sewing the game up, taking away his livelihood and those of many other professional boxers. "I mean, I gotta wife and kids," he says, "this is my thing, you know, this is my fackin' *job*, man, and they won't let me do it." So Keith has joined up with the new, and until recently semi-legal, UBO, and he kind of prefers it this way. He likes the fact that the tickets often cost a tenth of what BBC tickets do, that the fights are more evenly matched, that they tend to be "good scraps."

"Boxing for the people," he says, "not the fackin' toffs."

And as he is saying this, the iceman's clenched right hand is slapping against the palm of his open left one. It is a vaguely disturbing sound. Every time he does it, I find myself wincing. "I'm the best, Joe," *slap*, "the very best," *slaaap*, "you know what I'm saying?"

"Oh yes, Keith," I simper. "Yes, I think I do."

If you stood on the tenth storey of a block of flats and dropped a basketball over the side, which I know you wouldn't, I'm just saying, the sound it would make as it hit the pavement below would be a little bit like the sound Keith Bristol's hand is making now as it hits the palm of his other hand. A loud, heavy percussive *slap* sound, the kind of sound that has exclamation marks after it, the kind of sound in whose production you would not want your face to play any role whatsoever, not even a cameo. I mean, just *listening* to this guy talk is like getting punched. Getting punched by him must be like getting smashed in the head with a baseball bat.

In about two hours time some poor wide-eyed greenhorn called Geordie Boy Jackson is going to get into a ring downstairs with Keith Bristol and try to hit him so hard that he falls over. When I ask the iceman if he is at all worried by this prospect, he looks at me like I've just puked my dinner up on his trainers. Then he pinches his nose and begins to laugh. He has an oddly high-pitched laugh, for such a big man. *Hee, hee, hee*, he goes, "no mate, nah, I'm not too worried."

"So you're a good bet?" I say, feeling stupid now, because he's laughing so much. "The other guy has no chance?"

"Well, yeah," he muses, stroking his chin, "I suppose he 'as *some* chance, yeah." He looks over at me and grins. "If 'e comes into the ring with a fackin' loaded gun, he has a chance, yeah."

Downstairs, Ritzy's nightclub in Streatham is beginning to fill up with punters. Streatham is a very fine, if rather excitingly paced, suburb of South East London, and Ritzy's is to its happy environs what *Les Deux Magots* was to the *Rive Gauche*.

When I reveal our destination to the taxi driver, however, he practically breaks into tears and starts talking about his poor widowed mother. I form the impression that he isn't too fond of

Streatham in general, or Ritzy's in particular, for some reason. He quips, in fact, that Ritzy's is the kind of establishment where the bouncers search you for knuckledusters on the way in, and if you don't have any, they are so relieved that they beat the shit out of you. He is clearly joking, of course, just in case Ritzy's owners, legal advisers or admirably civilised *clientele* are reading, but oddly enough he isn't laughing, as he pulls up outside, nods at the long queue of big-boned men at the front door, and counsels, "I'd be very careful if I was you, mate. I really farkin' would."

"I'm a journalist," I tell him, nonchalantly. "I'll be fine."

"Oh right," he sighs. "You're a journalist. Well, I'm sure that'll get 'em shaking in their shoes."

Unlicensed boxing. Now, to me, this phrase conjures up dingy liniment-smelling basements, greasy fivers changing hands in corners, drugs, corruption, the wrong person's piss in a greasy test tube, fat horseshoes sewn into boxing gloves. I am looking forward to scurrying down an alley, up a metal fire escape, knocking three times and saying the Fat Man has sent me to check out the action, although, there being rather a lot of me to love these days, since I came to live in London and started eating steak and kidney pie, there is always the danger that I will be mistaken for the Fat Man myself.

But Ritzy's turns out to be very far from a basement. Rather, it is something of a classy joint, a cavernous purple and pink barn of a place, glinting with strobes, sweeping with spotlights, glittering with spiral tubes of neon. There are various bars and plush burger stalls, at the highstools of which you would not be surprised to see Del Boy and Rodney Trotter discussing business. There are perhaps 1800 punters crammed in to Ritzy's, about two thirds of them male, and some of them, it must be noted, already the worse for drink. But there is an air of efficiency and relaxed control also. Reg Parker, the promoter, is wandering around quietly telling everyone what to do. There are security men all over the floor, with arms as thick as tree trunks and tattoos adorning their faces. The place has been fenced off into differently priced seating areas. A video camera has been set up in the DJ's box. The whole event seems to be well organised.

Down on the dancefloor, where the ring has been erected, there are two paramedics from the Saint John's ambulance brigade, two doctors and one of those machines for starting your heart when it stops. It is all very impressive, although for one short instant you do admittedly wonder whether you would see these pieces of medical equipment in Ritzy's nightclub any busy evening, whether it actually has anything to do with the boxing.

I look up at the ring. It is big. It is a lot bigger than a boxing ring looks on the telly. The blue ropes are the breadth of your wrist. I feal fear. The muscles in my throat tighten. Just looking at that ring makes me want to urinate with anxiety. On my way upstairs to interview Iceman Keith Bristol in his dressing room, I reflect that this is really no way to make a living. But Keith doesn't agree. "Men have to fight," he shrugs, "it's their nature. It's better to do it here."

I'm back down on the dancefloor now, and the people are starting to cheer. The stocky litle MC gets into the ring, wearing an antique tuxedo, a black bow tie and cuban heels of such spectacular height that even Marc Bolan would have baulked. The sound system is belting out "War" by Frankie Goes to Hollywood, and all around me people are singing along, punching the air, going "what is it *good* for, absolutely *nothing*." Most of them are young, the men in smart jackets and ties, others in garish tracksuits, or brightly-coloured shirts and baggy jeans, the women in heavy makeup, tight skirts, lycra leggings.

The MC picks up a microphone and begins to strut around the ring like a bantam cock overstuffed with illegal hormones, kicking the flex out of his path, neck jerking as he reads silently over his notes. He trots forward and then back, as though he is attached by elastic to one of the cornerposts. His name is Harold Stevens, someone tells me, but he is universally addressed as "Aitch." Calling him "Harold" would be a serious mistake, you feel. It would be a bit like meeting the Queen and calling her Betsy.

"Gentlemen, gentlemen, if you please," Aitch intones, "Jemmenplease." The presence of a significant number of ladies on the premises seems to be slightly overlooked. You sense that Aitch has not been reading his Camille Paglia. The first bout is nonetheless briskly announced, a welterweight contest between Sav "Wild Thing" Austin and Southpaw Tony Barlow. The crowd stand up and roar as Sav and Tony come dancing down the aisle and into the ring.

Sav is a pretty fellow with the kind of figure that makes some of the women in the audience point and take photographs. He looks fit and strong, but not particularly wild, as he preens and pouts at his admirers. Tony Barlow looks mean, a lot more serious. But he too has his enthusiasts. As he jogs around, loosening up and swinging at the air, a young woman beside me murmurs yearningly to her friend, "fuck, Geena, imagine him goin' down on you." Geena sucks at her large glass of Coke. "Oh, Christ, *don't*," she gurgles. "I'll wet meself in a minute."

The bell goes for round one. The two young men circle, neither seeming to want to strike the first punch. Then Barlow jumps in, suddenly looking the more determined of the two. He tries a few jabs, a heavy swing, then Sav lands a good right to the side of the face. The crowd screams. Barlow retreats. Sav comes forward again, trying to connect punches to the body. "Fucking *crease* him, Sav," someone shouts, "bang 'im, son." Austin attempts to swing a wide left hook, but it's blocked, and Barlow pounds in a heavy right to the body. The two guys thump seven shades of shimmering shite out of each other for two minutes, then round one ends, to a tumult of whistles, screams and hollers.

A young brunet. woman in a black tasselled bikini climbs into the ring and begins to walk around it — if "walk" is the appropriate verb for what she is doing — smiling, sticking out her chest and holding up a card with the number 2 emblazoned upon it. Now, I don't know if you can imagine the reaction of a thousand semi-intoxicated South London men when a semi-naked woman climbs into a boxing ring and does this, but I will ask you to just put down this book for a second, close your eyes and do your best. The only printable example of the ensuing dialogue is "coo-ee darlin', you're farkin' fit, ain't you?" (Now that I think of it, there were actually quite a number of speculative enquiries regarding the state of the young woman's health.) I sit by the ringside watching her, trying to imagine what amount of money it would take for me to remove my clothes and teeter around a boxing ring in white stilettos, swinging my cellulite-ravaged arse and pouting at a room full of horny and over excited ex-pugilists. (If anyone has an offer, by the way, I do have an agent.) My heart goes out to her, and, it must be said, just about all of her goes out to us. It turns out to be by far the bravest performance of the evening.

After they hose down the crowd, the bell goes for round two. Sav comes out like a fast moving train, and lands on a powerful straight right to Barlow's abdomen. Barlow clings on to him, shuffling back to the ropes. "Smash the cunt," somebody shouts, "garn Tony, bust 'im, do the bizz." Barlow bursts out, punching hard, but he's not too accurate. The crowd are going crazy now. You feel that if you were in Mexico, rather than Streatham, they would be crying "ay caramba" and throwing hats in the air. Barlow circles, trying to get control, looking for an opportunity to load his left hook. Suddenly he sees it. He swings. Sav ducks and grins, dancing back. The lace on his left glove has opened. The referee pushes him into his corner and the second ties it up. Sav charges back in, flailing. End of round two.

The ring girl clambers in and does her stuff. The ref grins sympathetically as she passes him. Sav's seconds are smearing his face with vaseline, trying to patch him up. They're counting off points on their fingers, shouting. He nods furiously, sucking great mouthfuls of air into his lungs as he listens.

At the start of round three, Sav comes out fast again. His back is burnt with rope marks. Both men are looking tired now, as they dance around, working their jabs. Barlow is punching efficiently, clocking up points. They drift into a neutral corner, panting, weakened again, holding each other up as the crowd boos. Then Sav catches Barlow in a headlock, and on the ref's blind side, pummels the side of his face, four, five, six times, and the people roar with applause. The fight ends. Barlow wins, by a unanimous points decision.

"Both fought their 'earts out for us," Aitch observes. "Nice warm round of applause now Jemmen, for a sporting contest."

The second bout matches Welterweights Jimmy Smith and Wayne Weeks. They're both tough and lean, better boxers than the first two. They move through round one with grace, athleticism and astonishing speed. Weeks's hands are fast, his feet light. He gets the measure of Smith pretty quickly, slipping in and catching him with constant and severe body blows. In his corner at the end of the round, Smith already looks beaten.

His assistant second is a fellow boxer, a very pleasant and amiable chap called Russ Ford, to whom I've been chatting earlier. Russ works as a gardener for his local council, but he's just won a UBO championship title and is looking forward to boxing full-time. He thinks boxing is good for kids, toughens them up, keeps them out of trouble, teaches them to look out for themselves. Boxing isn't dangerous, he laughs, it's not half as dangerous as "real life." Russ does not know how prophetically correct those words will turn out to be. Only ten days after tonight's entertainment, an electronic grass strimmer will explode in his hands, covering a third of his body in first degree burns. He will spend seven weeks in hospital and will not box again for a very long time. You're pretty safe in a boxing ring, as he said that night. It's real life that gets you every time.

Russ bellows a last instruction. Round two begins and Smith belts in with a smooth jabbing action. Weeks counters furiously, trying to lay in the heavy hooks. Punches connect and every time they do the crowd shouts. But the fight slumps again after a minute. A man beside me says they should be having a fucking war, these two, but instead they're having a rest. Suddenly Weeks seems to go up three gears. He throws a right to Smith's chin. Smith falters. Weeks senses his chance, steps forward, teeth clenched, his fists hammering with the speed and precision of a heavy-rock drummer as he batters Smith to the canvas. One minute forty of round three, and the first knockout of the night. The crowd are up on their feet roaring their approval. Weeks dances around the ring, waving.

Queen's "We Will, We Will Rock You" comes bursting out of the speakers as Aitch announces the middleweight bout between Paul Morton and "Iron Man" Darren Corville. Corville has a lot of supporters and that seems to spur him on. He moves like a machine through the first two rounds, dodging, weaving, throwing in heavy cuts and hard straight lefts. The bout ends in round three, as Morton goes down, tries to get up on the count of eight, falls backwards against the ropes and fails to make the count. But they embrace then, the two fighters. They smile and laugh and hug each other. "There's no overtime in this game," as somebody said to me earlier. "You go out to win, and you'll do anything, but you want to be a sport too."

Sport. Well, I'm not used to this amount of physical violence on a Tuesday night, so, feeling the need for refreshment, I go to the bar, where I get chatting to a young Scottish-Asian bloke who is down in London driving a minicab. He was at the last UBO fight, he says, there was a real cracker of a scrap between Jimmy Cable and Darren Corville. He loves boxing, this guy says. He's in a gym and he boxes a bit, and he wants to be a professional some day. He has a head the size of a beachball, and every visible inch of his arms is covered with tattoos. We have a beer and he tells me that he has just got out of the slammer in Glasgow, where he has served three years for A and B. This stands for assault and battery, as it turns out. Effing H, I say.

We chat all the way through bout four, while Super middleweight Eddie Burnett does his level best to chop down relative newcomer, Lester Patoveccia, a last minute substitute for reputed megabruiser Paul Stockton, who is ill. Lester acquits himself with some style, but he hasn't got the stamina of his fully-trained-up opponent. He lasts until the end of the match, but then loses. Still, I'm surprised that it is a unanimous decision.

"Oh well, if he hadnae had a fuck last night," my friend chuckles, "he woulda creamed 'im."

Whinnying with nervous laughter, I ask him whether this old myth is true, about boxers abstaining from carnal activity the night before a fight. And it *is* true, apparently. This particular bloke — who is a mere amateur — lays off the horizontal rhumba for two whole weeks. "Makes me more aggraissive," he explains, before almost taking a chomp out of his beer glass. He then confides, for some reason, that he's had some particularly thorough sex with his Irish girlfriend, Janet, that afternoon, which is why he is feeling so relaxed tonight. I punch him playfully on the chest and quip that I'd hate to have met him if he was tense. He nods at me. "Ay," he says. "You wuid."

We get a bevvy, then sit down together and watch the fifth bout, a cruiserweight contest, between Roger "AJ" Lee and Wayne "The

Duke" Gibson. This one turns out to be a veritable slugfest. Right from the bell the two men are pounding into each other, brawling like off-duty squaddies at a bar-extension. A great right from Gibson sends Lee staggering, but he lunges again, dancing and swerving, lashing out a right upper cut. There are no jabs in this fight, no finesse, just swings, hooks, cuts. Neither man wants to take a backward step. It's toe-to-toe stuff all the way, and the crowd are on their feet, roaring and waving their arms. Gibson's left eye is completely closed before the end of round one. The doctor is called to his corner and he shakes his head. The fight is over, but Lee agrees to give his unlucky opponent a rematch soon. As soon as they find his eyeball and pop it back in, I guess.

My Scottish friend leans over and taps me on the arm. "What's the dafference between Bing Crosby and Walt Disney?"

"I don't know," I say. He winks.

"Bing sings," he chuckles, "but Walt fuckin' disnae."

Johnny Boy Rambo and Darren Burford are up next. I look around the frantic audience and notice a young woman's face in a state of almost religious ecstasy as she watches the fight. She is holding her hands up, squeezing slowly at the air, gnawing hard at her lip as her eyes follow the boxers around the ring. Her fingers clench and unclench and as Darren Burford is pushed up hard against the ropes, the tip of her tongue moves to the corner of her mouth and she laughs out loud. Johnny Boy Rambo connects with a strong cut to Burford's face and a shower of sweat spatters the screaming ringside crowd. He drives in again, straight and heavy through Burford's guard. Burford is trapped in the corner now, the ropes biting into his back. "Give 'im combinations," a man behind me is screaming, "combos, Johnny, punch his fucking lights out then get 'im downstairs." It's a close bout but Burford is a little too heavy on his feet and Rambo gets the result in the end.

"Handa now," Aitch announces. "The main event." Men and women rush in from the bars carrying plastic glasses of beer. Up on the balcony people stand up and look over the edge, clapping. The song "The Final Countown" begins to blare.

Iceman Keith Bristow comes skipping down the stairs of the Ritzy, wearing silky blue shorts, flash boots and a dangerous smile. He lopes down the aisle through the crowd, high fiving, waving, grinning at people he recognises. His trainer lifts the ropes and Keith scurries underneath and into the ring. The crowd roars as he starts briskly shadowboxing. He jogs from foot to foot, stretching his neck. The women in the audience are wolf-whistling and cat-calling. He leans back his head and shakes his long arms, blowing hard through his pouted lips, snorting, snarling. He looks, as they say in South London, open for business. He lunges forward and begins to pummel the air again. The crowd goes berserk. I feel sorry for the air.

Geordie Boy Jackson is no ballet dancer himself. He's big, thick-armed, nasty-looking, and he comes into the ring with a scowl on his face. The ref calls them both to the centre and gives them the patter, arms around their shoulders like a benevolent uncle in a Norman Rockwell painting. Jackson chews hard as he eyeballs Keith, their foreheads almost touching. He looks like he's about to head-butt him. The bell goes.

"*Kill* the fucker, Keith," someone yells. "Take him *out*."

Jackson lands the first punch, but Bristol shrugs it off. They circle, dodging back, landing tentative blows. They're feeling each other out now, they've never fought before. They're trying to guess what's coming next. "*Murder* 'im, Keith." Jackson moves in but Bristol parries well, the punch seeming to slide off his neck. His arms are so long that Jackson just can't get through. Bristol side-steps. Jackson strides in again and attempts to put a few jabs together. But then suddenly, twenty five seconds into round one, the iceman strikes.

He catches Jackson a vicious upper left to the face and the Geordie staggers to the ground. "*Yes*" the crowd screeches in one voice. The ref starts a count but Jackson gets up, reeling, his gloves to his eyes. Bristol skips over, connecting hard with Jackson's body. Another thirty seconds and the kid is chewing the canvas again. But he gets up, as the crowd holler and whoop. Bristol steps forward almost reluctantly. He punches Jackson four times on the side of the face. The kid collapses, gets up on his hunkers, topples, falls onto all fours, head lolling. "Get up," the people yell. "Get *up* and bang 'im." The referee is close to stopping it. The kid gets up again, taking wild and frantic swings, like someone trying to swim but sinking further down into the sea. Bristol moves in, pounding at his chest and head, then pushes his shoulder, and the kid's legs just seem to crumple beneath him, although once again, he tries to stand. But the ref steps over, grabs Jackson and propels him into his corner. He comes back and holds up Bristol's glove. In two minutes and thirty two seconds the main bout of the night is over. There is a tornado of booing from the crowd. The ice man dances around, grinning. He has barely broken into a sweat.

The evening ends in an odd kind of anti-climax. Aitch gets into the ring and calls for "a lovely hand for the game loser" but nobody claps. "The Final Countdown" comes on again, as Jackson climbs out and wanders disconsolately off in the direction off the dressing rooms, head hanging, his arms down by his side. He looks like he doesn't know where he's going; he looks lost. People knock back their drinks and begin to file out of Ritzy's in untidy lines, muttering about the last bout being some kind of fix. The security guards are huddled together by the ring saying that Reg the promoter is furious, that Geordie Boy's people didn't tell him the truth about his record and that Reg isn't going to pay him. As I go to leave, one of the guards comes over and smiles. "Enjoy that, mate?"

"Yeah," I say. "Except for the last one."

He scowls. "Mmm. Wasn't really pucker. Dunno what occurred."

He nods at my notebook. "What magazine's this for then?"

"*Esquire*."

"Oh yeah. *Esquire*. Write for them much, do you?"

"Sometimes."

"Yeah, must be good, writing?"

"I suppose so. Yes, it's OK."

He looks around and glances up at the ring. "Better than the fight game anyway. Better way to make a living."

"I don't know. I'm sure it isn't."

He purses his lips and whistles softly. "I'm fucking sure it is," he says.

"Well, I'll send you a copy," I tell him.

"Yeah," he laughs, "OK. Send us a copy. Yeah, let's see what the intellectuals make of us peasants in *Esquire*."

I look at my watch and tell him I have to go.

He glances around at the ring again, then turns back to me, staring into my eyes very intensely, as though there is something else he wants to say. He shakes his head. And then, very suddenly, he puts his thumbs to his chest as though he is wearing braces. "Oh well, if you're drivin' 'ome, be careful," he says, smiling as he begins to caricature his own accent, "but you're in Sarf Farkin London 'ere, mate, so if you're *walkin'* 'ome, be double farkin' careful, squire, know what I mean?"

"Land of Hope and Glory" begins to play over the PA system. Up in the ring, Iceman Keith Bristol is still dancing around, chatting to his trainer. He's so full of energy that he can't seem to stop moving. He looks like he won't come down for hours. His girlfriend is standing on the other side of the ropes watching him. The house lights come on. The music is turned off and there's an weird echo now in Ritzy's nightclub, as the last of the people leave, still grumbling. "Yes," I say, and try to laugh. "I know what you mean."

"'Arry," he grins, "knowharamean, Arry? awight 'Arry?" and he turns and walks slowly away and begins to fold up the chairs.

Part II: How To Be Irish In London

I went to live in London in 1986 and I stayed living there for quite some time, and it often used to occur to me when I lived in London, as, indeed, it does now from time to time, that it can't be easy being a queen. The poor old dear has had one *annus horibilis* after another. The kids are splitting up, the palace is falling down, the mother is on the gin. It is all like a particularly atrocious episode of *"Eastenders"*. My own *annus* hasn't been exactly *mirabilis*, but compared to poor old Betty's, it's been a bowl of cherries.

It must be tricky being Betty these days. Imagine being married to Phil the Greek for a start. The man has all the charm and tact of a disgruntled yak. He once referred to the Japanese as "slant-eyes." He allegedly mistook the Prime Minister of Tanzania for a doorman at the Ritz Hotel. Kingsley Amis once said that sex was a great cure for a hangover, which, indeed, must be the case, because if you thought Kingsley Amis was going to make love to you, you'd certainly avoid getting drunk in the first place. But the thought of being rogered by old Prince Jug Ears would have you taking the pledge for ever, I think.

Betty deserves so much more, I feel. She is such a wonderful person. As parasitic multi-millionaires go, she is definitely one of the best. She stood up to Mad Maggie on apartheid. She is skittish and funny, the only member of her family with her wits about her and something like a brain. Former Australian Prime Minister Bob Hawk tells a good story. He was having an audience at Buck House one day, just him and the queen, and a couple of those fat little corgi dogs that should be hollowed out and turned into slippers. Midway through the conversation, one of the corgis suddenly farts loudly. "Oh my God" Hawk says, "the corgis." The queen stares at him for a moment. She takes a sip of her dry sherry. "Who else?" she replies.

The breakup of Charles and Diana's marriage must have been hard to take. John Major had to announce it to the House of Commons, and hearing him pompously intone in his nerdy little voice "their highnesses are still very fond of each other"- with the assembled sycophants all nodding and going "hear, hear" — was absolutely bizarre. In the jargon of psychotherapy there is a concept called denial. This is where you refuse to acknowledge things which you find too painful. My sister Eimear often tells me that I am "living in denial," to which I always reply "oh no I'm not." But John Major is certainly living in denial. John Major needs to talk to my sister Eimear. She would sort him out.

Chaz's status as future head of the Church of England will be unaffected, Major said. But I'm afraid the C of E simply does not want the head honcho to be running around town with leggy supermodels on his arm. Prince Charles is barking anyway. He is quite simply several chevrolets short of a funeral. He is more comfortable talking to his trees than his family, and that is the only sane thing you can say about him.

Princess Diana might be Queen one day, we are told. Yeah, right, and monkeys might fly out of my butt. Don't get me wrong now. I would certainly be in favour of this. After all, any royal court ruled by Princess Di is going to be made up of disco dancing surfing champions and former members of Duran Duran. If anything will finish off the Royals for ever, it is the notion of Princess Diana being a Queen.

The Royal family are widely regarded as clowns now. The only one of them people like is Princess Anne, and that's just because she looks good in jodhpurs and she's been on "A Question of Sport" a few times. John Major was wrong when he said he was expressing the sympathy of the whole country on the breakup of the fairytale marriage. People simply do not care any more.

I only saw the Queen once in all my years living in London. I was walking down the street one day, when somebody told me she was going to turn up at her bank just across the way at any minute. There was a large crowd waiting on the pavement, as she stepped out of the limo. But nobody cheered. There was silence. She took a few steps towards the crowd, thinking that they just hadn't recognised her. Still nobody applauded. They stood and watched, in silence. I couldn't believe it.

A newspaper report the next day tried to describe the look on her face, as she turned and went into the bank. But it didn't get it right.

I was there, and I saw it. It was a look of blank fear. *The Sun* quoted a passer-by. "I just saw a crowd and stopped," he said. "If I'd known it was the Queen I wouldn't have bothered."

It was during my years in London that even the *Sun*-readers decided they didn't want the Queen any more. The castle really was burning down.

It was a pretty interesting time to live over there, because the Queen wasn't the only Londoner having problems. A few nights after the day I saw her, I was on my way home from a party, when a strange and memorable thing happened to me. I was standing on the platform at Charing Cross Station when I saw a young man that I thought I recognised. He reminded me of my brother, actually. He had the same build, the same haircut. I approached this young man. I was curious about him. I got up very close beside him. Then I could see that his clothes were shabby. His face was grey, the colour of porridge. I knew then that he was not my brother. I knew he was a homeless person.

Suddenly he fell forwards onto the platform, his arms flailing. People did nothing at all about this. People raised their newspapers to their eyes. He seemed to roll forwards a little, so that he almost fell down onto the track. After a moment, two young women approached him. I went to help them get him up on his feet. We got him up, and he started moaning with pain. We brought him out to the street, and then the two women went away.

I gave him some money for a cup of tea. I wanted to get away from him, I am ashamed to say. I wanted him to take the money and leave me alone, but he looked up at me then. "Would you be able to come with me?" he said. He was Irish. He just wanted someone to go for a cup of tea with him.

We walked up Saint Martin's Lane to a late night coffee place near Leicester Square. We got some tea, and he ate a bit of soggy toast. He had a very bad cough. He kept wincing in pain whenever he coughed. He was shaking badly.

He was from Athlone, he said. He'd had a bad row with his father. His mother had run off somewhere, and his father's girlfriend had moved into the house, and there had been rows. He had been beaten up by his father, and he'd had to get away. He hadn't been in London for long.

We talked a bit about Irish music. He liked the band Something Happens, he told me, he had seen them play a few times. He kept shuddering and shaking and coughing. He hadn't eaten anything at all in a few days, he said.

He asked me what I did for a living, and I told him I wrote books, and that sometimes I wrote for newspapers. Which ones?, he wanted to know. *The Sunday Tribune* was one, I said. He nodded. He'd sometimes read *The Sunday Tribune*, he told me, and he liked it. He took another sip of the hot tea, and his hands trembled again. Did I know Paul Kimmage, *The Sunday Tribune* sports reporter? No, I told him, I didn't. That was a pity, he said. Paul Kimmage wrote great articles in *The Sunday Tribune*.

I tried to ask him about his life in London. It was the loneliness that would get you, he said, rather than the cold or the hunger. It wasn't the begging, or the way you had to shit into plastic bags, because they wouldn't even let you into the pubs to use the toilet. It was waking up in a doorway at six in the morning, freezing cold, and knowing that you wouldn't talk to a single person all day long. He said it was a terrible thing to wake up by yourself, in your filthy clothes, and to know you'd have to walk around all day, until it was time to go to sleep in a doorway again.

I tried to give him more money, but he didn't want to take it. I insisted, and in the end he took it. Then a terrible thing happened. Suddenly, his face crumpled up and he started to cry. He started to sob, the way a child would. His face screwed up and he hung his head and wept. I put my hand on the back of his wrist and he grabbed my hand and squeezed it hard, still crying, without looking at me. I was very close to crying myself. He said he just didn't know what he was going to do. He kept looking around himself, with a look of utter confusion and fear in his face. "I'm only hanging on by my laces," he kept saying. Hanging on by my laces. He was about the same age as me. He was absolutely despairing.

Our so-called leaders should know that any night of the week you will find young people from every corner of our country, over in

London, all hanging on by their laces in a city where they're treated like scum. They are hungry and cold. They have absolutely nothing. Our political leaders should think a bit about that, while they're discussing their beautiful options with each other.

He was from Athlone, he said. His second name was Foley. He asked me, next time I wrote anything in *The Sunday Tribune*, to put in the paper that he was alright, that he was making out OK in London, and that he said hello to anyone in Ireland who knew him.

It wasn't the only time I met homeless people in London. I should tell you that I had spent a little time in New York one Summer, and there were so many homeless people in that city that competition had set in, and they had developed remarkable strategies for extracting assistance from the public.

One day as I was moseying down Bleeker Street in downtown Manhattan, honest to God, a homeless man wearing nothing but his underpants and a pair of boxing boots jumped out in front of me, tapped me on the shoulder and pointed up at the sky. "Jeez, dude," he cried, breathily, "check that *out*." "What?," I said. He nudged me hard in the ribs. "*Look*," he insisted. "Look up, man. Is it a bird? Is it a plane?"

"I don't know," I said. He pulled a lipstick out of his trunks, quickly scrawled a large "S" on his chest, then held out his hand to me, beaming. "No, it's Superwino, man! Now gimme a greenback."

Over in London, the poor were not quite as creative, although their plight was just as scandalous. (In London, for example, homeless people are twenty times more likely to be sexually assaulted or murdered than other members of the public.)

One night, anyway, I went to review "Sunset Boulevard" for *The Sunday Tribune*. The theatre is in the Strand, an opulent part of the city, and the audience seemed to be very rich. Certainly, there was a long line of limos outside, the like of which you would not even see in Charlie Haughey's driveway. And after the play, as the limos roared off, the homeless people were huddled in the doorways all along the Strand, wrapping themselves in newspapers and polythene bags, trying to stay out of the rain.

I was just wandering along the street by myself, trying to think of what I would say about "Sunset Boulevard" in the paper the next Sunday when a middle-aged woman came up to me with a baby in her arms. She handed me a note. "I am refugee of Bosnia. Help me. All my family are killed in Sarajevo."

Well, I felt sorry for this woman. Anyone who lives in London gets to know pretty quickly when people really are poor. There's a desperation in the face, an awful darkness behind the eyes. It's a thing actors never get right. When people are utterly poor they do not look excited. They look hopeless and frightened and half-dead, the way this unfortunate woman looked.

I patted my pockets furiously but had no change. I had spent every last bob on purchasing a large gin and tonic at half time. With anything written by Andrew Lloyd Webber, I find, you do tend to need chemical stimulation if you want to last until the final curtain. I was embarrassed that I couldn't help. I apologised and went to walk on. She reached into her pocket and handed me another note. "I have nowhere to sleep and my child is hungry."

I didn't know what to do. So I told her about this hostel I knew for homeless people, where a girl I knew used to work. She didn't seem to get what I was saying, although gradually I formed the odd impression that she did understand, but was pretending not to. I took out a pen and drew a map for her, on the back of her note, indicating the whereabouts of this hostel. And I walked on.

The Bosnian woman began to walk alongside me, staring at me all the time. As I quickened my pace, she broke into a trot. I began to get a little uptight. And she began to run along beside me then, panting and coughing, chattering away in what I presumed was the Bosnian language. Suddenly, she thrust out her hand and grabbed my lapel. "Look," I said. "I'd love to help you but I really have no money. I'm sorry." And then a strange thing happened. She stepped back from me, this Bosnian lady, and put one hand on her hip. Her upper lip curled into a sneer. "Ah would you fuck off with yourself," she exclaimed, "sure you're only a fucker anyway." A telling moment.

She was from Dublin, this poor woman. But she was pretending to be a Bosnian refugee, so that she could beg enough money to eat.

Thus, the homeless were having to develop their thespian skills, on the streets of John Major's London. And people say the Tories don't do enough to encourage private initiative.

Even though I like being back in Dublin these days, I still go to London a lot. In fact, I passed through again just recently on my way home from holidays in Spain. The last weekend of the holliers was a bit of a *lost* weekend, I must admit. All I remember is sauntering out into the Barcelona streets on a Friday night at seven o'clock for a quick half a shandy and waking up face down in the gutter on Monday morning with my shirt pocket full of vomit — mine, I hope — , my plane ticket between my teeth, my trousers round my ankles, my wallet empty as the Taoiseach's brain and the words "Adios Bambino" written in scarlet lipstick across the front of my spectacles.

I got to Heathrow on a Monday afternoon and immediately rang a taxi, a shameless extravagance, yes, but I was so laden down with plastic sombreros, wind-up flamenco dancers and electronically clacking maracas that I felt the tube was not an option. It was a bank holiday in Blighty, so taxis were scarce. When the driver finally arrived I walked towards him, clutching the aforementioned souvenirs, whistling "Una Paloma Blanca" and proudly flaunting my extra large I LOVE THE COSTA DEL SOL T shirt. "Allo Mate," he said, "where you fackin' bin then?"

"Swaziland," I said.

The driver was in a sociable mood. As we pulled out of Heathrow he flipped an Elvis Presley cassette into his tape machine and smiled at me in the mirror as he joined in on the chorus.

You ainna nuthin but a houn dawg

Cryin awla time

You ainna nuthin but a houn dawg

Cryin awla time

You ainna never caught a rabbi

And you ainna no frind a mine

He glanced at me then, with a grin so cheesy that you could have melted it down and spread it on toast. "Sunbathe, didya?" he said, "in Switzerland?"

"Yes," I said, removing my earplugs.

"Not very farking brown, are ya?," he said. "You're not even fackin' pink, mate."

"Only politically," I said.

"Did you get sand up ya bum?" he enquired.

"Sorry?"

"Sand up the ole Khyber Pass," he said, "When you wuz on the ole beach?"

"No," I said. "I don't think so."

"HAHAHARR," he tittered, "Fackin' awful tha' is, when you get sand up yore aws, innit?"

I was more than happy to concede that this would be a very distressing turn of events, yes.

"I got sand up my aws on Sat'day," he confided. "Went to Margate with the ball and chain. My jaxi is really givin' me gyp as it 'appens, knowwaramean?"

"Oh, is it really?" I said. "How very sad."

Crossing the Thames at Vauxhall Bridge we passed a crowd of skinheads who seemed to be spending the bank holiday having some kind of mass meeting. Many of them were wearing swastikas. As we sped past, some of them waved at us and did Nazi salutes. Others had huge snarling dogs on lengths of twine.

I sat back and peered at the unrolling bombsite that is South East London. I had just returned from a country whose history had been blighted by forty years of fascist dictatorship. I thought about the bloody hatred this had brought to Spain. Yet here were these dribbling cockney meatheads in their brand new doc martens, slapping each other on their lederhosen-enclosed bottoms, waving their arms in the air and chanting about the Farverland. The whole shagging shooting gallery of them had the combined intelligence quotient of a hamburger.

But it's serious now, what's going on in London. Statistics show that one in every three young men has a criminal record, and, be assured, I am not talking about "Tubular Bells" by Mike Oldfield. The teenagers on my street are carrying knives and wearing Hitler

T-shirts. Fascist chic. When I was fifteen, if you had an Elvis Costello tape or a skateboard you were the coolest thing since the Antarctic Ocean. But to be cool in South London these days you have to carry a machete. It was funny to be back. It was odd. I was glad I wasn't staying too long.

It is a cliché that violence breeds violence, but when you live in England for any length of time you can see why people say that. Societies reap what they sow, and in a country where a Prime Minister could proudly proclaim that there was no such thing as society any more, it was clear that one day things were going to fall completely apart. One warm Friday afternoon, in a quiet shopping centre in Bootle, on Merseyside, they did just that.

I lived in England for seven years, and in that time nothing I can remember ever shocked people the way the murder of two-year-old James Bulger shocked them.

It was something to do with the unspeakable helplessness of that child's situation. It was something to do with those video photographs of the boy being led to his death by people he thought he could trust. It was almost unbearable. We felt heartbroken for the poor child and his parents. Yet there were other reasons why this killing shocked people so utterly. It had to do with the deepest primal fears in all of us. It plunged us back into a nightmare world, where the very people who want to guide us through the forest turn out to be the wolves who destroy us. Somehow we carry this dread into adulthood. And then the fear is made flesh by the blurred images of a child in a shopping centre on a Friday afternoon in Liverpool. It was so ordinary, and so devastating.

We didn't have to be told what his mother must have felt like, because somehow we knew. We didn't even have to be told what the poor child must have experienced, because we remembered how it felt to be lost and afraid ourselves, no matter how briefly, when we were children. That was the point about poor James Bulger. In some way, that child was all of us. I don't have children myself, but each time I saw those photos, I thought about my five-year-old nephews. I thought about the children of friends and colleagues. I kept thinking the obscene thought, how would I have felt, if this dreadful thing had happened to one of them? I felt cheapened and sick that I'd been made to think like that.

There were new calls for the death penalty. The liberal press argued that this solves nothing, that it isn't a deterrent, that it springs from a desire for revenge. Personally, I'm opposed to the death penalty too. I think the price we pay for our freedom is the toleration of the intolerable. Civilised societies are predicated on the humane notion that people are basically good, that they will usually act in civilised ways, that even when they do not, they will be treated with decency. That's how I feel.

But if James Bulger had been my son, I'm not so sure I would have felt like that. I'm sorry, but I know that if he'd been my son, I would have wanted the person who had done this thing to be killed. Worse, I think I would have wanted to pull the trigger or squeeze the syringe or press the button myself. Worse still, I think I would have wanted this person to feel fear, and helplessness and pain first, and that then, only when he was as terrified as that child must have been, would I have wanted him to be killed. I'm not even the tiniest bit proud of this. But I'm just telling you honestly, because maybe it shows how deeply we are all degraded by human cruelty. How, in England, in those terrible weeks after that child died, we were all so easily sucked into instincts that were barbaric. This happened and in one instant we were back in the jungle. There were mobs wandering the streets of Liverpool, chanting "murderer" at innocent children. Only in time did we see that we had to resist. There was no other choice. The poet Auden wrote "we must love one another or die." He understood the terrible dilemma of human experience, that we must triumph over evil by not becoming evil ourselves.

I was in Nicaragua once, and I met a man who had been tortured. He had been beaten, whipped, castrated, slowly, ruthlessly, logically broken down. After a time, he told me, he had become an entertainment to his torturers. That was the word he used. An entertainment. They would delight in discovering new ways to hurt him. Following the Sandanista revolution this man became a government official. He could have easily arranged for his tormentors to be killed, but he did not do this. He told me that his vengeance had been to forgive them. He summoned them, one by one, and he forgave them, and then he let them go back to jail. I couldn't understand it then. To be honest, I still can't, not fully. But I know that man was right to do what he did. He was a Marxist, an atheist, a human being. And he knew that remaining human sometimes means digging down to that part of us that still cries out for decency, even when the world seems to be falling apart around us.

The killing of James Bulger was one of those terrible times.

But there were other terrible times too, during those years in London. The IRA regularly planted bombs in the city, and friends often told me how difficult they felt it was to be Irish in London at times like that. I was in an odd position, I suppose, because being a writer I spent most of my time at home. I didn't have an office to go to every day, so I would sometimes not be exposed to the reactions my friends experienced. But they kept telling me how the IRA made them feel ashamed. They said it was no wonder the British hated the Irish. You couldn't really blame them, they would say, it was all because of the Provos. But I was never so sure about this.

One thing is that I have enough shame for my own actions, thank you very much, without worrying about those of the IRA. But another very important thing to know about many British people is that they do not like foreigners very much. They do not even like each other very much, if the truth be known. The Scots hate the English. People from the South hate people from the North. But the one thing that really unites the disunited kingdom is the notion that foreigners are basically naff. A tory minister was asked recently about Turkey's application to join the EEC. "Well, let's face it," he sniffed. "They're not really, are they?"

The English very frequently find foreigners "not really." Alternatively, they find foreigners very funny. In Britain, if you don't understand something, you humourise your ignorance. This can reach surreal proportions. On BBC television there is a hugely successful show called "Allo Allo." It is a comedy about the nazi invasion of France. While the synagogues of Europe burn once again, it must take a truly spectacular objectivity to find fascism and anti-semitism funny.

I remember an incident that happened to me while I was living in South East London. My sister Eimear, who is a painter, had an opening of an exhibition of her paintings in Dublin one Friday night. I couldn't get home for the party, so the day before I went to the florist's shop in Lewisham, where I lived. I wanted to send Eimear a bunch of flowers, as a congratulations.

Now the woman who runs this shop is a Cockney, and I'm afraid Cockneys just bring out the worst in me. It is wrong, it is prejudiced, I know, and I am working on it, but I have to tell you honestly that as far as I'm concerned, Cockneys should be just rounded up and made to live on an island somewhere. Dublin had Joyce. Paris had Sartre. This is a culture whose main contribution to the world has been "My old Man's A Dustman."

"Allo darlink," the florist leered, "awight?" She had a face like a well-spanked arse, and an accent that would have made Bob Hoskins sound like the Queen Mother.

"I'd like a bunch of flowers please," I said.

"OOOh yew 'ave sarch a larvely voice, Dearie," she said. "Yew've made me come over awl fanny."

"Thank you" I replied.

"I don't moind foreigners when they 'ave noice voices," she reassured, "like, when yew can undestaand 'em." She leaned closer to me, then. "Not like those farkin' Pakki bastards," she grinned.

"What?" I said.

"Yew know," she cackled, "them nig nogs. Now ah'm not a racialist or anyfink, bur I mean, reaaally, they come over 'ere and they caan't even spaik the farking language, can vey?"

Needless to say, I cancelled the flowers. I felt angry and enraged, I really did. I had friends who were Pakistani, and I knew many of the local Pakistani shopkeepers, and a gentler kinder group of people you couldn't meet anywhere in the world. I tried to put what the vicious old bat had said down to experience. But later that day I had a meeting with the features editor of a magazine. He told me about a piece he had published recently on the black sprinter, Linford Christie. "Yes," his boss had sighed, when he'd seen it, "the article is OK, but really, shouldn't we have had someone British?"

Linford Christie is a world champion who has won gold medals for Britain. But Linford Christie, because of the colour of his skin, is also considered "not really."

Each year, there are between sixteen and twenty racist murders in London. This year there were well over two thousand race attacks. *Searchlight* magazine has documented the neo-nazis who are currently working in branches of the British civil service.

I know Irish people working in England who get racist abuse every day. An Irish man I know recently asked his boss for a reference. The reference came back the next day saying "this is to certify that X's use of semtex is excellent, and he makes the best letter bomb in London." But it's all a larf, you see. Only a giggle, so shut up and take it, Paddy. Laughter, in Britain, has always played a vital role in the cultural legitimisation of hate.

But the Irish in London should not take it any more. Our grandfathers and uncles built that city. We are as entitled to be there as the children of the black men and women who worked beside them. We have been demonised for long enough. Before, it was because we were drunken fools. Now it's because we're killers. It is time that those of us who don't support the terrorists put a few of the facts on record.

Britain created the Irish problem. Britain sustained it. Britain continues to be one of the most ignorant and xenophobic societies on the face of the earth, and we should keep telling them that until they get the message.

Not that I'm a racist or anything. Some of my best friends are English actually. It's just that sometimes, I have to confess, I just don't know if I'd want my daughter to marry one. (That's a joke, by the way. I don't actually *have* a daughter.)

It is not that the English don't have their good points. They do indeed. Most of them are moderate and tolerant. They can even be polite and diplomatic when they want to be. Witness, for instance, their weird attitude to swear words. The English understand the power of the curse very well, and most of them swear occasionally, in private. But they really don't think swear words should be used in the media. They tend to have strong feelings about it.

I remember well the Sunday morning in London when BBC radio reported in shocked tones that John Major had "used an unparliamentary word" to describe some of his colleagues. The entire nation must have wondered what this unspeakable word was. In fact, Mr Major had merely said that three members of his cabinet were "bastards." Well, of course, the next question that sprang to mind was which three? Because it was with some difficulty that we might have picked out just three "bastards" from such an assembly of unbridled and irredeemable illegitimacy.

But Major had legitimised the word "bastard." All through the following week, solemn newsreaders and glinting-eyed reporters intoned the word into cameras, trying hard not to snigger. It was suddenly OK to say "bastard." It was Prime Ministerial. Mrs Thatcher's former secretary, Bernard Ingham appeared on the news and tantalised the horrified public when he revealed that even that demure and gracious lady's language had been "pretty robust" on occasions.

By the following Thursday, more tales of Major's scatological outpourings were filtering through. Radio 4's *Today* programme reported coyly that the PM had used "a well-known Anglo-Saxon word" in an off-the-record conversation with Jonathan Dimbleby. "Fuck" they simply meant, a word which, incidentally, is not Anglo-Saxon, but which is so powerful that it cannot be mentioned over the airwaves, even when a Prime Minister has uttered it.

This seems to me a terrible pity, a sad impoverishment of political life. We are lucky that Irish politics have been greatly, if sadly too occasionally, coloured by the use of such sturdy and frank language. Who can forget Mr Charles Haughey's delightful 1985 interview with *Hot Press* magazine? It was more full of obscenity than a play by David Mamet. There were "one or two fuckers" Mr Haughey confided, who he would like "to throw over a cliff."

A number of American leaders have similarly shot from the hip. President Roosevelt said famously of the pro-yankee Nicaraguan dictator, Anastasio Somoza, "he may be a son of a bitch, but he's our son of a bitch." And on one occasion John Major was quoted as concurring with the shrewd adage of Lyndon Johnson that it was better to have one's political foes "inside the tent and pissing out, rather than outside the tent and pissing in."

But perhaps the king of Prime Ministerial rudeness is the Australian, Paul Keating. His cabinet meetings are always linguistically exotic occasions. "Now listen mate," he once said, to John Browne, Sports Minister, who was proposing a 110 per cent tax deduction for contributors to a foundation, "you're not getting 110 per cent. You can forget it. This is a fucking Boulevard Hotel special, this is. I go out for a piss and they pull this one on me. Well that's the last time I leave you alone. From now on I'm sticking to you like shit to a blanket." In parliament, Mr Keating has been similarly enthusiastic. "You stupid foul-mouthed grub," he once bellowed at opposition member Wilson Tuckey — whose name sounds obscene enough in itself — "shut up! Sit down and shut up, you pig!"

"You fraud," he once accused another member, "you disgraceful, disgusting fraud." The speaker of the house promptly intervened, saying "The Prime Minister must withdraw those unparliamentary remarks." Keating retorted, "of course I will now withdraw them. 'Disgusting' is not unparliamentary, you clown."

There was a lot of fuss about this in Australia but I really do not know why. We don't like it when politicians use mystifying jargon words that the rest of us don't understand. In that context, surely we don't have the right to expect them not to use clear and appropriate words that the rest of us use quite often. Fair play to Mr Major, I remember thinking that day in London. He may be making a b****x of the economy, the little ****, but he's f*****g-well advanced the cause of the English language.

But I was often to reflect on the fact that words really can get you into trouble in England. I found this out quite forcefully one morning while researching an article on the Irish prisoner Frank Johnson, who is currently serving a murder sentence in a Kent prison for a crime he says he did not commit. I was interested in Frank's case, and I wanted to find out more about it. The resulting telephone conversation went as follows:

BRRRRRRRRRR. Ring ring. Ring ring.

Hello? Is that directory enquiries?

Yes? Which number?

I'm looking for Liberty please.

Aren't we all sir?

No. I mean, Liberty, the civil rights group. They're like Amnesty International, you know? They deal with miscarriages of justice.

Oh right. Just hold on, sir. I'll look it up for you.

Thanks.

Hmmmm. In London, are they?

Yes, they are.

Ah yes, here it is. Just hold on.

Electronic voice: The number you require is 071 734 1234.

Brrrrrrr. Ring ring. Ring ring.

Hello?

Hello, is that Liberty?

Yes, it is.

Hello, my name is Joe O'Connor, and I write a weekly column for a newspaper in Ireland.

Oh yes?

It's called *The Sunday Tribune*.

(Nervous titter) *I've never heard of it.*

No. Well, you see, I'm interested in writing about this guy, Frank Johnson. He's Irish and he's in jail for a murder he says he didn't do.

Heavens, I see.

He says he was framed by the police.

Oh dear, does he?

Yes, he does. He's been in jail for seventeen years now and there's a campaign getting going for his release.

Oh, that's nice.

Yes. One of the Birmingham Six is involved.

Oh that's good, isn't it? There's really too much of that sort of thing these days. It's awful really, when you think.

Yes, it is.

Irish, is he?

Yes, he is.

Well, they don't get a fair trial, do they. It's awful. The poor man. What did you say his name was, Joe?

Frank Johnson.

The poor man.

Yes. Anyway, do you think I could speak to someone about his case?

(Anxious pause) *Ermm..whom did you have in mind?*

The person who's in charge of his case there.

Beg pardon? Do you mean here?

Well yes, you see I read that Liberty was taking an interest in his case.

Are we? Are we really?

Yes. It was mentioned in an article in *The Guardian*.

Was it?

Yes it was. Duncan Campbell wrote an article about it.

Duncan?

Duncan Campbell. The investigative journalist. He said you were handling his case.

Are you sure, Joe?

Yes, I am.

You read that Liberty was taking an interest in his case?

I did, yeah.

I haven't heard anything about that.

Well, could I speak to your press officer maybe?

Alright then, hold on a mo?

OK, thanks.

(Tinny electronic version of "Für Elise," teedle-eedle eedle eedle-um, dee deedle *dum*, dee deedle *dum*, dee dee dee *dum*, dee dee dee *dum*, dee dee dee *dum*, dee dee dee *dum*..)

Hello? Can I help you?

Yes. My name is Joe O'Connor and I write this column every week for *The Sunday Tribune* newspaper in Ireland. I was just saying to your colleague that I wanted to find out a little more about the case of Frank Johnson. He's serving a life sentence at Swaleside Prison in Kent for a murder that he didn't do. I was wondering if you could give me a quote about it?

Er..Well, Joe, I don't really know.

Just something small would do.

Well, errm, I suppose, if he's innocent, as you say, let's all hope he's released soon.

And I could quote that, could I?

Well, I suppose so, yes. I mean, I don't really know. I'd have to check with my boss. Could you phone back later today? He's at a conference.

Don't you know the case I mean?

Er..not really, Joe no.

No?

I can't say I do, really, no.

This is Liberty, isn't it?

Yes.

Liberty. The civil rights group?

(Pregnant pause)

Well, no Joe. This is Liberty. The department store in Regent Street.

(Even more pregnant pause)

I think you have a wrong number, Joe.

(Pause so pregnant it's about to give birth to quads)

Oh, right then. Sorry.

Thank you for calling anyway, Joe.

I'm sorry. God, this is embarrassing.

(Relieved giggle) *Oh that's alright, Joe. Always happy to help the press here at Liberty.*

In England, take note, you always have to very careful about what you say, and how you say it.

The day before I came home to live in Ireland again, after seven years, I suppose I was feeling a little tender. For all its many faults, I loved London. For me, it had been a place of escape, of hard work and great fun, of mainly generous people, of good friends, of professional colleagues who had done nothing but help me, of racial mix and almost magical glamour. There were so many memories, some awful, but most of them unforgettably wonderful. I was walking up and down Lewisham High Street, feeling moody and speculative, when I saw a sign for a karaoke bar.

It's a funny thing, but the Irish need very little encouragement to sing in public. The English, however, need all the latest in international technology.

If ever we needed proof of the cruelty of the Japanese nation, surely we need look no further than the pursuit of karaoke singing. And yet the English have taken to karaoke, as my friend and publisher Dermot Bolger would say, like Hollywood Indians to whisky. It's weird. But karaoke is as popular over in Blighty as terminal boredom is in Portlaoise.

According to the *Concise Oxford Encyclopedia*, (eds. Sacho, Vanzetti and Drabble, 1979) the word "karaoke" is actually derived from two quite obscure 14th Century Japanese words, "karao," meaning "a young male singer with dreadful acne," and "oke," meaning "wearing white socks."

Anyway, I was pondering all this while passing my local pub that last afternoon in London, when my attention was drawn to a large rudimentary notice in the window. "KARAOKE LUNCHTIME SPECIAL!!, CHEAP NOSH!!! ALL DRINKS 80p!!! IT'S BLOODY MAD!!!!." Well, I was immediately tempted. I thought that anyone who could put that number of exclamation marks on a poster had to be offering something pretty exotic.

I entered the establishment with bated breath. The place looked like the lower deck of a coffin ship. People were jammed into the kip in a manner that would have made sardines weep with sympathy. There was a chubby little fellow with a pony-tail on the karaoke stage at the back. If the enthusiastic cries of "garn, Keith, *garn*, ya fat farking bawstidd," were anything to go by, the gentleman was something of a local hero. He was wearing a pair of jeans at least seven sizes too small, with the result that his monstrous pink buttocks were being forced upwards, and were protruding above his waistline like tumescent pillows. ("The Dagenham smile" this phenomenon is called, on London building sites.) He had on a shirt so lurid that at first I thought he had vomited fifteen pints of assorted fruit juices over himself. Keith shimmied up and down the stage, undulating his ball-alley of a backside, waving a pint of lager in the air, singing *"Don't You Want Me, Baby?, Don't You Want Me, Oh?"* I gazed up at him. The answer to his question, I felt, was a categorical "Not really, thank you."

I went to the bar and got a drink. Half way through the second verse Keith put down his microphone. The crowd roared. I began to feel nervous. Keith opened his shirt, licking his lips. He then lifted out his enormous breasts, fingering his nipples, pouting, still singing. He picked up the microphone again, wedged it firmly between his ample mammaries, squeezing them tightly together so that the flesh actually gripped onto the microphone. He bowed his head and continued to sing, unperturbed by the ensuing round of frantic applause. You don't see feats of such intelligence and skill in South London just any day of the week.

A fellow turned to me, nodding in the direction of the stage. "Farking maad," he grinned. "Maad fat funking bawstidd, innee?" I concurred that this indeed seemed to be the case, yes. My new friend's lower lip curled up over his top one, sucking away a moustache of beerfroth. "Ere, mate?" he hissed, blearily. "You want an E?"

"What?" I said. "An ecstasy?" he explained. "Twenty nicker?"

"Ah, no," I replied. "I feel ecstatic enough already, thanks."

He nodded and shrugged, gaping back towards the stage. "Garn, Keith, *garn*," he cried. "Get yore *thruppenny bits* out!" He turned again. "Ere," he smiled. "You know what else 'e docs?"

"No," I said, "what?" He leaned towards me, looking impressed.

"He only bleeding farts the tune of 'God Save The Queen'", he whispered. "'E did it a few minutes ago an' all. *Hur hur hurr*. Pity you missed it. Was really farking fanny."

I sighed deeply and finished my drink, glancing back up at the stage. Keith was spilling lager over his hirsute saucer-sized nipples now, then raising them to his lips and sucking them. The crowd was going crazy. There were about a hundred young people in this pub, all cheering, clapping, absolutely plastered, high on ecstasy, singing karaoke songs and watching one another fart the national anthem. It was the middle of Friday afternoon.

As I left the pub and closed the door behind me, I realised I was kind of glad I was coming home to Ireland. Sometimes, you see, when I lived over in London, I couldn't help getting the feeling that England was headed for very big trouble.

Part III: Living In A Black And White World

Outside the marble and chrome entrance to the Savoy Theatre it looks like the Rolling Stones have just trundled into town. The queue for the last few tickets is stretching down the pavement and spilling over into The Strand so that the traffic is beginning to jam. Car horns blare. A lorry driver reaches his fist through his window and shakes it, shouting.

All along the street, clipboard-wielding reporters are jabbering into television cameras. Scores of photographers are milling around the theatre door. Men in windcheater jackets and hushpuppies are shuffling up and down selling T-shirts and posters. One of the posters has a large union jack, a cartoon image of Nigel Short with his foot crushing Gary Kasparov's throat, and a slogan that says "THERE'LL ALWAYS BE AN ENGLAND."

Inside the theatre, almost all the seats are full. Most of the audience are young or middle-aged men. There are hardly any women. Some of the men have stacks of fat books about chess, laptop chess computers, magnetic chess sets, binoculars, stop-watches, chess clocks. They show each other their paraphernalia. One man explains how his computer uses the same software programme as Kasparov's, how his wife nearly chucked him out of the house when he told her how much it had cost, but how it was worth it. And although each seat has a headphone set built into it, over which an in-house commentary will be broadcast, a man in the next row has brought a miniature television set so that he can watch live coverage of the match on Channel Four.

White light glows from the elegant stage. There are two large computer-generated chessboards on the wall at the back, and the floor of the stage is tiled in black and white so that it too looks like a chessboard. At the front there is a table and two chairs. Short has chosen a 19th century walnut chair from Simpsons club. Kasparov insisted on a modern steel and leather effort that would not look out of place on the bridge of the Starship Enterprise. The table has a chess set laid out on it, two notepads, and a chess clock with two faces.

The clock is important. Championship chess is played not just against an opponent but against time also. Each player has an allotment of two hours. When he makes a move he presses a button on his own clock, which stops it, and automatically starts that of his opponent. Each player must make forty moves in two hours. If he fails to do this, a small flag attached to his clock drops and he loses the game, regardless of how many pieces he has lost or gained.

The lights go down suddenly and there is a burst of excited cheering from the audience. Nigel Short can be seen pacing up and down in the wings. Photographers flood in to the stalls. Grandmaster Raymond Keane comes on and announces the challenger. There is tumultuous applause.

The greatest player in the history of British chess wanders onto the stage with a diffident beam on his face. He is slim, lanky. awkward in his movements. He looks as though he has just woken up, so bewildered is his stare. He has on wire-rimmed glasses, a grey suit, a grey shirt, a grey tie. He looks like a Tory MP. He grins and sits down at the table, stretches his neck.

The master of ceremonies announces Gary Kasparov. The applause is polite and restrained. The champion bounds on with the exuberance of a puppy in a TV commercial. He is a tall handsome man. His white suit is smartly cut. He shakes hands with Keane and then, briefly, with Short, whose face is set in a scowl. Kasparov is a bundle of nervous energy as the two players pose for the cameras. His fingers pluck at the sleeves of his jacket, run around his shirt collar as the flashbulbs click. Nigel grins.

Both players have been preparing for months, with the dogged commitment of heavyweight prizefighters. In interviews, Short has stressed the importance of his physical fitness. He has been swimming and working out in the gym every day. Kasparov has been weightlifting, jogging, boxing, eating a high protein diet. His dinner consists of a large portion of smoked salmon followed by two steaks.

The pre-match media battle has been vicious. Each player has vigorously rubbished his opponent at every opportunity. Kasparov has predicted a quick humiliating defeat for the Englishman. Short has accused Kasparov of being a former member of the Communist

Party, of being a creature of the Soviet regime, of being unrespected by his chess colleagues. "It's no secret that I just don't like the guy," he said recently. "The trouble with Kasparov is that he just didn't get enough spanks as a child."

The editor of Rupert Murdoch's *Times* newspaper — the event's sponsor — makes the first move for Kasparov. Short replies. They each move out central pawns, then knights, in a standard opening. Kasparov brings out his bishop next and Short advances another pawn. Short tends to move quickly. He then folds his arms and stares away from the board, towards the back of the stage. He's refusing to make any eye contact with Kasparov, refusing even to pay him the credit of looking concerned about what the champion might do. Kasparov is unperturbed. He takes more time to make his moves. He purses his lips, stares at the pieces. On his fifth move, Kasparov castles, moving his king into safety. Short castles shortly afterwards, on his seventh move, and Kasparov looks suddenly thrown. It's an unexpected ploy. Kasparov declines the main gambit line and moves out another pawn to gain a small but important advantage. Short is forced on the defensive. He has no choice but to guard the weakened pawns on his queen's side. Kasparov tries to build an attack.

Unlike most grand masters, the world champion makes no attempt to hide his feelings. His face often twists up into frustration and annoyance. He clenches his fingers, gnaws his lip. You can almost hear the cogs rotating in his head. Short has deftly closed off his left flank now, and the quick defeat predicted by Kasparov is obviously not going to happen. The game settles into a defensive and closely manoeuvred rhythm. Pieces are moved around in the centre of the board. Pawns are advanced, tentatively staking out territory. Twenty five minutes in, Kasparov moves his queen's pawn.

The audience are having difficulty getting their headphones to work properly. The volume is way too loud, and the commentary can clearly be heard echoing around the auditorium. The in-theatre commentator refers to Kasparov as "Kazza," prompting a communal guffaw from the audience. The players look up and glare.

People nudge each other. The auditorium settles into silence. You can hear the clocks on the stage ticking out the time, but apart from that there is no sound except for the rustling as some of the crowd leaf through their chess books. If you were to move a cough sweet from one molar to another the sound would seem like a volley of rifle fire. After the first hour, all the pieces are still in play.

By move fifteen the game is concentrated around the centre of the board once again, Short continuing to move with a brisk efficiency, Kasparov still seeming the more thoughtful of the two. A flurry of aggressive activity follows and by move seventeen all four knights are taken. But it's a defensive game. It's careful, studied. The players are feeling each other out, using the hundreds of hours of home preparation to try to locate tactical flaws. They move, hit the button on their clocks, write down the details of the move in their notebooks. The in-seat chess computer is predicting a probable draw.

Half way through, the game is finely balanced. The centre of the board is blocked and each player's weaknesses are roughly evening out. But then slowly, inexorably, the contest seems to slide towards Kasparov. He's eased his queen and his castle into strong positions. Short is getting rattled. He starts to take more time with his moves. His head bobs. Kasparov seems to find the waiting unbearable. While Short is considering his strategy, the champion sits slumped forward with his hands over his ears as though trying to block out some dreadful noise.

For three and a half hours the game is cautious and considered. Then, suddenly, Kasparov launches a frenzied attack on Short's king. He sacrifices an important pawn to get into a potential checkmate position. There are gasps from the audience. The in-seat computer is predicting a win for Kazza in two moves. Short barely manages to slide his king out of trouble. Kasparov looks shocked. He peers at the board as though it's just burst into flames. The computer is predicting a draw again. Kasparov glances up and appears to mumble to Short.

The man beside me is speaking through clenched teeth. He thinks Kasparov is offering Short a draw, but that Short is turning it down. Short evidently believes he can win. People around me begin to rise to their feet.

Short has sixty seconds to make ten moves. Kasparov has two and a half minutes to do the same. Even if Short doesn't win, he looks to be in an almost certain drawn position. All he has to do is make all his moves without falling into a defensive error and he'll draw, inflicting a heavy psychological blow on Kasparov's hopes.

People in the crowd are standing on the chairs now, speaking urgently but under their breaths. "Go on Nigel. Go *on*. *Stuff* him, Nigel." They are willing Short on, but they know that they cannot cheer, because if they do they will distract him. So the theatre is filled with an intensely odd sound; the sound of two thousand people, all whispering. A man in front of me puts his fingers to his eyes and turns away, visibly trembling.

On the stage, the players are moving their pieces so quickly now that you feel sure one of them will make a mistake. This is Kasparov's favourite style of play. He loves nothing better than to put his opponent against the clock. He doesn't even think about his moves then, he has said, he just slides the pieces around by sheer instinct. The players move, slap frantically at the buttons on their clocks. There are only a couple of seconds left on Short's. If the hands get to six, his flag will fall and he will lose. He stretches out his fingers, hesitates for a fraction of a second, moves his king. He makes for his clock. It's all over.

Pandemonium breaks out in the theatre. People are shouting and cheering. One man thinks that Kasparov has lost. He says he saw Kasparov's flag fall. Another says it wasn't Kasparov's flag that fell, but Short's. He starts arguing with a teenage boy beside him, saying that Short has thrown the game away. He says he blew it all on the fourteenth move, and he gets out a book and starts pointing to a little diagram of a chessboard. "He should have played bishop to G4," he says, "attacking the queen." The boy is adamant that this is wrong, that Kasparov is the one who has blown it. "Move 36," he insists, "if he'd done rook to E7 it was bloody checkmate." The man with the portable television thinks that both flags fell at the same time.

But the man who saw Kasparov's flag fall is dancing around, throwing his arms around the man beside him, shouting out that Nigel has won. It's unbelievable, he yells. Nigel Short has beaten the greatest player in the world.

Nobody knows for sure what has happened. Karpov is gripping the armrests on his chair as though trying to break them off. He looks wide-eyed, exhausted, pale grey with tension. The audience is going crazy. There is cheering and whistling, loud and frantic clapping.

The two adjudicators, Yuri Averbakh of Moscow and Carlos Falcon of Barcelona, come to the players' table with clipboards and pens in their hands. They exchange a few words with Short. Short nods, stands up, grins broadly at the crowd. When they see him smiling, they roar with applause again. "Yeesssss!"

Some of the audience try to start a chant — "Eng-land, Eng-land, Eng-land" — but it doesn't work, because everyone else is too excited to chant in unison. They are whooping and yelling. Judge Averbakh steps forwards and a chorus of shushing echoes around the theatre as the official announcement is awaited. "Well done Nigel," someone shouts. "Shhhhhhh," comes from the balconies.

Averbakh shakes his head. "I have to announce," he says quietly, "that Nigel Short has lost on time before making his fortieth move."

Kasparov punches the air with elation. Short picks up his notebook and slopes off the stage. The audience are stunned, open-mouthed and silent. They can not believe it. After three hours, fifty nine minutes and fifty nine seconds of play, Nigel Short's last hesitation has cost him the game. People sink back into their seats with their heads in their hands.

The world championship lasted for eight weeks. Nigel Short and Gary Kasparov did this again, every Tuesday, Thursday and Saturday for two months, twenty three times, over 138 hours of chess, before Karpov emerged as the greatest player in the world and collected a cheque for over a million pounds.

But back in the theatre that hot afternoon, nobody knew that this would happen. They had scented English greatness, and that was what was on their minds. "I don't know how Nigel does it," the man with the portable television said. "Just looking at that makes me want to lie down."

"Yes," another man said. "But he's different, isn't he? He's like a machine."

"A hero," muttered the man with the TV. "A fucking hero."

"Mmmm," said the second man, "That's what I meant." He paused and looked down at the empty stage, where Gary Kasparov was sitting alone, head bowed, arms folded. He looked at him. He smiled.

"Hero is better," he said. "You're absolutely right."

Chapter Four
Great problems of the Twentieth Century

Part I: Europe.

I was in Spain recently, with my brother John, and the scorching weather was more draining than a speech by the Taoiseach. But the trip did have its educational moments. One night we found ourselves in a sado-masochism disco-bar where the drumbeat nearly knocked the fillings out of our molars, and the tightness of the manager's trousers was in inverse proportion to the looseness of the punters' morals. The floorshow was absolutely intriguing. Suffice it to say, when the staff put on their rubber gloves, it was not to do the washing up. Caligula himself would have barfed at the antics.

But I felt tense. There is something dreadful about being on holiday. It is only good and healthy because like all such things it is unpleasant at the time but retrospectively worth the endurance. I am not just talking about the frantic rush before you go, the exhausting screaming sessions with your loved ones about the peseta rate and the ERM, the annual removal of the floorboards in the course of the fourteen hour search for the passport. I am talking about actually being on holiday.

You wake at 6am, vile-tempered and hungover, after ninety minutes of sleep. You stagger down to the square and order a coffee. The waiter brings it. You sip. You think: begob now, here I am, relaxing. So this is relaxation, you feel, as you start to wonder whether the special branch will come around in your absence and confiscate your flat because you once signed a Troops Out petition. You chew your nails. You look around. The German vegetarian couple you keep bumping into try to speak to you. You ignore them. The way they grin at each other over the croissants makes it clear that human beings, unlike public toilets, can indeed be vacant and engaged at the same time. You try to read one of the fat difficult books you bought when you were sulking at the airport. It turns out to be written by a fat difficult author. You do read, for five whole minutes. But you can't concentrate. The heat is broiling your braincells. Another sip of coffee. Fourteen hours to fill before you can go back to bed.

You try to write a postcard. You bought fifty postcards of squiggly designs at the art exhibition yesterday. But you can't think of anybody to whom you can send them. So you look through your address book. You realise that you have no friends really, that for some reason nobody likes you. You become unselective as you pore through the pages. Pretty soon, everyone you ever kissed in your life is going to get a postcard. That makes three. You try to write the cards without mentioning the weather, but you can't. So you write "weather here, wish you were wonderful," tittering so much at the sheer Wildean wit of it all that you practically gag on your *cafe con leche*. You write your cards. You then realise that your ex-girlfriends will compare notes at the next coven meeting and place some appalling hex on you for putting the same remark on all three cards. You tear them up. Another sip of coffee. Thirteen hours and fifty minutes until you can go back to bed.

The medieval cathedral turns out to be a deeply unpleasant experience. What do you care for naves? Far from transepts you were reared. Why does the bust of the baby Jesus look like an evil pensioner? What is that funny smell that European cathedrals have? What would happen if you stuck your head through the confessional curtains and stretched your lips with your thumbs and shrieked *"EEEARGHHHGGH"* at the priest, or, better still, at the grey-haired old penitent?

And beaches. All these svelte foreigners flinging off their ganzees and foostering about in the surf like lobotomy victims. You, however, are so flabby that you keep on every stitch while sunbathing, because if you did not, you would be hit on the head with a bottle of champagne and launched by King Juan Carlos. You spend the whole afternoon in a sordid pickle of sweat, sexual frustration and sunstroke and carry home enough grit in your socks to build the foundation for an airport. You go to the bar and get plastered again, and try to dance the cha-cha-cha with a muscular off-duty police-woman from Valencia. The one in Cork, that is, not the one in Spain.

Wish you were here, indeed. Wish I was there, more like it.

Part II: The Crime Wave

One night recently, I got home around midnight in great form. It was one of those nights when you want to sit up for a while and think about life. If I had a garden I would have strolled out to look at the stars, ponder the meaning of love and then pee contentedly into the bushes. But in the absence of a real garden, I dug out a tape of the recently departed Derek Jarman's stunning film "The Garden" and I tried to put it into the video machine. It was then that something became clear. Not only did I not have a garden. I did not have a video machine either.

It did not occur to me for some time that I had been burgled. I spent ten minutes looking around for the video machine. I asked myself aloud where I had put it. I even looked in the wardrobe. (Anything lost ends up in my wardrobe eventually; I found Glen Miller in there last year.) But no video. I thought I was going bananas. I closed my eyes, feeling finally destined for the place where the doors have no handles.

Slowly, I became convinced that someone had merely borrowed my video machine. Mentally, I went through the various keyholders to my flat, their multifarious spouses, exotic sexual partners, dubious associates, laconic sidekicks, ungainly co-conspirators in sin both mortal and venial. Degenerate riff-raff all, but I still could not imagine any of them tumbling in, filching the video and leaving again, without at least burning a message of thanks into the wallpaper with a funny cigarette. I was astounded.

Now, I suppose it is just possible that some of you may not actually have a key to my flat, and have thus never visited it, so allow me to tell you that it is on the third floor of a very tall building. Unless one is a member of the SAS, there are only two ways in; the front door, and the back window. The door had definitely been locked when I'd gone out. So, gradually, with Poirot-like cunning, I deduced that villains had clambered up what must be the longest ladder in Christendom and entered my gaff through this third floor window, which was, I now saw, open.

I sat in a chair for at least half an hour. I could not believe that I had been robbed. I smoked one cigarette after another, feeling the muscles in my throat beginning to tighten with rage. It is important to state, at this point, that politically, I am a radical wishy-washy liberal. I am in favour of the armed masses storming Leinster House immediately, once they offer to pay for any damage. But I must confess that all such enlightened sentiment went out the window almost as fast as the fecking video. If I could have caught the thieves, I would gladly have gagged them, strapped them into a chair and repeatedly played them at high volume the greatest hits of The Carpenters, with extra gratuitous blasts of "Please Mister Postman" and "There's a Kind of Hush (All Over The World Tonight")".

A character in Samuel Beckett's novel *Murphy* curses not just the day he was born, but also, in a flight of imagination, the night he was conceived. This I did. Reader, I hollered. I seethed. I stormed up and down, pronouncing obscenities that I thought I had left in the playground. There was no part of the human body left unmentioned. The language in my flat was as ripe as a Portarlington boarding house tomato, and almost twice as blue.

It's not the Watergate break-in, I know. And yes, it is only a poxy video. But it just drove me stark staring crazy to think that somebody had been into my flat without my knowing about it. It was very odd, thinking of these guys being in my room. Now I've had to get the locksmiths out, and my poor flat looks like the basement vault of a Central American dictator's *palacio*. And the worrying thing is not exactly that my flat was burgled, but how I felt about it. Weird stuff. Out of proportion, somehow. Stuff I'd rather not be feeling at all, if you want to know the truth.

Part III: The Nature of Time

As I write, Autumn, like an amorous rottweiler with an unspeakable erection, is once again all over us, and one of the things we shall each have to do is indulge in the annual communal madness, the putting back of the clocks. Every year it is the same. The clocks go back an hour at two a.m. on a Saturday night/Sunday morning, we spend all Sunday afternoon wondering whether this really does mean that we got an extra hour of sleep or not, the automatic timer on the video recorder is shagged for the best part of a week, and three whole months later, the guys who fix the big clock on the town hall tower finally get around to catching up, just in time for Christmas, when what the clocks have to say does not matter very much, and then Spring, when the clocks all go forwards again.

Why do we do this? What is the point? What is time? What is existence? (What *is* Marty Pello out of Wet Wet Wet and who cuts his hair?) Well, Albert Einstein's work, of course, is very important to a true understanding of the nature of time. It is a little difficult to explain in simple terms which a lay person would understand, but I've done a good deal of research work on it, and basically — if you'll forgive the scientific jargon here — Einstein's theory of relativity states that time seems to go a fuck of a lot more slowly when you're with your relatives.

All this timepiece-tampering palaver would give you the dry heaves. Really, what difference does it make? I mean, you can take six a.m. and put your clock back by an hour and call it five a.m. You can call it half past two, for that matter. You can call it Archbishop Lorenzo Ignatius McCarthy the third, if you like, and bring it home for tea and sandwiches and a cuddle on the couch afterwards. But it's still six o'bloody clock, and that's that.

People say it's all to do with not wanting the poor little kiddies to be shuffling along to school in the dark. Well, when I was going to school the amount of light made precious little difference on the scale of things, I can tell you. It was not nearly so important as the poignant fact that the only people who would snog me at the Friday night disco in Prez had faces which would have curdled milk, that my best friend was an invisible Martian called Mickey, and that some of my teachers were of a psychiatric profile which would have made Hannibal Lecter seem like Uncle Bulgaria out of The Wombles of Wimbledon. Take it from me. If there is one thing young people are not particularly interested in, it is the relativity of day to night. As sure as one follows the other, young people will always have something else on what we might euphemistically term their minds. We are talking, after all, about the generation that made Mister Blobby a star.

So why do we indulge in this strange communal madness of clock-changing? Our noble Celtic ancestors marked the passing of the seasons by biting the heads off chickens, chanting mystical mantras at the sun, dancing naked hokey-cokeys around dolmens, smearing each other's nipples and genitalia with mead, shagging each other silly, then slitting each other's gizzards in ritual sacrifice, and building Newgrange. Now *that* I can relate to. That seems to me a much healthier approach.

On the pavement just outside my old flat in South East London there is a flagstone with a groove carved into it, and an inscription proudly proclaiming that this is the line of zero longitude, the Greenwich Meridian. If you were to stand out there for long enough — which you wouldn't want to do these days, because the local hoodlums would have the eyeballs out of your bonce without missing a beat of "We Are Millwall. Nobody Likes Us But We Don't Facking Care" — you would see that this line runs over my former back fence, across my former garden and through my former bedroom. It actually runs right through the centre of my former bed. When I lived there, I was very happy about this line. It meant that on the rare occasions when I did get to sleep with somebody, the earth may not have moved, but at least it divided into two, which, you know, was something to talk about over breakfast, before handing over the busfare home. It also meant that when I did cohabit, myself and the ball and chain kipped in different hemispheres, which I always thought would be a really sound basis for any long-term relationship. In addition, when sleeping alone, it meant that I could have a foot in both camps. I could wake up in a different half of the world every morning. Indeed, I could roam from east to west and back again in the middle of the night, simply by rolling over to scrutinise the alarm clock, or, in the cold Winter evenings, by getting up to grope about for the bri-nylon cardie, the woolly leg warmers, the electronically heated rollers and the catering-size tub of Vic chest rub.

But I was still not happy. I don't think it's right. It is oddly characteristic of the English that having spent the last five centuries barging their perfidious way into every single country that had the poor taste to be inhabited by foreigners, wiping out most of the natives and briskly barging back out again with great sackloads of ancient artifacts, they then decided they wanted to colonise time itself! Honest to God, is Wales not enough for them? How can you trust a people who would want to *own time*?

Greenwich Mean Time?! What an amazing nerve. It is absurd. Wherever you go in the world, time is calculated not by where you actually *are*, but by how far away you are from Greenwich! The further away the better, in my book. Listen, Greenwich is very near where I used to live in London. I spent a good deal of time in Greenwich over the years, and, hey, Vegas it ain't. Greenwich is actually a dreary little dump on the southern banks of the Thames, full of deranged blue-rinsed old dears whose rubbery faces have been lifted more often than pub toilet seats, sitting in twee cafés where the menus have little line drawings of Pepys and Keats and Percy Bysshe Shelley on them (what kind of name is that for a grown man anyway? *Bysshe*?) prattling on about the blacks and the Asians and the price of zimmer frames and the almost compulsory nature of sodomy these days.

Greenwich Mean Time, indeed. Just imagine if we had tried that caper in Ireland. Dublin Mean Time. BallyJamesDuff Mean Time. The County Cork Meridian. Imagine, even, if any other town in Britain had tried it. Solihull Mean Time. Glasgow Mean Time. Stoke Newington Mean Time. Would they have got away with it? Would they be a laughing stock? Would a one-legged duck swim in a shagging circle and would His Holiness the Pope kiss tarmac? I think so, yes. Time is running out for Greenwich. The poor old clocks should be left exactly as they are.

Part IV: Money

My financial life is an utter disaster. The rest of my life — emotional, political, psycho-sexual etc — is merely a cataclysmic misery. But the money end of things, now that is serious. My problem is that I have pretty much the same economic planning ability as El Salvador. My tax is a mess. My invoices are a veritable Gordian knot of confusion, grief and disorganisation. I feel these days like a very large flamingo. No matter what way I turn, there is always a very large bill.

I am broke as the ten commandments. I am skint as a pox doctor's clerk. Church mice come up to me in the street and offer me their spare change. My creditors are hounding me. My cash card has been swallowed up more often than a potent tranquilliser in suburbia. My credit card has been declined more forcefully than the offer of a brisk no-questions-asked shag at a nun's convention. The bottom line of my telephone bill looks like a telephone *number*. When I was a wide-eyed and credulous nipper, they used to tell us in maths class that you could not multiply infinity by two. Well, they were wrong. I've seen it done; the answer is written on the bottom line of my phone bill.

Recently I went to see an accountant. After I had finished weeping and gnashing not only my own teeth, but also my Grandmother's lime-encrusted dentures, which I had specifically borrowed for the occasion, the accountant talked me in off the ledge, sponged me down and explained calmly that as a self-employed person I could claim various expenses against my tax. I had recently bought a word-processor, for instance, and I could claim for that, and for part of my telephone bill also, once I had the receipts. Receipts were the key to human happiness, she seemed to feel. Receipts were everything. The answer to the speculative question, *tsch*, life, what's it all about, eh?, was "receipts." On the last day of judgement, when we were all queuing up at the pearly gates, Saint Peter would not be asking for lists of prayers fervently said or good and charitable works piously performed or fleshly temptations successfully avoided, but, rather, for our VAT returns, our national insurance numbers and, above all, our receipts.

"Receipts?" I guffawed, "what? Them annoying little bits of paper you get when you buy something? Heck, I just chuck them in the bin. Is that not what everyone does, no?"

My accountant tittered with the air of a woman beginning to suspect the presence of Jeremy Beadle in an ante-room. "You're having me on," she said.

"*Au contraire*," I replied. She went a bit quiet.

"Receipts?" I scoffed, "Don't make me laugh. Into the garbage with them, faster than a hot snot from a headbanger's nose."

She peered at me at this point, as though I had just broken wind.

"Your cheque stubs, then," she said, her face paling to the colour of cream cheese. "Surely to God man, you keep your cheque stubs."

"Well," I said, "not exactly." I told her I threw my cheque stubs away, and in any case I rarely filled them in, because the only time I ever actually wrote a cheque was when I was half-plastered at three a.m. in some subterranean fleshpot and gagging for another bottle of Moroccan Beaujolais before doing the funky chicken with some inebriated and dribbling psychopath.

"But your bills," she gasped. "You have your bills though. You wouldn't throw *them* in the bin, surely to the Sacred Heart?"

"Er, yeah, Marie," I explained. "You see, when I get a bill I write a cheque. Then I throw the bill away. This means the bill is gone, and I can start my life all over again with a clean slate."

I tried to explain that, as a lapsed Roman Catholic, paying a bill was the fiscal equivalent of going to confession for me. Paying a bill was a process of self-purgation, and just as a forgiven sinner wants to forget all about his past wickedness, a bill-payer does not want to be reminded of long-gone and only faintly remembered pleasures. But she didn't seem to understand.

The journalist Claud Cockburn was a wonderful man, who wrestled all his life with impecuniousness and poverty. He had a fine way of dealing with bills. Whenever one came, he put it in a large barrel beside his desk. No matter how urgent, into the barrel it went immediately, to join its comrades in the tumescent mound of red-inked final demands. Once a year, he would reach in, lucky-dip-style, and extract three bills at random. These he would pay.

On one occasion the bank wrote to him to say they had not been paid any interest at all for quite some years. He wrote back, explained his system, the intrinsic natural justice of the barrel approach, the extraordinary organic beauty of it. But the best bit was at the end of his letter. "If there's any more of your nonsense," Cockburn concluded, "You, sir, are out of the game!" I don't know what readers will make of this. Especially readers who are accountants. But I think I might give it a lash anyway.

Part V: The Aging Process

Horror of unspeakable horrors, this year I turned thirty. I am so depressed. I will never see twenty again, except, perhaps, on a hall door, or an IQ test. My younger brother took time out from listening to mindrotting rap music to send me a card with a dinosaur on it. "Don't think of yourself as old," it said, "THINK OF YOURSELF AS ANCIENT."

For months now, people have been tittering "oh well, the big three-oh, eh? It's all downhill from here, fnar, fnar, no more horizontal hokey-cokey for *you*, eh grandad?" If one more brain-damaged imbecile offers me sympathy for being eight years past my sexual peak, there will be two thumps. Me hitting him, and him hitting the deck. There will then be a soft popping sound, as I uncork my jumbo-size bottle of hormone replacement pills.

I remember my dear father being thirty. I was six at the time, and I thought thirty was an utterly vast age, that my beloved old Dad was some sort of latter-day Methuselah. But on mature reflection, this was not because *he* was thirty, but because he was five times the age *I* was. If my father was a hundred and fifty now, I would be similarly bewildered, as he would be too, I feel sure, given some of the colourful things up with which he has had to put.

But now I keep thinking it *is* a vast age. Thirty whole years. Ten thousand nine hundred and fifty days. Two hundred and sixty two thousand, eight hundred hours. Where have they gone? I keep thinking, a third of my life is already over. *Half*, probably, given the amount of chips I eat.

The thing is, I couldn't wait to be thirty. I counted the seconds. Your twenties are for stumbling into trouble, I told myself, for getting tragically drunk at indifferent parties, for staying up late and discussing abstruse books you've never read, for trying correctly to pronounce the word "Jamiroquai," for believing that human nature is basically good, for trying to make sense of the world's absurdities, for asking yourself just what is the *point* of The Progressive Democrats, for finding Vic Reeves and Bob Mortimer even remotely amusing, for learning to put on a condom without reducing yourself to hot tears of agony, for buying records by angst-ridden English rock bands, for entering into mind-blowingly destructive relationships with people who despise you, for sitting in acid-house nightclubs and fervently pretending to have a good time while some festering disc-jockey *manque* snogs the living tonsils off the person you came with.

But your thirties, ah, your thirties. You glide into maturity with the stately grace of a galleon. You have attained wisdom. You are not interested in MC Hammer or 2 Live Crew or Suede, (either the fabric which sets your teeth on edge, or the band which does the same). You think flares are what you shoot into the sky when your trawler is about to sink, not embarrassing trousers worn by odd people in Manchester. What care you for scrawny Kate Moss, when your own febrile adolescent fantasies were fired up by the leather-clad posterior of Olivia Newton John in *Grease*? Your illusions have disappeared in direct relation to your pimples. It's a swings and roundabouts thing.

People keep telling me that thirty is the end of everything. They keep wittering on about all the great things people have accomplished in their twenties. Bobby bloody Moore, for instance, had captained England to World Cup victory by the age of 25. Well, OK. Emily Bronte had written "Wuthering Heights" (29), YEAH, OK, I KNOW!!! Van Morrison had recorded "Astral Weeks" (22!), *ALRIGHT, SHUT UP, I GET THE BLOODY POINT*. And Mozart. Oh yes, here we go, Wolfgang Amashaggingdeus Mozart, as sure as a sixpence, he'll always gets dragged out at times like this. It's the only thing Mozart is *any* bloody good for, if you ask me; making thirty-somethings feel bad. The unspeakable little scumbag had knocked out twenty five major works by the age of sixteen! When *I* was sixteen I wouldn't even take out the bins once a week for my mother, and there *he* was, penning symphonies in tights. Well, I bet he had no friends in school. I bet Mozart was always the last to get picked for football.

Adolescence may be good for wig-wearing wimps like Wolfie, but that doesn't bother me. Heck, no. Because writers generally do their best work as they get older. Samuel Beckett was a well-developed forty-eight when *Waiting for Godot* was premiered.

Finnegans Wake came out when James Joyce was a positively wrinkly fifty-seven, although, admittedly, premature dementia had set in by then, as that particular novel is the literary equivalent of wandering the streets with a four-year-old Dunnes bag on your head and screeching at passers-by about how you're picking up *Radio Free Europe* on your fillings.

And I mean, look at Jesus, for Christ's sake! What age do you think Jesus was when he set out on his mission? He wasn't an ecstasy-crazed teenager with undropped testicles, a light fleece of fuzz on his neck and ludicrously expensive trainers on his feet, was he? No. He was *thirty*. And if it's good enough for the son of God, it's good enough for me.

So, thirty is OK. Mature, I think is the word, rather than vintage. I'm not sensitive about it, honest. Now, where's me zimmer frame and me surgical stocking, nursie? And sluice out that colostomy bag, will you? I'm going down the post office to enquire about the bus pass.

Part VI: WB Yeats and dealing with Christmas

The smell of the mistletoe, the roar of the dry sherry. Christmas will all too soon be all over us once again. Personally I don't feel so hot about this. Personally, in fact, I feel as uneasy these days as a circumferentially challenged turkey in November.

Do not get me wrong now. Your present scribe is no Scrooge. Your present scribe was born to be wild, babe. Be fully assured, wherever there is a hokey-cokey line, a half a lager shandy, a string of tinsel and a communal chorus of *Wombling Merry Christmas*, your present scribe will not be found wanting. But, such riotously merry times notwithstanding, would you ever tell me this? Is there not something just poxy about the whole idea of Christmas?

The whole frantic run-up, the hideous lights going up earlier every year, the rush, the bother, the traffic, the abysmal carol singers, the enforced cheeriness, the annual attempt to get off with some long-fancied colleague half way through *Feed The World* at the office Christmas party, only to discover, as the alcohol begins to wear off, that you have been drunkenly wearing the face off your own reflection in the steamed-up and puke-encrusted mirror on the wall of the pub jacks. And you wondered how you were doing so well all of a sudden.

And the Christmas shopping ritual! You find yourself in the subterranean toy section of some department store that you haven't been in since the Mammy bought you your last pair of short trousers. You have a hangover the size of Ireland. You can barely walk in a straight line. This is not because you are still intoxicated. It is because you have so much leftover change in your pockets from last night's gargling session that you are weighed down like a prize racehorse. Thus handicapped, you are trying to buy a prezzie for the five-year-old niece who hates your guts and bursts into tears whenever you enter the room. You feebly attempt to sort out your Sonic the Magic Hedgehogs from your Teenage Mutant Ninja Turtles. You linger a while outside Santa's grotto, watching the kiddies canter out and merrily rip the paper off their presents. "What did you get, then?" you say, tousling the hair of one cute little fellow. He bursts into tears and pisses all over your trouser leg.

And the songs, good God, the Christmas songs. Cliff Richard warbling about puppies and yule logs and international peace. George Michael singing *Last Christmas I Gave You My Heart* ("But This Year I'm Giving Sony a Law Suit"). John Lennon's unspeakably turgid *So This Is Christmas and What Have You Done*? The answer being, in his case, half a pound of cocaine and a couple of tabs of acid.

Well, maybe I'm being too hard on Christmas. The clergy tell us that it is supposed to be a pious Christian occasion. Of course, this is nonsense. Christmas is a modernised pagan celebration of the winter solstice. It did not even exist in the Christian calendar until almost AD 500, and scholars still differ greatly on the actual date of Christ's birth. But the pagan origins of Christmas are important in explaining why people over-indulge at yuletide now. At heart, Christmas is about the body as much, if not more, than it is about the soul. And if God does exist, I suspect He wouldn't mind that too much.

I was in Barcelona last year, as I think I may have told you already, (and will, no doubt, be telling you again) and I went into a shop which sold figurines for Christmas cribs. They had all the usual characters, the Virgin Mary, the baby Jesus, cows, etc. But my eye was caught by another figure, a little bald man with his trousers around his knees, squatting. He had an expression of bliss on his face, and he was, well, crapping. I don't want to dwell on the details, but take it from me, the statue was extremely anatomically correct. He was *El Cagador*, the shopkeeper explained, a traditional figure in cribs in Catalonia. She said he symbolised God becoming flesh, the human body functioning even in the midst of the miraculous. *El Cagador* was absolutely essential to a true understanding of Christmas, the shopkeeper said. I liked that idea. And before anyone gets offended and sees blasphemy where none is intended, let them remember the wise words of Yeats next Christmas: "Fair and foul are near of kin, and fair needs foul I cried." If there *is* a yuletide message, I guess that's it. And even if it isn't, it might still be a good line to try out at the office party.

Part VII: The Communications Revolution

Recently, on moving back to live in Dublin, I caved in to personal and professional pressure and reluctantly bought myself an answering machine. This will make some people deliriously happy, but I am not one of them. I am not happy at all. I loathe answering machines. In the entire wretched arsenal of postmodern cultural tortures, the answering machine ranks with the ubiquity of the nintendo gameboy, the still current popularity of The Beatles' *White Album* and the widespread availability of the lime-flavoured ribbed luminous condom. All poignant signifiers that humankind is basically finished.

It is not the first time I've owned one of these infernal devices; I purchased one the week I moved to London some seven years ago. It seemed to me, carbuncular and wide-eyed wannabe, that buying an answering machine was a very London thing to do. I knew nobody back home in Ireland who had an answering machine. God, I thought, as I unwrapped it and plugged it in, far from answering machines we were all reared, back home on the Shamrock shore. Back home in Ireland we had to, like, answer the telephone ourselves when it rang! I mean, good Christ, what kind of drooling undignified savages were we?!! But look at me now, Ma, my telephone calls being answered for me, and *by a machine* too, never mind one of your servants! By a machine, mother!! Ah, the eighties. What a decade.

I also thought that if I had an answering machine more people would ring me up. I thought having an answering machine would make me friends. I thought it would be a substitute for going out to pubs, engaging strangers in conversation on the bus, taking up a nightclass or pursuing loose floozies around indifferent discobars. I suppose I thought my answering machine would come with messages included. I thought I would stroll in from a hard day's graft and find dozens of enticing messages just waiting to be answered. There would be offers of easy money, of philosophical enlightenment, of unconditional love, of slippery and gymnastic sex; there would be invitations to sup with accomplished novelists, revolutionary thinkers, lithe supermodels, nymphomaniacal slappers recently released from long spells of solitary confinement. Alas, no. There is nothing quite so crushing as having an answering machine and galloping home with your tongue flapping out of your beak with anticipation, only to find that the little digital display is insistently spelling out the digit zero. Why does it not just flash up the words "sad fucking loser" and be done with it?

Eventually, when you live in a new city, you do actually meet people. The wrong people, yes, mad people with throbbing veins in their foreheads, people who would make Beavis and Butthead seem like epigrammatic Wildean sophisticates. But still people. Well, mammals at any rate. The answering machine then becomes a source of unadulterated misery. For every pleasant message you receive, there are four vicious diatribes from the various plankheads you are trying to avoid for emotional reasons, or those to whom you owe large sums of money; in my case, often the same thing.

After a few years of London life, my answering machine simply broke down. (It was either it or me.) It could still receive incoming messages alright, but it stopped letting me put my own message on it. People would ring up and get ten seconds of utter silence followed by a crackle, an intense panting sound and a long piercing scream. I think my callers must have thought I was trying to be Pinteresque. (In fact, come to think of it, my answering machine *was* offered its own short season at the Gate Theatre, Dublin.)

Anyway, when I last moved back to live in Ireland I didn't bother to bring my old answering machine with me. I left it there in my old flat in lovely Lewisham, where no doubt it is still exuding its air of profound menace, playing merry havoc with the social life of the new tenants and confusing my old bank manager, whose life, I convinced myself eventually, would not be significantly improved by the knowledge of my new address.

Now, horror of horrors, I've been forced into getting another one. I mean another answering machine (sadly) as well as a new bank manager (even more sad). I'm fed up with it already. Like most things which are advertised as convenience devices, answering machines are an almighty bloody nuisance. What's wrong with just not answering the telephone? What's wrong with taking it off the hook? Or unplugging it? You might miss something really important, my so-called friends tell me. Oh yeah, right. Like, Michelangelo would never have painted the ceiling of the Sistine Chapel if the Pope hadn't phoned him up and left his number. "*Per favore* Mick, give us an auld bell back, I might have a bit of a nixer for you, OK, me auld chiner, *ciao*, oh janey, there's the bleep now, God bless."

The answering machine is a creature from the lowest pit of purgatory. In any decent society it would be banned. And if my old bank manager is reading this, there's no point in thinking that just because I've got one now, you can suddenly get me. I'll be out if you ring, I swear to God. I'll be gone. I'll be in South America. Promise. (I won't really. I'll be standing there, watching the spools turn, laughing.)

Part VIII: Bored Failte

I told you there about moving back to Ireland, and leaving my answering machine behind me in Pagan London. It was a happy day for me, seeing the city of my birth and boyhood again. But one thing you notice on returning to Dublin after a spell abroad is the inexplicable but undeniable fact that there are more crashing bores strolling the avenues of our capital then there are caps on a debutante's molars. I do not say that all Dublin people are bores. Not a bit of it. Most Dubliners are great company, full of jizz and strange mischief. But Holy Mother in Heaven, do we have our share of fellows — and usually they *are* fellows — who would make you want to sprint out and purchase a gallon of emulsion purely in order to slap it on a jacks wall and watch it dry rather than engage them in even a millisecond's intercourse?

You have met, I assume, The Man Who Knows All About RTE? "*That* place? Hah. Pull, pull, pull, that's what gets yeh up the shaggin ladder above in that kip, sure that's well known. DID YEW NOT KNOW THAT, begob, I'm surprised at yeh, and yew a college man. Sure, the fingers udd be worn off yeh with the pullin, oh yeah. It's no wonder yer wan, Olivier O'Leary upped and offed ourra the gaff." And his cousin, The Man Who Didn't Get Into The Civil Service? ("Ah well, I didn't have the right connections, if you get me drift. Them buckos look after their own. If you're not in The Knights you may forget about it.")

Quite ubiquitous these days is The Man Who Followed Irish Football For Years But Wouldn't Go To A Match Now If You Paid Him. "No, I would *not*, are yew jokin' me? Sure Janey, it was great years ago below in Glenmanure Park, ye'd be there all be yerself in the stand and the gaiters bein freezed off yeh be the cold, ah yeah, yer balls'd be the size of peanuts, but now that was fookball. And that's not fookball they do be playin now, sure it's gone too poplar now, all them yuppies, all them Ole Ole-heads, sure they're not real fookball men..."

Then, horror of horrors, there is that unspeakable creature: The Man Who Has A Good One For You. "Is it yerself? C'mre to me,

I've a good one for yeh now. I went to a pub on the moon one time, burr I didn't like it, no atmosphere, dja geddit? The wife, right, she's a face on her like the supreme feckin court, no appeal, ha ha ha. She has teeth on her like the ten commandments, all broken. HA HA HA. No. C'mre to me. These three thick culchies, right, they go into a bar in Jerusalem, HA HA HA, and the first culchie says..."

Next we have The Man Who Does Impressions at Parties, The Man Who Thinks Charles Haughey Should Be Persuaded to Come Back (For The Good of the Country), The Man Who Does Not Want You To Get Him Started About The Farmers, The Man Who Invites You To Guess How Much Them Slacks Cost Him in the Sales ("No, go on, have a guess, they're corduroy mind, none of your rubbish"), The Man Who Told His Boss A Thing Or Two, The Man Who Thinks We Should Hand The Country Lock Stock and Barrel Back To England (And Pray To The Holy Mother They'd Take It), The Man Who Thinks Christmas Has Gone Fierce Commercialised, The Man Who Thinks There Is No Need At All For the Bad Language in Roddy Doyle's Books, (a close relative of The Man Who Is Not A Prude, But.) Also, we have The Man Who Knows That Mary Robinson Is Not What She Seems, The Man Who Was Beaten To A Pulp Every Day of His Schooling Be the Brothers (And Divil The Bit of Harm It Ever Did Him) and The Man Whose Friends Have Been Telling Him For Years That He Should Write a Book About His Life (Only Nobody Would Believe It). He is among the worst, this last monster. He is to be feared. "I could tell yeh stories about yours truly now pal that would raise the fookin hairs on yer neck. But yeh know what? Yeh wouldn't believe them!!"

Trotting after these chaps is The Man Who Would Feck Off Out Of This Priest-ridden Country If Only He Was Ten Years Younger, The Man Who Knew Brendan Behan Well, The Man Who Still Has His Health ("sure that's the main thing, isn't it?") and The Man Who Misses the Old Days When Chizzellers Had To Make Their Own Fun. ("I got a ball of silver paper for me birthday every year until I was twenty seven, and I was happy as a pig in shite.")

The king of Dublin bores, of course, is the talkative taxi driver, the withering pox be upon him and his. How many of us have had to endure the following turgid monologue?

"Taxi? Howya boss, sit in there and take the weight off yer brains. Purr on the auld seat belt, willya like a good man. Where are yeh gointeh? Ratmoines? Game ball. We're off. Listen, do yeh know any jokes? C'mere, I've a good wan for yeh. I wouldn't say the auld wan is ugly righ?, but she fell asleep in the gairden wunst and the dog buried her. HOOHOOOHOOO. Did yeh see that airticle on the paper there about Ballymun? Towerblocks? Are yew jokin me? Don't be talkin. *Ballymun deproived*? Me bollix. On the pig's back up there. Don't talk to me about deproived, when I think abou' that place I want to gawk. Hot watther? Way ourra that don't make me laugh. Leave it flowin all day up there. Don't pay a bean for it. And free heat. Up there once, wait till I tell yeh, collectin a fare I was. Middle of winter, and do you know wha? Guess. Strippin the feckin clothes off themselves with the free central heatin. Like the beach or sumpin. Like shaggin Rimini it was. Deproived me howl.

Darndale, that's the same. Deproived. Yer man from the Labour Pairty is never off the television abour it. And what that prognosticatin' bowsie would know about deproived now you could write on a stamp. I seen him ownee the other night outside Lillie's Bordildo and him bein lurried into a joe maxi blue mowldy with the dhrink and singin Sean Southa Garryowen and the hair on him like a madwoman's fanny and a nurse with him and the frock on her up to her wishbone. Oh Jem Larkin is back in the saddle right enuff. But no, deproived is the latest. Jaze it would make you throw the head altogether. I mean, them houses above in Darndale is lovely. The ones with the arches. They're after winnin' every award in the bewk. The arkitexture is ownee bleedin rapid in them. And do yeh think *I* can afford arches? I can not, not even in me fookin shoes. Far from arches that shower was rared. Lovely houses. But fallin apairt now a course. Anywhere else they'd be grand, but it's the Woild West up there. Mad commanches they are. You would need your tomahawk up there.

Some people are just ignorant. Jairseeful Mazes, yeh can give them nuttin. The wild dogs that do be roamin around up there, sure they'd take a lump ourra yer arse yeh wouldn't fit inteh yer hat. Yeh see a thing or two now Boss, in the taxiin' trade, I don't mind tellin yeh, but up in shaggin Ballymun beejaze yeh'd see characters danderin' about the place that'd straighten the hair in yer oxters. And as for the smell up there, in the lifts, don't get me stairted. Disgoostin. No respect for a pairson's feelins." (Pause while driver enthusiastically evacuates contents of nostrils into dubiously stained kerchief.)

"And I wouldn't mind ownee they're *set up* out there. They are laughin at the rest of us, they are *scutterin themselves* laughin, I'm tellin yeh. Free heat, free butther and free yew name it, firin' the free grub inteh themselves good-oh, me same poor deproived buckos beyond in Ballymun, oh bedad, every last wunna them on the rock and roll and havin childers left and right to get money and you never hear about *that* from the arty-farty Labour Pairty, oh no. They wudden know *how* to work. Wudden know what to *do* with a tool. And there they are, feckin themselves over the balconies! Nuthin else will do them bar leppin the balconies. The ingratitude of it. I was ownee sayin to the war department there last night, Monica, sez I, the *ingratitude* of them hop-o-me-thumbs beyond in Ballymun is what gets me, sure it's no wonder this country is a laughin stock. They do break their howls laughin at us in England you know, Monica. They think we are bleedin hilariousness pairsonified.

And do you no what she sez to me? *DO YEH*?!!! Sez she, they ARE deproived. Annoyin me, yeh know? Hoppin the ball she was, ourra badness. Moi grandfather fought for Urland, sez she, and I'll tell yeh this Jack, he never thought when we gor our freedom we'd put up places like Ballymun. *When* did your grandfather fight for Urland, sez I. Wasn't he in the post office in 1916, sez she. He *was* alright, sez I, he was buying a fookin stamp. Ah well, don't be talkin. Here we are anyway, Ratmoines wazzen it? What's this is the damage, sure we'll call it the even fiver, yeah. Tankin yew. Listen, c'mere to me, I hope I didden bore yeh to bleedin tears, did I? Wake up. WAKE UP YEH EEJIT!!!"

Something should be done about this pantheon of Dublin superbores. Perhaps we could round them up and export them to Holland, as vengeance for knocking us out of the recent World Cup? Although, come to think of it, I've been to Holland and over there, you know, bores are actually...oh, never mind.

Part IX: Learning To Say You're Sorry

There is a man in New York called Mr Apology. He is a carpenter by trade, but when he is not knocking out sturdy chairs and attractive coffee tables, Mr Apology is providing another useful public service. He is turning himself into the conscience of America.

The deal is that you call Mr Apology's phone number and tell his answering machine your darkest secret. It's very simple. You ring the machine and let it all out. It can be serious or trivial, whatever you like. Your time is unlimited. Other people then call in and hear the tape of you getting it off your chest. You can call back and hear their recorded advice, if you like, but it's up to you. (Mr Apology makes no money out of this, by the way.)

I rang Mr Apology myself recently, and I must say it was the most fascinating half hour I've spent on the telephone in years. The recording first cautions "if you wish to confess to a major crime, please call again from a public telephone, as the police may try to trace your call." There then follows as much public breast-beating as you can possibly take. Fraud, theft, bestiality, gluttony, sloth, it is all marvellous stuff. One man who works in a well known hamburger chain confessed to regularly "dicking the French fries," whatever that may mean. (Philip Roth, in *Portnoy's Complaint* writes about masturbating with a large chunk of liver, "I fucked my family's dinner!") Another apologist, *who was married*, felt guilty for having regular *and* consensual sex with his adult sister, ("I guess we're just, y'know, closer than other brothers and sisters.") Another man was bragging, rather than apologising, for having slept with many of his clients' wives. I had fully intended to leave a confession myself, but my own sins were not half as interesting as those of the other callers. And then something occurred to me. Not one of these apologies sounded genuine. The callers were real alright, but I felt that they had invented their wrongdoings. Which was even more fascinating in a way.

A friend of mine is married to an Indian woman, and is learning Urdu at the moment. When I asked him how it was going, he shrugged and said, "OK, but sari seems to be the hardest word."

And how very true that is. Still, one thing the Roman Catholic Church and the West Midlands Serious Crime Squad have in common — well, one of many things actually — is the shrewd professional understanding that given the right circumstances people will always want to confess, whether guilty or not. This fact can get you into big trouble. The American writer Tobias Wolff has a salutary tale about an encounter he once had with a fellow author, the late Raymond Carver. In the middle of a pleasant evening, Carver suddenly broke down and told Wolff he had been an alcoholic for years. After Wolff had sympathised and bucked him up, a strange thing happened. "Listen Ray," he found himself saying, "I've got something to tell you."

"Jesus, Toby, of course," Carver replied. "What? What is it?" Wolff hung his head in shame. "This isn't something I want people to know about. But Ray, I used to be a heroin addict."

"I couldn't stop myself," poor Wolff tells us. "Ray's surprise and horror were even greater than my own, and I found them bracing, inspirational. What I know about heroin can be engraved on the head of a pin. So I improvised. I let my invention run riot over Ray's credulity until I was satisfied that I had topped him...I made him promise once again not to tell anyone."

Wolff brooded for weeks, until the next time he saw Carver. He told him there was something he should know. "What's that, Toby?" Carver asked, no doubt in eager expectation of being regaled by further lurid tales of "horse," "chasing the dragon" and "heavy vibes." Wolff confessed that he had never taken heroin in his life, and that he had no explanation for inventing such a yarn. Carver was gobsmacked. The two sat in silence for some minutes, Wolff feeling extremely guilty for having deceived his old friend. But the lie wasn't the problem. Eventually, shame-faced, Carver made a confession of his own. He had "told a few people." Actually, he said, he had told everyone he knew. "But Toby," he pleaded in mitigation, "I swore them all to secrecy."

"From that day on," Wolff recalls, "we never spoke of it. But now and then other people, some of them complete strangers, have given my cryptic words of sympathy and encouragement."

Confession is a very dangerous activity, you see. Guilty readers take note and be warned.

Chapter Five
Jesus and Me

A Wopbop A Loobop A Lop Bam Boom

Shortly after I came back to live in Ireland, the Brother arrived up to the digs one night with a face on him the length of a wet Sunday in Kinnegad. Something was clearly on his mind. He sat out in the good room ruminating, while I foostered around the kitchenette like a deranged bluebottle. I do not often have guests to dinner, but in the case of The Brother I am always happy to jemmy open a tin, incinerate the contents and scrape them deftly off the pan. It is nice to make the little effort, after all.

After I had fed and watered him, plates licked and satisfied burps having been exchanged, The Brother came clean on what had him so astray. "Your nose is never out of a book," he said, "so tell us this, how long is Lent?" I replied that it was forty days and nights. "It is in its hat," he scoffed. "Course it is," I countered. "Our Lord spent forty days fasting in the desert, you prattling heathen eejit, and that's what Lent commemorates."

"Lent is not forty days," he said. "Get out your fake filofax and count them up, Burger-Head." So I did. And he was correct! From Ash Wednesday to Easter Sunday is a whopping forty six days! I was astounded. All my natural, I had thought Lent was forty days long. And now it was longer, by nearly a seventh! I've heard of inflation, but saints alive, this was a bit much.

We talked for an age about the matter, The Brother and I, but no clarification could we find. He then confided that he had been so discombobulated by the conundrum that he had consulted his parish priest. The noble PP had said that in the old days "time was measured differently," and that the modern equivalent of forty days was forty six days. An admirably inventive explanation, although clearly balderdash. Calendars have changed, yes, but a day has always been a day, after all. For forty days to equal forty six days, a biblical day would have to be nearly thirty hours long. Which means that Monday would last until six o'clock of a Tuesday morning, and Tuesday would pant on until the midday Angelus on Wednesday, and so forth.

I tried to explain this to The Brother, but do you think he'd see it my way? After a while, I suggested we ring another holy man and get a second opinion. This we did. The curate whose evening we interrupted was a genial cove. He said the biblical forty days should not be taken too literally. Many petro-gallons of midnight oil had been expended by the scholars on the subject, and the consensus was that "forty days" merely meant "a long time." So, the bible might be inaccurate on this point? the Brother asked, horrified. Yes, the good priest said, indeed.

Well, things were getting worse. Forty days, it now seemed, might be anything from a week up! We sat there pondering. Then, suddenly, a dreadful glint appeared in the fraternal eye. "Blast it anyway," he cried, "we'll give the archbishop a buzz." Now, I was absolutely against this, but nothing would do the Brother bar going straight to the top. Out to the phone with him, quick march, and he dialling up the palace. "Can I speak to himself?" he says, the pup. Silence. "Are you a member of the archbishop's family?" the priest on duty enquires. For one awful moment I thought the Brother was going to say yes, he was his eldest son. But God be praised, he didn't. "No," says the bro, "it's merely a spiritual enquiry," and he proceeds to outline our plight.

The archbishop's secretary explained that Lent lasted from Ash Wednesday to the Wednesday of Easter Week, and that Holy Thursday to Easter Day was "the triduum," if you don't mind, not part of Lent at all! But this unsatisfactory explanation still means that Lent is forty two days, not forty. Also, that Good Friday, of all days, is not part of Lent, when surely to the hokey it is. In addition, the bishops's man said the devotee could be excused fasting on all the Sundays in Lent, and, also, on Paddy's Day. This reduces the required total to a measly thirty five days' abstinence, not the biblical forty, never mind the hefty forty six of the calendar.

The point is, depending on who you ask, Lent is anything from thirty five days up to forty six. It is agreeable to see Mother Church accepting the inevitability of consumer choice, I suppose. Although God be with the olden times, all the same, when people knew for sure what was expected of them.

It is easy to poke fun at religion, of course, which is why, no doubt, we do it. But seriously, no *seriously*, I have always been interested in Jesus, just as I feel sure he has always been interested in me. As the most influential figure in human history, we certainly can not know enough about him. Since writing a few articles about Christianity myself last year, I have been doing some more reading on the subject, and I must say it has been very enjoyable and illuminating.

For most of us, the four gospels are the main source of information about Jesus's life. In purely historical terms they are fascinating but infuriatingly incomplete and mutually contradictory documents. Part of the reason for this is that they were not written contemporaneously with the life of Christ, nor even for many decades after his death. Mark is the earliest gospel, dating from about 80 AD. Matthew was written in the 90s, John around the turn of the first century and Luke around 120 AD. Taken together they present the familiar narrative of Christian belief; Jesus was the son of God who became human, performed miracles, preached belief in his own divinity and in the forthcoming end of the world, was crucified and came back from the dead before ascending to heaven. But in fact, there is a much earlier source, which implies that many aspects of this narrative are fictitious.

Some time ago, scholars noticed that the gospels of Matthew and Luke only coincided when they followed the pattern laid down by Mark. They already knew the much later date of John, thus, they could deduce that of the remaining three gospels Mark must have been the earliest. It was also clear that Mark had included in his gospel almost all of an earlier document, some kind of handbook, a collection of the sayings of Jesus. Through careful study, scholars were able to isolate which parts of Mark had been based on this earlier source, and even to produce a separate text of that source. They called this document "Quelle," the German word for "source," or Q, for short. Since then, early copies of material very similar to Q have been discovered by archaeologists, proving the textual scholars correct. (A number of English translations of Q are available. A very readable one is included in *The Book of Q and Christian Origins* by Burton L.Mack, Professor of New Testament Studies at the Claremont School of Theology.)

Q first appears in 50 AD, a mere twenty years after Jesus's death. Unlike the gospels, it is almost exclusively concerned with Jesus's sayings rather than his deeds. (There are no miracles recorded in Q, for instance, whereas Mark in particular is full of spectacular supernatural events.) Thus, Q can justifiably be seen as the most accurate picture of what Jesus actually said, and what his earliest followers actually thought.

As such, Q represents a great challenge to the traditional view of Christianity. There is no mention of resurrection in Q. Jesus makes no claim to be divine, or even to be a prophet. There is no injunction to the apostles to set up a church, and there is absolutely no papal or episcopal authority established by Jesus. In fact, a close reading of Q suggests that the early Jesus movements were not actually Christian at all. Q implies that the early followers of Jesus did not see him as the long-prophesied Christ or messiah, but, rather, as an enlightened preacher whose teachings, often expressed in riddles, aphorisms and puzzles, were mainly social rather than spiritual. They did not see his teachings as an indictment of Judaism. They did not regard his death as divine. Clearly, the Q people did not believe that Jesus was the son of God, nor that he rose from the dead. And they certainly did not worship God in his name.

Q is a powerful argument for the contention that Christianity is in fact a mythologized religion. It implies strongly that later New Testament scholars must have embellished the words of the historical Jesus, as recorded in Q, with well-known mainly Syrian and Greek myths about the destiny of a divine being, his martyrdom and resurrection, which would have circulated widely through the intellectual world of the time. If the conventional view of the origins of Christianity are correct, and if Jesus was actually Christ, then how do we explain how his first followers failed to see this themselves? Q begs such vitally important questions. They should be answered with honesty by the modern day custodians of Jesus's message.

But I suppose these people have other things on their minds. I had cause to fly over to London on business recently, and when I got to Heathrow, the taxi driver offered to put my case into his boot. I warned him that it was very heavy. He scoffed, manfully. "You wonna see wot vem farking arabs 'ave in their cases, Mate, if you fink this is farking 'eavy. All their farking gold I s'pose, har, har, har." It was wonderful to be back in multi-cultural, tolerant London.

The extraordinary thing was that the country was in the grip of feverish religious debate. The pubs of south east London were full of beerbellied treble-chinned men, discussing transubstantiation, sacred ritual, the divine succession of Christian ministry. It was quite extraordinary. Everyone in London seemed to be talking about women priests.

Now, let me explain my own position. Up until recently, I was utterly opposed to women being ordained. This was not a sexist stance. I was utterly opposed to men being ordained, also. Of course some priests are very nice fellows, and I am lucky enough to number one or two of them among my friends. But the world has quite enough priests in it already, without women wanting be priests too. A novelist friend of mine says there should be an embargo on promising young Irish writers. There are quite enough of them now, he feels, and we don't want any more for about ten years. I felt the same way about priests.

Still, I figured, if we have to have priests — and I do mean if we absolutely *have* to — I suppose they may as well be women. Maybe if priests had periods, they would not go blathering on blithely about wombs, with the cosy familiarity one usually associates with American tourists blathering on about Jury's Irish Cabaret. I am looking forward to seeing a pregnant bishop also. That will be a great day for Christianity.

Now, I have been reading the new Catholic catechism. It says that couples who have sex before marriage are "in grave sin." It says that contraception may *sometimes* be allowed within marriage, but only the allegedly "natural" method. It is apparently OK to use biology to prevent pregnancy, but not physics or chemistry. That's the thing about priests, you see. You're just getting to like them, and they start on about this auld guff.

As for sex outside marriage, can I just point something out? Sex outside marriage is going on in every little town in Ireland — in my experience, in fact, the littler the town, the more sex there is. Portarlington on a Friday night, for instance, is like Weimar Berlin. Enfield, County Meath, is a veritable Sodom and Gomorrah, or so I have been told. Straight sex, gay sex, kinky sex, underage sex, before marriage, after marriage, in bedrooms, under bushes, in presbytery parlours and bus shelters. A woman I know assures me that you haven't lived until you've had a Garda in the back of a squad car, and I believe her. The point is, it is going on. There is a simple reason for this. It is that people are at their most human when they are involved in the pleasure and humility and vulnerability of sexuality. If there is a God, he was doing us a big favour when he doled out the pheromones. People who are genuinely religious know this. They do not get hung up about it. They have better things to be doing.

On *BBC Radio Four* recently I heard an interview with an Irish nun called Sister Colette Riley. Sister Colette was a laughing, happy woman. She had studied reflexology, a form of massage which concentrates on the feet. It is based on the notion that every body part has a corresponding part in the foot. Sister Colette now spends her time in homeless people's shelters, massaging people's feet. Sometimes their feet are very dirty, she said, but you have to remember that people are entitled to their dignity. It is hard for people when they live on the streets, she said. It is hard for them to look after their feet.

When she was asked if there was any scientific basis for reflexology she laughed and said she didn't know, but that it was a great comfort for people to have their feet rubbed anyway. Just to be touched by another person was a great comfort. The interviewer asked why she did all this. Sister Colette Riley paused, as though she could think of nothing to say. "Well, I love them," she laughed, softly. "I suppose it's because I love them."

Jesus Christ washed the feet of beggars and lepers. He did not tell people who to sleep with. I listened to Sister Colette Riley's beautiful laugh, and I suddenly realised why women priests are such an absolutely marvellous idea. And a woman pope, now *that* would be really something.

I mean, can I just say one thing here? I actually like the present Pope. I think he is a very great man. I deeply admire his dress sense, for instance, even though in his more excessive moments he does admittedly wear garments which would give Dame Edna Everage a migraine. Still, the guy has style. And he has done more for the aviation industry than even Alcock and Brown. If the Vatican State Travel Agency gives out air miles, I think we know who customer *numero uno* is going to be. Yes, The Pope has his faults. He was an indifferent goalkeeper when he played for Poland, for example. Jesus saves, true, but the same can not be too readily said of His representative on earth. And yes, he has bizarre opinions on Hell and angels, and he obviously had some dreadful experience with a woman early in life, seeing as how he clearly dislikes them so much. Perhaps, like myself, he got his tongue caught in a teeth-brace during his first kiss, and had to disentangle himself with the aid of a teaspoon? Well, if that is so, he has my sympathies. You see, basically, I understand him. The Pope and yours truly have been through a lot together.

And I hope his reign will continue for a long time. There is talk that the next Pope is being groomed already, that he will be a certain Cardinal Martini. (Will he, I wonder, be known as "the most beautiful Pope in the world"? Will he be available for Holy Mass, "anytime, anyplace, anywhere?") But I hope that doesn't happen. I want to hang on to JP Mark II.

I keep in touch with the Pope regularly. You see, I had cause to write to him some time ago, regarding a private and rather delicate family matter. A certain rather hotheaded relation of mine had rather publicly torn up a photograph of Il Papa. So I sent him a sincere apology and a big roll of sellotape, and I got a very nice postcard back. Since then, we have kept in touch, The Pope and I. As readers will know, His Holiness has a great love of The Young People of Ireland, or so he tells me anyway. So it pains me to say this. But I have one bit of advice for The Pope. Would he ever just *stop*?

I mean, *I know* he's a pontiff. *I know* he's supposed to pontificate. But, sweet merciful leg of the lamb of God, would he ever just STOP, about contraception being akin to murder, and all that auld blather. "Veritatis Splendor," the latest papal encyclical, is a criminal waste of good trees. Is it too late, I wonder, to get it pulped into toilet paper, or something useful? "Veritatis Splendor" brings a new meaning to the phrase "papal bull." Contraception, the same as murder? I mean, yes, admittedly, anyone who has ever tried to put on a condom at three in the morning, half-stocious, with a bellyfull of chicken vindaloo, fingers frantically fumbling in the pitch-blackness of a Rathmines bedsit, would agree; sheer bloody murder is the only word for it, (or so I have been assured). And any poor unfortunate woman who has ever tried inserting a diaphragm, only to have it spring back across the room with the velocity of a thermonuclear missile and nearly take the eye out of the cat before shattering the double glazing, will concur: contraception is certainly not *pleasant*.

Contraception, like the Roman Catholic Church, is messy, slippery, sometimes embarrassing, often exhausting, vaguely disturbing and, ultimately, difficult to dispose of. In an ideal world we would not need it, but the world, sadly, being created by the Pope's boss, is not ideal. Would his holiness ever just take that up with Him upstairs, and leave the rest of us alone? I mean, contraception is evil? Pull the other one, Your Holiness. Somebody should go through "Veritatis Splendor," carefully taking the word "not" out of every sentence that contains it, and inserting the word "not" into every sentence that doesn't. I'd like to apply for the job, actually. I think I'd be damn good at that kind of thing.

In Ireland, of course, you have to be careful criticising the Catholic Church, because people do get a tad upset. I remember once writing something in *The Sunday Tribune* which provoked a number of letters, taking me to task for being disrespectful and scornful. I mean, all I said was that Jesus had no friends and no sense of humour. Four separate accounts of this guy's life, and did he ever come up with one single gag? No, he did not. Jesus was less funny than Bob Monkhouse, and that is saying something. But my article was not intended to be scornful, nor, I believe, did it read so. It merely asked a number of honest questions about the dominant myth of our culture. Well, OK, maybe it was *a bit* scornful. But only in fun. I admit it.

Mr Murphy wrote a scorcher from Cork to call me, flatteringly enough, "the devil incarnate." Believe me, readers, if I was the devil incarnate I would have been flapping my way down to the city by the Lee to haunt Mr Murphy as frequently as possible. And incidentally, Mr Murphy, if you are reading now, the word "bollocks" has two Ls. You are obviously not a Roddy Doyle fan.

Dr O'Brien from Blackrock, Co Dublin, wrote a detailed letter, countering my claim that Jesus was close to few women. He quoted me the scene of Mary Magdalene washing the feet. This, to the doctor, indicated that Jesus did have women friends. Now, I wonder does the doctor encourage his own women friends to wash his own feet with any regularity? What it indicated to me was that Jesus treated women like second-class citizens, which is, interestingly enough, the way the Roman Catholic Church treats them now. If I ever have the pleasure of meeting the good doctor, I look forward to having a good argument about the other points which critics of Christianity have raised; the disturbing character of Jesus, the pernicious, corrupt and violent influence of the Christian churches through the ages. But let us turn to the central question of the resurrection. Let us try to look objectively at the available evidence.

The gospel of Matthew has Mary Magdalene and "the other Mary" going at dawn on Easter Sunday to the tomb of Jesus. There is "a great earthquake." An angel appears, rolls back the stone and sits on it. As a result of this apparition the guards on duty at the grave "trembled and became like dead men." The women leave. On the way home, they meet Christ, who gives them a message for the disciples.

Mark tells a very different story. Mary Magdalene, Mary "the mother of James" and a third woman, Salome — unmentioned by Matthew — go to the tomb. There is no earthquake, no mention of any guards. When they arrive the stone has already been rolled back, a conflict with Matthew, who has the appearing angel doing this. When they enter, they see a "young man sitting on the right side," inside the tomb, *not* outside, as in Matthew. There is no apparition of Christ here, no message to the disciples. In direct contradiction to Matthew's gospel, the women, in fact, "said nothing to any one, for they were afraid."

Luke omits Salome from his account. He has Mary Magdalene, Mary the mother of James, a woman called Joanna — who is unmentioned by Matthew and Mark — and "other women" visiting the tomb. Again, no guards, no earthquake. "Two men" appear in this version, not one, as in Matthew and Mark. Contradicting Mark completely, Luke informs us that the women "told all this to the eleven, but they did not believe them."

John's version is different again. Mary Magdalene goes to the tomb alone, finds that the stone has been removed, runs to find Simon Peter and "the other disciple." These three go to the grave. No Mary, no Joanna, no Salome, no other women, no guards, no angel moving the stone, no earthquake. The two men enter the tomb, find the body missing, then "go back to their homes," leaving Mary Magdalene alone. Two angels promptly appear to her, contradicting Matthew and Mark. Then Jesus appears, but she does not recognise him, "supposing him to be the gardener." A man whom she knows well enough to wash his feet appears to her, and she thinks he's the gardener. Odd, that.

Let me be specific. The gospels completely contradict each other on (a) who went to the tomb, (b) what happened when they got there, (c) what happened when they left. That is to say, on the very central event of Christianity, on which the entire myth is based, they cannot even get the story straight. Any objective person would be suspicious about this and would conclude, I suggest, that the story of the resurrection is quite simply the most spectacular non-event in history. And when millions of human lives have been utterly ruined by the propagation of this myth, I contend that we would be far better off not celebrating it.

But to each his own, I always say. I have friends who are religious people, and very nice they are too. Indeed, a young couple who live quite near me in Dublin are born-again Christians. They're terribly nice. I like them, really. It's just that they insist on dropping the occasional note into my letter box, telling me that I too can have "a personal relationship with Jesus," as though Jesus is the kind of auld shipmate with whom one might go for a game of pool and a natter about Bosnia of a Friday evening. And every so often, when I pass their gaff, I can hear them praying in tongues.

It's an extraordinary sound. Now, I have lived next door to odd people in my time. I have lived adjacent to opera singers with lungs that could suck the air out of inner tubes, and guitar players of such astonishing inability that they made Jimi Hendrix sound like Brahms. Once I lived above two enthusiastically sado-masochistic lesbians whose principle delight in life was to flail the living bejayzus out of each other every night from seven thirty to eight forty five. Their bruises, cuts and seeping abrasions were so appalling that whenever I met them on the stairs I mistook them for members of the Birmingham Six.

So I have heard sounds coming through wallpaper, let me tell you. But praying in tongues takes the biscuit. Like, you're sitting there trying to watch the telly or you might have just got out of the bath, and be feeling all pink and squishy and vulnerable and all of a sudden — *akha rhama llama phooey bop abop a ringo awaayayyoyeah* — the sound of praying in tongues comes rattling up the ventilator shaft, like the backing vocals of an early Little Richard track. God now, it makes it very hard to concentrate on the Countdown conundrum.

The other night I was trying to heat myself up a defrosted lean cuisine — ah, the joys of single living — when my cooker started to tremble like a recovering alcoholic and belch out great clouds of smoke. When the electrician arrived, I skipped downstairs with the agility of a young goat to let him in. These very nice people were kneeling on the grass in front of their flat — "the lawn," they insist on calling it, although I have seen more verdant growth on teeth — with a couple of their friends, praying in tongues. Suddenly, they all stretched out their hands and put them on the head of one bemused young woman, and started chanting "cast *out* the demons, Lord, yesssah, *cast* them away, *into* eternal fire," (It is an odd characteristic of born-again Christians, in my experience, that they always put the stress on the wrong word in a sentence.) Well, I was quite puce with mortification. The electrician was standing very still, aghast, pinching his nose, a look of numbed and disbelieving panic on the rest of his face. They had a barbecue going in the background, with a couple of greasy bloody steaks sizzling away, and they were kneeling, eyes closed, performing exorcisms on each other, praying in tongues! *Soomee mahoonalalala bonie soomee obbabobbabobba shimmie moronie shimmie*! Well I was going to ring the police. I mean, this is shagging Donnybrook, after all. This is not Waco, Texas.

Upstairs in my kitchen, as he regarded my cooker with the pursed lips of a man who knows that he is on forty pounds an hour plus VAT, the electrician was confused. He asked me what these people had been doing on the lawn, and I explained that they had been praying in tongues. What was this? he enquired. This was when the Holy Spirit or divine paraclete filled the faithful elect with the love of the Lord and allowed them to praise the divine being in the secret and elusive poetry of the cherubim, I said. "Jayzus, go way," he replied. "Is that right?"

He just couldn't get his head around praying in tongues. He was a Roman Catholic, he confided, and he couldn't imagine the Pope praying in tongues. I said I couldn't imagine His Holiness actually having a tongue at all, for some reason, although, heaven knows, he uses it often enough, to the widespread and obvious satisfaction of the faithful.

But, I must admit, when I saw those people praying in tongues, it brought back bittersweet memories. Because when I was young -and this is a terrible confession — I too was a member of the clap-happy brigade. I attended a Catholic boarding school, and the only way one could be occasionally excused from study was if one joined up with the school prayer group. Thus, I found the Lord.

And it wasn't too bad. Other teenagers who grew up in the seventies drank cider and smoked pot and had oral sex with each other in supermarket car parks and on the beaches of our fair land, or so I am reliably informed. Indeed, I am told that this kind of thing still goes on, that if one were to wander down Dollymount Strand any Friday night and yell, loudly, "Get out here Darren and put your drawers back on this minute!" one would nearly be stampeded to death in the rush. But I never did any of these things. I spent most of the late seventies at prayer meetings, in stuffy rooms with posters of sunsets on the walls, holding hands with people I didn't even know, grinning like a lobotomized clam, rattling a tambourine with a little picture of the Holy Child of Prague on it, and singing along to "Jesus Wants Me for a Sunbeam."

But it had its compensations. I liked it very much actually. I'd recommend it warmly to all sensitive teenagers. Because being a born-again Christian, I found, was a great way to meet girls. Sensitive girls, intelligent girls, girls to whom one could talk, and who knew the words to "Seventeen" by Janis Ian. Girls who wore long batik dresses and played nylon-stringed guitars and wrote epic poems about their pimples and their parents' lack of understanding. Girls, above all, whom one could walk to the bus stop when the prayer meeting was over and make some frantic attempt to snog. I met my first girlfriend at a prayer meeting. She preferred Bob Dylan to Janis Ian. This was initially very attractive. But then she preferred Bob Dylan to everybody, really. In the end, she preferred Bob Dylan to me.

Still, it really wasn't too bad being a born again Christian. It became apparent quite early in this spiritual journey that the greater one's proficiency at praying in tongues, the greater the chances that one's own tongue would be located half way down the oesophagus of a fellow worshipper by the end of the evening. So I babbled and burbled with the best of them and the spirit did indeed move in mysterious ways.

As I sat alone in my flat that evening, having forked out a hundred quid to the electrician, and forked in perhaps half a pound of stodgy lean cuisine, it all seemed such a long time ago. And as the sound of the praying kept coming up from the garden, *weelea, weealaaa, urghaoopeedoo*, it occurred to me that really I should think about renewing my membership. Get out my tambourine and join downstairs. Become born-again all over again. Awopbop-aloobob Alop-bamboom.

Chapter Six
Stayin' Alive: How to be Healthy

A friend who is a doctor recently took one look at me and suggested that it might be a shrewd career move to avoid dying of a stroke or an immediate heart attack. So I went out straight away and joined a gym in Dublin. You see, I have been neglecting my body for quite some time, as, for some reason or another, has just about everyone else. I have no desire to become superfit exactly, merely to be able to barge my way up to the bar five minutes before closing time without collapsing from exhaustion. Also, I find that my daily constitutional — over to the shops to buy cigarettes and ice cream — has become a little more tiring of late, and, you know, these little danger signs can be telling.

When I was a teenager I was actually thin. My pert *gluteus maximus* was quite frequently compared to two eggs in a hanky. These days it would be more readily likened to a couple of rugby balls in a durex. Back then, I always looked young for my age. I remember an aunt telling me, when I was one year old, that I didn't look a day over zero. Now, sadly, I resemble the portrait which Dorian Gray hid in his famous attic.

I know where my problems began. When I became a student and moved into a flat I began to neglect my health. It started with the odd hamburger in the Belfield restaurant. Pretty soon, on my rare trips to the supermarket, I had devised five criteria which had to be considered before any foodstuff product could be purchased. (A) You had to be able to eat it in three minutes, using only a fork, while pogoing around to "White Riot" by The Clash, "Mirror In The Bathroom" by The Beat or "Free Nelson Mandela" by The Special AKA. (B) You had to merely add water to it in order to render it edible. (C) It had to be more full of plastics than Elizabeth Taylor's face. (D) You had to be able to use the container afterwards as an ashtray. (E) It could not, on any account, be lettuce.

I am now paying for the sins of my youth. Still, I must confess that I have no real desire to be skinny. Freud maintained that the purpose of psychoanalysis was to replace destructive neurosis with ordinary human misery. Similarly, for me, joining a gym is so that I may become just averagely unfit again, rather than terminally knackered.

The joint to which I belong is run by two very nice women, and the ambience there is relaxed. This is a good thing. I have investigated joining gymnasia before, but I have always felt very uneasy in them. Any time I have ever been to a gym it has been full of silent bowsies with big muscles and necks thicker than their heads. I have no stomach for that kind of thing. It is, *ochón*, the only way in which I have no stomach.

But ah, how easy it is to fool oneself when one is overweight. Take the weighing scales, for instance. Most people stand on that infernal machine. But for too long now, my own method has been to hang suspended by my knees from the shower rail, like some class of exotic and almost certainly flightless bat of South American origin, and to then press down on the scales with my hands until the desired weight is reached. I am the only six stone man in Ireland whose confirmation suit does not fit him any more.

Yet I have always had this ambivalent feeling about physical exertion. If God had meant us to jog, for instance, why weren't we born with Reeboks instead of feet? Does the bible say anything about aerobics? No, it does not. Jesus may have cleared the temple, but we may be sure it was not with a pole-vaulting stick. And when Moses came forth, it was not in the hundred metres hurdles. Still, I suppose the day has come. I must get over my doubts.

The fags will have to go too, I guess. Look, I smoke. I know what I'm talking about. I am smoking now, even as I am writing this. A smouldering fag is wedged between my nicotine-stained fingers as I type, pitiful creature that I am. If I could smoke while shaving, I would. Once or twice I have smoked in the bath. A former girlfriend once asked me if I would mind only smoking after we had made love. Within a week, the pure creature had almost died of sexually-induced exhaustion.

There has been mucho baloney in the newspapers this year about a new book which came out in America — where else, where else? — extolling the merits of smoking, and saying how glamorous and existentialist it is. Now listen here, smoking is about as sexy as

Ronald Reagan in a wetsuit. Dear reader, give up the weed. I may be struck down by a bus while jogging tomorrow, and after some of the things I have done in my life, I will have a good bit of explaining to do in the great hereafter. If just one of you gave up the coffin nails on my account, a hefty slice might be removed from my spell in purgatory. Please? Don't make me beg.

You know it's bad for your health. You know the way sucking on a burning scrag of rotting leaf is not the best way to stay young. You know the way you wake up every morning spluttering like an orgasmic walrus. And the way they will one day have to remove a large section of your lung and replace it with a device which looks like a small accordion. And the way this device, which should be getting digitally manipulated by Sharon Shannon on a regular basis, will actually be doing your breathing for you.

But the worst thing about smoking is not what it does to your body. It is what it does to your mind. You are going to a party, say. What is your last thought as you exit the lodgings? Do you have enough fags? No, probably not. Better stop at the huckster's shop and get another hundred. Right. All set. But hang on! Everyone at the party knows *you're* the heavy smoker. They'll all ask you for cigarettes, when it gets late, and they're drunk, and they're singing "The Boys of The Auld Brigade." Better double back and get a few more packs. Now, do you have matches? Pat your pockets. Better get a few more boxes. Some shifty fecker will probably nick them. You get one of those big boxes. Strap it to your thigh with an elastic band, in case you lose it. Now. Do you have your lighter? What if it runs out of fuel? Get some just in case. And a few cigars. And a packet of cigarette papers. And a pouch of Old Jack Tar's Thick Cut Yo-Ho-Ho Shag. Calm down. You're grand. You're only dropping in for an hour, after all.

You arrive at the soirée weighed down like a pack mule. You find a corner in which to stand. You light a cigarette. All the other smokers are in the same corner, in a fume of despondency and noxious stale Major smoke. The host is staring at you like you're some class of leper. He gave up the coffin nails in '87, oh divil the bit does he miss them. Oh, bedad, it's done him wonders. He can taste his food now, he is libidinous as a young goat in Spring, his once black lungs are as pink as Nancy Reagan's hair. You nod. You grin. Your fag end is getting longer as you listen. Can you flick it on the carpet without being seen? Do you flick it into a wine glass? Do you flick it into your matchbox and then surreptitiously slide the lid closed, only to cause a small explosion some moments later?

You get drunk, because you feel so bad about smoking. You go home feeling miserable, having had a row with your host's spouse, about Fianna Fail, or the international situation, or nicorette patches. You sit sulking in the living room, watching the testcard, trying to persuade yourself that you had a good time. You smoke your last cigarette. Slowly. Down to the butt. You sad druggy loser, you then *smoke the filter*! You make a cup of tea. Maybe the evening wasn't so bad after all. But you begin to panic. You don't have one for the morning!! All the shops are closed now!! Your palms sweat. You notice the aspidistra on the windowsill. You tear off a few leaves and roll them up in a five punt note. You light up, sit back and take a big puff, feeling sexy, existentialist, cool as Jean Paul Sartre in a snowstorm. You're an adult, after all. Have another big suck. Sure, God now, isn't it the most sophisticated habit there is?

Well, as my teachers used to say, you're only fooling one person, and that's your little old self. Give it up, won't you? Give the ciggies the elbow. Just do it and see how you like it. *I* will if you will, I swear to God and all the blessed angels. (I won't really. I'm only saying that.)

You see, I am all in favour of health, really. Of course it is not just our lungs and hearts which bother us these days, but our minds also. The other afternoon I was having a coffee in town when I overheard a conversation. A nice-looking young man and woman were sitting at the next table, holding hands and *talking to each other about their therapists*. Now, when I lived over in London, therapy was all the rage. You were nothing if you were not trotting along for a weekly sob-in with some syrupy-voiced and medically unqualified person about your emotional problems. I will cheerfully admit that I tried this caper myself for a while, in the almost admirably stupid belief that pain is an emotion we grown-ups shouldn't ever have to experience. I could have bought a Porsche with the money I spent to discover I was wrong.

And now I get the feeling this therapy stuff is catching on over here on Saint Patrick's blessed isle. It's sad. Of course people who have real mental or emotional disorders need help. They need psychiatrists and psychologists, professionals who have demonstrated their commitment to healing by actually doing the odd exam on the subject. But what wounded people need like a moose needs a hatstand is half-baked sycophantic platitude, which is all most forms of "therapy" have to offer.

The most popular therapy in Britain and the US is "inner child therapy," a pseudo-religion of self-obsession which contends that we are all basically children, doomed to repeat patterns of "abuse" practised upon us by our evil parents. It is very popular with middle class kids who find life a tad tricky, probably not so popular in Bosnia or East Timor, where the texture of people's suffering is not nearly so postmodern. But if you're the type who has too much time on your hands, and if you want someone to assure you that you're only humourless and dull because Mom and Pops didn't buy you that nose-job for your graduation, inner child therapy really is the thing.

How is dysfunction measured in this ideology? Take a look at Charles Whitfield's book *Healing The Child Within*. "Do you seek approval and affirmation?" he chides. "Do you respond with anxiety to authority figures and angry people?" If you answer yes to the above — and let us face it, unless you are Charlie Bird, you will — you'll need to get your inner child sorted out. (Which means, in effect, you'll need to buy it a few more inner child books.)

Odds-on, they'll be written by one John Bradshaw, an American therapy guru who has become very rich by helping his readers realise how inadequate they are. Bradshaw's fame is now so great that it has caused his own inner child problems, he has confessed. And his way of appeasing his threatened inner child? "For the last few years," he has written, "we always fly first class." (If only there were more dysfunctional people in Ireland, Aer Lingus wouldn't be losing so much money.) Do you indulge in "inveterate" dreaming? Bradshaw asks, from his luxury seat overflying the landscape of human misery. Horror of horrors, do you "avoid depression through activity?" Why then, your inner child is practically barking.

In the therapy worldview there are no communal or societal responsibilities, only duties to the self. There is no personal failing that cannot be blamed on others. If you drink too much, snort coke or beat your children, it's not really you, it's your poor frightened inner child. "Hitler," Bradshaw writes, "was re-enacting his own childhood, using millions of innocent Jews as his scapegoats." Wonderful, huh? Belsen was all Herr and Frau Schickelgruber's fault. It is profoundly to be hoped that Mr Bradshaw and his airborne inner child write their next bestseller with their trousers down, so that we may hear what they have to say more clearly.

In the meantime, here is my own therapy guide in full. Put down this tome and go out for a long walk in the fresh air. If that doesn't work, get yourself a qualified shrink with a lot of experience and a little human understanding, not a John Bradshaw book. You'll be feeling better before you know it.

Not that vigorous exercise is a cure all for everything, you understand. A speculative and brave young journalist once asked Oscar Wilde if he was at all interested in outdoor sports. "Oh yes indeed," Wilde replied, "I have often played dominoes outside Parisian cafes." Good old Oscar. I am absolutely with him on this one.

There is a bizarre notion going about these days that the outdoor life is somehow good for us. Now that the Spring is here, not only are we fuller-figured men to be herded into gymnasia, cajoled into saunas, forced at gunpoint into health-farms. In addition, once these unspeakable humiliations are over, in whatever is left of our much-needed leisure time we are supposed to go wandering about like cretins through the countryside.

My friends keep telling me that it would be good for me to get the odd walk in the country. It would be "good" for me, they say, thus exhibiting a very dubious conception indeed of goodness. Pshaw, phooey and huh. If God had meant us to exercise at all, we would have been born with roller skates attached to our ankles, and the eleventh commandment would have been "Thou Shalt Put On A Leotard and Prance About Like a Fat Old Imbecile." I was brought up in a place called Glenageary, a suburb of Southside Dublin, where the only exercise anyone ever got was adultery, lawnmowing and going to the shops to buy cheap potent drink in the middle of the day. And as for the countryside, forget it. The countryside is for sheep, morris dancers and germs.

Some time ago I was invited by a charming couple I know to join a group of friends who were visiting their country house in the Catalan Pyrenees. The plan was to fly to Madrid and get the bus from there to the local town. Once there, I was told, I could get a taxi up the mountain to the tiny hamlet.

I got on the bus at 7 a.m., surrounded by a pack of vile-smelling English hoodlums who looked as if they would happily kick seven shades of shite out of you without missing a beat of "Olé, Olé, Olé." They spent the entire journey brushing the dandruff off their fake raybans, assembling intricate postmodernist sculptures out of their nasal detritus and trying to ignite each others farts with matches. I spent the whole journey reading the collected short stories of John McGahern. I feel sure there is a moral there somewhere.

Eventually we arrived at the town. I walked around a bit, noticing with a sinking heart that there were advertisements everywhere for all sorts of new-fangled and dangerous outdoor sports. White-water rafting, paragliding, cliff-jumping. I am serious. Jumping off cliffs is a sport now. Things are getting so bad that I fully expect swallowing a litre of paraquat and then shooting yourself in the head with a sawn-off shotgun to be a demonstration event at the Sydney Olympics.

Anyway, a very nice local man agreed to convey me up the mountain in his jeep. I will draw a discreet veil over this part of the journey. Suffice it to say that the roads were so swoonmakingly steep and my stomach so fragile that I was to wish more than once I had brought along either my brown trousers or a good strong pair of bicycle clips, or both.

I arrived at my friend's house at about 3 p.m., to much clapping of the back and hearty congratulation. The village is tiny; there are only six families and one telephone. (Which, I suppose on reflection, is better than having six telephones and one family). A walk all the way back down to the nearest river was immediately proposed. It would not take long, I was told by my so-called friends. I concurred immediately, feeling that this would confuse them, and also, that it would be best to get the vile and tedious exercise part over with, so that the drinking and dissolution could then begin in earnest.

Ten minutes later I was being led down the side of a ravine which was more sheer than a pair of President Mary Robinson's tights, staggering through piles of sundried cowshit, hypervenilating, clinging for dear life onto clumps of brambles and vicious flesh eating nettles, the major moments of my life flashing before me in murky colour, the sun screaming down on me, the mosquitoes regarding my pink raw flesh the way the Belles of Saint Trinians would have regarded an unattended ice-cream van parked in their playground.

I fell face forward into the river and bobbed about there like a harpooned whale, desperately trying to drown myself. When that didn't work I rolled around and floated on my back, staring in derangement up at the blue sky and wondering how any of this had happened to me. I thought I was going to die. "Bloody great, eh?" my friend called, repeatedly slapping his chest in a manner that would have made Tarzan look like a big girl's blouse, "fantastic to get a bit of the old country life, eh?" At this point, a few of the Englishmen from the bus emerged from the bushes in loud swimming trunks. They dived screeching and howling into the river. One of them surfaced just beside me.

"Can't beat it, huh?" he said.

"No indeed," I laughed, adding, albeit silently, "but perhaps I could beat *you*, smug Saxon bollocks, with a very large hammer."

Later that night, in the privacy of my room, I examined what was left of my sunburnt and ravaged body. I was a fetid mass of cuts, sores, scratches, bruises, hives, rashes, bites, pustules and grazes. I looked (a) like a medieval martyr after a particularly stressful afternoon on a crucifix, or (b) a person who had recently got off with Madonna.

It all had a certain novelty value, I suppose. But ever since then I feel uneasy being in the countryside. Those green fields brimming with life, that clean pure air. You look out over the beautiful view, the birds whirling around in the haze, the lambs gambolling in the fields, the locals gambling in the bingo hall, the sun delicately layering the dawn sky with the soft hues of scarlet and vermilion. And you feel you'd swap every single lousy bit of it for a smoky urban pub, a large gin and a packet of fags. *Glenageary Über Alles*. There is very little hope for the countryside and me. I shall have to pursue health in the city.

Women feel that they are victims of body fascism, but men have their own problems with which to contend. Let us face it, and face it boldly, having a penis is tricky. This has often pricked my mind, but one evening recently while on a brief trip over to London I went to have a Turkish bath with a male friend who is almost as vilely overweight as myself, and it occurred to me again with some considerable force.

Now, as I say, I am not very comfortable with my body. Admittedly, this may have something to do with the fact that my arse contains more cellulite than the front row of a Tom Jones concert. Still, I don't think I am alone. In England anyway, fear of the physical is almost the national sport. In England, one practically emerges from the womb in full evening dress.

The man in the lobby was fat as a fool and had nothing on except for the radio, his spectacles and a grin so cheesy that you could have melted it down and spread it on toast. "First time, boys?" he said. I gulped in the affirmative.

"How long then?" I said.

His eyebrows practically disappeared into his hairline. "Sorry?" he said, "bit farking personal, aintcha?"

"How long have we left," I stammered, "before you close?"

He looked at his watch, then reached down and absent-mindedly scratched his pendulous bollocks. "Oh, 'bout fifty minutes," he said. "Just get in there, strip off and relax."

Thus advised, we strode purposefully into the changing room, where all the members — and I do mean members — were spread out and displaying their talents.

Well, my friend threw off his clothes with the graceful ease of a Vaudeville showgirl. He then fell to the floor and started to do frantic push-ups, his breasts and stomach bouncing against the lino. I was a little less enthusiastic, I must admit. It took me twenty minutes to get my watch off, another ten to find a safe enough place for my socks. After that, the real trouble began.

My friend seemed to be getting into the groove. He began jogging up and down on the spot, hands behind his head, the tip of his appendage proudly slapping out a bossa nova rhythm against his abdomen. He was enjoying his nakedness, his return to the wild state. For one awful moment I thought he was going to start barking. I myself had got as far as my shirt buttons. To deal with the next dreadful stage, I had mentally developed a complicated arrangement which involved towels, Roman Catholic discretion and a good deal of hopping.

Anyway, when we had both peeled to the buff we stood there, gibbering in the cold. My friend began to whistle the William Tell overture, so utterly relaxed did he feel. I looked around the room, trying to admire the tiling, the sinks, the ceiling. But all I could see were penises.

It is such a rare thing to see a penis to which one is not personally attached that when one does, one is as curious as Galileo gazing at the moon through his telescope. Here were penises of all ages, sizes and shapes, organs of all colours, some grey, some black, others as pink as candy floss. The atmosphere was sedate. There was one extremely old man sitting in a corner. He had a cock the length of a docker's arm and balls the size of church bells. You could have made a very nice expandable briefcase out of his foreskin.

I wrapped a towel fervently around my waist and made gingerly for the steam room. A burly attendant stopped me and nodded at my towel. "You going in like that?" he said. I nodded, "I was going to, yes." He glared at me as though I had just vomited on him.

"Some of the blokes might think you wuz taking the piss," he advised. "You wouldn't want'em to think that, would you?"

He held out his hand and I gave him my towel. He glanced down at my shrivelling privates, pursed his lips and nodded, with the wearied air of a mechanic who has seen one too many brokendown cars. I stepped into the steamroom, blushing, sat down and began to be lightly sautéed. I wondered why I had been so unwilling to get my kit off but I really couldn't find any logical answer. I mean, my penis may not be the same length as an *Irish Times* editorial, but, you know, it's not quite as short as an *In Dublin* lonely hearts ad either.

Over in the steamiest corner, I could hear my chubby friend softly singing the Led Zeppelin song "Won't Ya Squeeze My Lemon Baby Till the Juice Runs Down My Leg," beating out a four-four blues rhythm against his corpulent thighs. I didn't feel well at all. I sat broiling in the steam, desperately counting the seconds until I could put my clothes back on. O Lord, O Lord, as the Old Testament has it, how hard it is to kick against the pricks.

Chapter Seven
Playboys on Crutches

The Secret World of the Irish Male.
Part I: The Sins of the Fathers

"Every woman becomes her mother" claimed Oscar Wilde, "that is her tragedy." He added, to stir it up a little more, "No man does; that is his." A neat gag, which perhaps means no more than it says. But another reading reveals a hidden truth. It is not that men should strive to become their mothers, but that they should at all costs avoid becoming their fathers. Fatherhood was always suspect in the Wildean worldview, and Wilde was far from alone in his suspicion. The possibility of mutating into one's own father was the force which kept Irish maleness fearful for centuries. It is a fear which still resonates powerfully now.

The Irish father-son relationship, recently explored in an RTE television series, is too often a fraught and extremely complex affair. In *Sons of the Fathers*, a spell-binding collection of frank and deeply moving conversations between Ciana Campbell and a number of Irish men, sons talked about their fathers with considerable bravery, compassion and affection. But at the dark centre of this mysterious love, in almost every father-son relationship discussed in the programme, a nagging and destructive anxiety was at work.

Last November in Boston I went to a show by the American-Irish comedian Denis Leary. "All these explosions we hear about over in Ireland," he said, "all those bombs and blasts on the CBS news every night, you know what they really are? They're not the work of the IRA. They're Irish men, just walking down the street and exploding with tension about their Dads."

It's only funny because it exaggerates a poignant truth. *Sons of the Fathers* revealed this unease with force. It was clear that having a father is tough for many Irish men. "He was a difficult man to get close to," recalled Bernard Ryan of his father, a warm but troubled man who left his family in heartbreaking circumstances, "I was never very close to him."

"I respected him," said Christy Fleming, of his own father, "but I was a bit jealous of him. It was important to get him riled up sometimes, to get a bit of attention. I regret not knowing him better." Niall and Dermot Stokes's recollection of their father portrayed a kindly man beset by tragedy. Maurice Stokes would often describe his role as a parent in a startling image, that of "walking down a beach, feeling the waves crash over you, knocking you down, and having to just get up again and keep going." Many of the fathers and sons in this programme would have known what he meant. Witnessing the strain of interviewees Ger and Tadgh Philpott as they recalled the afternoon Ger told his father he was gay was unforgettably painful. ("It was the biggest kick in the teeth he ever got," Ger remembered, before praising his father for coming in time to support him.) And to see Joseph Maguire come close to tears as he courageously recounted the love he and his father found quite late in his father's life — after what he called "an ice-age" of mutual misunderstanding — was devastatingly moving.

I'm very fond of my own father, Sean, I must say. In the thirty years I've known him, I don't think he's ever once let me down. We've been through a lot together and I think this shared experience has strengthened the bond between us. But we've also both been lucky enough to inhabit an age in which men have been permitted to discuss their feelings with a candour that would have been completely unacceptable even a generation ago. He's an affectionate, caring man. Sometimes I forget exactly how fortunate I am to have him. I don't mind saying that watching this series made me remember.

Replaying the tape of *Sons of the Fathers* I thought about Sean a great deal, because one his favourite jokes kept coming into my mind. A farmer has two sons who swear a lot. One morning, they come down for breakfast. "What'll you have?" the Da enquires of the eldest. "I'll have a shagging egg," the son says. The farmer smacks him in the face. "I said, what'll you have?" The son is nonplussed. "Erm, I'll have a shagging egg, please?" The farmer takes off his belt and thrashes his son up and down the kitchen. "Pup," he roars, "what did you dare say to me?" "I just said I wanted a shagging egg, Da." The farmer picks up a chair, batters his son black and blue and leaves him for dead. "Now," he barks at the other son, "what'll you have? And mind what happened to your brother." The youngest ponders for a moment. "Jesus, Da," he says, "I won't have a shagging egg anyway."

It's a joke that says a lot about the uneasy links between many Irish fathers and sons. The tragicomedy of their relationship is not that they are fated to dislike each other, but rather that they seem doomed, like many of the men in *Sons of the Fathers*, forever to talk at crossed purposes. "The programme is about people not being able to say things" commented series producer David McKenna, "but it's also about people not always needing to say things straight out."

All the men in the series seemed to have been close to their mothers. And indeed, at a cursory glance, Irish mothers generally have it a lot better than Irish fathers. Their importance is enshrined in the constitution, their influence celebrated in mawkish ballad and boozy come-all-ye. The traditional language of republican nationalism — with its emphasis on the maternal archetypes of Mother Ireland and the Shan Van Vocht — underscores this. Mothers appear time and again in political writings, poetic imagery and rebel songs. Patrick Pearse's last verse was written in the voice of his mother, with no reference at all to his father. In the patriotic song "Four Green Fields" the proud old woman appeals to her brave sons — and not her unreliable husband — to stop the invading stranger from stealing her territory.

In the Irish ballad tradition mothers are semi-sacred beings. Whereas fathers, when they feature at all, are often morally ambivalent if not downright disturbing figures. In one version of the famous 1798 song "The Croppy Boy," for instance, the soon-to-be executed narrator is betrayed by his father as he climbs the scaffold to die for the motherland. Reading the ballad tradition as a series of sophisticated familial metaphors, one thing becomes clear. The Irish political family is woefully dysfunctional. Fathers are absent. The struggle for freedom is a symbolic war by Irish sons for their virtuous, endangered and invariably single mothers.

So where were the fathers while all this was going on? Doing the real and non-symbolic fighting, I guess. Perhaps this is part of the problem. Not only were countless thousands of fathers in Irish history forced to leave their families for economic reasons, but whole generations of Irish men were brought up by their mothers, while fathers stalked the countryside fighting for independence, or went on the run, or were killed or imprisoned. Watching Niall and Dermot Stokes talk with pride about their grandfather being interned for his part in the 1916 Rising was heartwarming, yet it begged a set of uncomfortable questions about the historical effect of political struggle on the Irish family. Fighting the Tans was all very well, but sometimes you can't help feeling that if the Eamon de Valera generation had stayed home and changed the occasional nappy Ireland might have been oddly better off.

Culturally, this struggle for Irish national freedom often expresses itself in profoundly Oedipal terms. For if motherhood in our history is associated with revolution, fatherhood is often linked with authority. We see this most forcefully in the classic text of the traditional Irish father-son relationship, J M Synge's *The Playboy of the Western World*. In the play, Christy Mahon, a feeble youth, wins friends and sends his sexual stock-price soaring by boasting that he has murdered his cruel father. Far from being horrified or even mildly offended by this startling act of patricide, the villagers come to think of Christy as the epitome of bravery and style. More subversively, so does he. Murdering your father is good for you, the extraordinary message goes; it is only by doing this that a man becomes his true self, and, by implication, that a society achieves meaningful independence from the imperialism and oppression represented by fatherhood.

Like Christy Mahon, interviewee Joseph Maguire said in *Sons of the Fathers* that he was "intimidated" by his father. Bernard Ryan said of his own, "there would have been fear of him." (Ryan's interview was particularly memorable, both for its touching compassion and its repeated use of curiously distancing language. "There would have been drink involved," he said, for example, rather than "my father drank.") Indeed, all but a few of the interviewees spoke about fearing their fathers at some point. It seemed shocking, until you remembered that almost every aspect of our popular culture is imbued with this father-fear. It is even present in religious belief. The traditional popularity of Marian devotion in Ireland, for example, surely has a role in both causing and affecting this dread of the father. The old-fashioned idea that God was essentially a stern judge who was best approached through a supplicating mother was, after all, a peculiarly Irish one.

"He was always himself," Christy Fleming recalled of his father in the programme, "and I could never be myself." It was a succinct summation of the problem; the father-son relationship is at heart a tragedy of identity. Our literary tradition backs this up, providing us with many sober reflections on the ambivalent influence of the Irish father. The greatest Irish family saga of the century, *Ulysses*, has as its essential focus the yearning of sons and fathers to locate each other. Leopold Bloom, who has lost his only son, is drawn by fate to the young Steven Dedalus who cannot communicate with his own father, a bungling eejit, prickling with self-importance. For a few brief hours, Joyce allows fathers and sons to be at least symbolically reunited, but ultimately the relationship falters; the novel ends not with the new communion of men, but with the cascading celebration of womanhood that is Molly Bloom's soliloquy.

O'Casey's plays are full of incapable fathers also. Who would want an aulfella like Captain Boyle, the strutting eponymous Paycock? (The play ends with the assertion that it is better to have two mothers than one father.) In Wilde's work, fathers are often elusive, unreliable and shifty. In Brian Friel's *Philadelphia, Here I Come*, Gar's father is like Joseph Maguire's in *Sons of the Fathers*, "a somewhat uptight cold person [with] a lot of inner tension," a man who has no recollection at all of his son's most formative experiences. ("You and me," Gar observes, damningly, "we embarrass each other.") More recently, John McGahern's brilliant novel *Amongst Women* has at its tragic centre a father who runs his family with military efficiency and who cannot bear to even refer to his rebellious son by name. The ghost of Paul Durcan's father haunts much of that poet's fine work, from the devastating piece "Father's Day" in *The Berlin Wall Cafe* to the harrowing collection,

Daddy, Daddy. And Colm Toibin's *The Heather Blazing* is an exquisitely poignant voyage through the topography of the Irish family, revealing the emotional disasters accidentally unleashed every day in the hallowed name of the father.

Poor fathers. We wouldn't be what we are without them. Again and again in *Sons of the Fathers* Irish sons made this point. They admire many of their fathers' values, or, at least, their courage and tenacity in expressing values which their sons find utterly repugnant. But perhaps it is more interesting to ask, would our fathers be what *they* are without us? For we create our parents' personas at least as much as they create ours. We shape their lives, their moralities, their attitudes, their aspirations, their compromises and sacrifices. Perhaps we sons deserve the fathers we have, for if we do not quite mould our fathers in our own images, we certainly squander enough energy in the attempt, and Philip Larkin's famous account of what Mums and Dads do to their children works just as well when put the other way around. "You fuck them up, your Mum and Dad. You do not mean to, but you do."

Ultimately, if *Sons of the Fathers* reached any definitive conclusion it was that Wilde's father-mother saying was broadly correct. The programme left the viewer with the sense that becoming a good father oneself is somehow linked to the pain of learning to regard one's own father as a distinct human being, not as a perfect role model. The interviewees who are now fathers themselves all implied this, that we Irish men must at least try to view our fathers with something like the compassion we expect from them. We should recognise their separateness and give them a break. It's a convincing case. Because it must be pretty frightening, to borrow that haunting image from Niall and Dermot Stokes's Dad, to find yourself walking down that storm-battered beach with a small and vulnerable version of yourself for company. It must be lonely being a father. And as the waves crash around you, and the wind begins to howl again, it must be an eerily disconcerting sensation to feel the sands shifting once more beneath your uncertain feet.

Part II: Irishmen and Alcohol: A Love Story

Irish men can be difficult to deal with. Let me tell you about a friend of mine. One night last month I met him for "a few quiet drinks" after work. Ten hours and many pints later we were thrown out of the dingiest nightclub in the Western world for being drunk. I took him home, listened patiently to his inane babbling and his slurred choruses of "Let's Talk About Sex, Bay-Bee, Let's Talk About.. ungh... You and Me" and tried to fill him full of black coffee. Eventually, he fell face forward onto the carpet, tried to get off with it, puked, and lapsed into unconsciousness. I threw a coat over him and went to bed.

Next morning, the living room smelt like a low-rent brewery. My friend lay twisted up in a knot on the shag pile, red-eyed, filthy, dishevelled, reeking of lager and stale cigarette smoke. He looked like downtown Beirut on legs. I asked him how he was feeling. "Brill," he grinned. "Great night, eh?"

I know Irish women get drunk too. I've read the statistics. Two out of five Irish women prefer alcohol to sex. (It's been just my luck to have gone out with both of them.) If I had a penny for every time a Dublin taxi driver has told me there is nothing more dreadful than a drunken "bird"- "Fookin' hell, pal, they're bleedin' worse than a bloke any day. Some of them young wans would suck the feckin' gargle out of a dishcloth" — I would be a tax exile in Switzerland now. But, generally, female drunkenness is not the all-embracing inebriation of men. You do not, for example, see sozzled mobs of leering raucous women rampaging down O'Connell Street on the night before a rugby match, dropping their drawers at passers-by, singing "Way-Hay and Up She Rises" and humorously wearing stolen toilet seats around their necks. Rarely do you see a woman lying in the gutter, blithely redecorating the pavement with her rapidly fermenting gastric juices. I cannot recall the last time I saw an intoxicated gal tottering around a Dublin pub at ten minutes past closing time, swilling back a cocktail comprised of the varied contents of the leftover glasses. But I have seen men do all these things. Why?

Are women simply more civilized than men? Are they intrinsically more moral? Surely this is a very unprogressive argument. To say that men are vile scumbags, and that they return to their natural state when alcohol seeps through the facade, is to say that men are incapable of reform. It is to say that men can not, by their very nature, be soft, sensitive and caring. Which is demonstrably untrue. I mean, look at Derek Davies.

Some of my feminist friends have informed me that Irish men get drunk because they cannot express themselves properly while sober. Irish men are so screwed up, the weary old argument goes, that they cannot tell you they love you until they have a gut-full of Jack Daniels or Castelmaine XXXX. But isn't that a little rash, as the celebrated actress said to the bishop?

For a start, I have no problem at all with men being emotionally repressed. It all depends on the emotions we're talking about. Hatred, jealousy, paranoia, violence, are all well worth repressing. If male emotional repression means that fewer men will beat up their wives, hey, I can live with that. Women should repress those emotions too, in my book.

But perhaps I am untypical. The men I know are all "new" men. They have read their Germaine Greer. They can watch those television advertisements for feminine hygiene products — "with wings" — without tittering, blushing or flapping their arms. The men I know are nurturing, kind, balanced, at one with their inner children, kind to stray puppies. They talk about their feelings *all the time*. Indeed, the men I know seem to do nothing *except* talk about their bloody feelings. Me included. I often sense that the reason my women friends keep trying to get me drunk is that they want me to lighten up, stop droning on about Sylvia Plath's poetry and how awful PMT must be, and simper admiringly about football and supermodels instead.

These days, men have no problem at all expressing themselves. I think the reason we drink to excess is much more complex. The songwriter Richard Thompson has a poignant song called "God Loves A Drunk." It says "The drunk is just trying to get free of his body, to soar like an angel among the high heavens." Not exactly *Top of the Pops* material, I know, but there's some truth to this.

Alcohol gives Irish men a powerful short-cut to spiritual enlightenment not required by women. Male drunkenness is a residual ...erm... hangover from the ancient era when alcohol was used in religious ritual, (as it still is, in all the Christian churches).

Men drink themselves silly because they are cut off from the natural forces and life-rhythms which women possess. Women's bodies have built-in calendars, with the result that women are connected to time and history in a way that men can never be. Women also possess the power to confer life. They give birth and thereby continue the race. Thus, in evolutionary terms, us men are pretty unimportant, and deep down we know it. So we drink in an effort to get back in touch with the life-force, to tune in to the great cosmic power of the universe, to commune supernaturally with the divine omniscient spirit of time, space, creation and knowingness. Kinda deep, huh? And if you believe that for even one short moment, mine's a large one, please, with a little pink paper umbrella and a packet of Tayto.

Part III: The Truth Always Hurts:
Irishmen and Lies

I have another friend. He is to lying what Michelangelo was to fancy brushwork. He is the original, the undisputed world champion of falsehood, the old master of the porky pie. Most people lie sometimes, usually for personal gain, or to prevent a loved one's feelings being hurt. Not this guy. He lies for absolutely no reason. He just likes it. He just finds it amusing. I have heard him tell people that he works for IBM or RTE or MI5, (when actually he does not work at all. He is, as he says himself, "still contemplating entering the workforce.") Without so much as a light blush, he has told people that he used to go out with Naomi Campbell, Michelle Rocca and Kate Moss. Simultaneously. ("Yeah, used to get pretty tricky actually, tellin' auld Naomi to get her drawers on and slip out the back way when Kate was coming up the stairs, y'know? Bit of a moody auld wagon, Naomi is sometimes. Kate's a sweetheart though, give you the shirt off her back.") The guy is utterly shameless. He has told people that he is related to the Royal family, to Bill Clinton, to Mother Teresa of Calcutta. He has told people that he is the proud owner of a brand new Jaguar XJS, when, in point of fact, his only means of transport is a bedraggled ladies bicycle he found late one night upon staggering drunkenly into a skip outside his house. (That's a bicycle which is itself bedraggled, by the way, not a bicycle for ladies who are bedraggled.)

There is no end to this man's deceit. Once — this was probably the worst time of all — I heard him telling an American woman we met in a Dublin pub that he used to be in U2 before Bono became the lead singer. "Oh yeah," he shrugged modestly, "I'm still really good mates with the guys, you know, I still hang out with them all the time. Great guys, really great guys. They're coming round Sunday actually for a jam."

Only once in my life have I confronted him about this. As soon as he had come out with some preposterous untruth, I looked him in the eye and said "You're lying, aren't you?" He denied it. He tried to look hurt, something which all Irish male liars learn to do very convincingly. He denied it for about half an hour, and then he told me how disappointed he was that I could *possibly* think that about him. ("Disappointed" is another telltale word in the Irish male liar's vocabulary. If an Irishman ever tells you he's disappointed by what you've just accused him of doing, you were right, he's doing it, probably very often, and probably with your best friend). Finally, almost on the point of tears, he said, lip trembling, that he had never lied to me in his life, and that he "just didn't believe in lies" (which is, incidentally, the biggest male lie of all.) Finally I wore him down. He admitted it. "But why?" I asked him. "*Why* do you have to lie all the time?" He peered at me as though I was some kind of recently escaped lunatic. He shrugged. "Why not?" he said.

This guy is unbelievable. But that's the awful thing. He isn't really. The terrible thing is, he is actually so credible. He could tell you that day does not follow night, that black is deep cerise, that Albert Reynolds is a credible leader for Ireland, and you would find yourself nodding in fervent agreement. I think it is partly to do with the way he looks. He is unfeasibly handsome, perpetually tanned, with pronounced cheekbones and a noble aquiline nose. His eyes have just the right hint of practised doe-like innocence. To call him a liar to his face would be like calling Bambi a potential venison steak. I mean, he fools *me* sometimes, and I've known him since we were seven, when he used to lie to our teacher about not having done his homework because he had been savaged by an escaped lion on the way home from school. (Once, he caused a terrible scene when he burst into tears during the morning prayers and told the teacher that his father had died of a heart attack over breakfast that morning.) I mean, I *know* what a lying cheating scumbag he is, but sometimes when he goes "oh yeah, listen, I meant to tell you, I met that Claudia Schiffer in a club in town the other night and we're going out for a curry and a good bop in Bad Bob's on Friday" I find myself believing him. It is all very strange.

I suppose the main reason I believe him is that men are such liars anyway. Give your average possessor of a pair of gonads half a chance to evade, distort, exaggerate, deceive, misrepresent, equivocate or slander, and he will. Irish men just like telling lies. It helps them pass the time. They will tell lies that make themselves look good — "I love you, darling, and I'd never dream of fancying anyone else," for instance — but, amazingly, they will also deliberately tell lies that make themselves look worse than they are. "I had fifteen pints of Guinness last night, and half a bottle of vodka, and then I had a kebab on me way home and I spent half the night puking me bleedin' liver up and when I woke up I was paralysed from the neck down and me right leg had been hacked off with a chainsaw, and I'm doin' it all again tonight coz I'm a mad bleedin' terrible bastard, I really am."

The problem is that most men's lives are so boring, dull and meaningless that the odd flaming spectacular untruth helps to jazz them up a bit. Women lie too, but much more rarely, and, usually, for a definite and quite narrowly focused reason. Women do not lie as a hobby, the way men do. This is because women are better at fantasising than men. Women's brains are more complex, more sophisticated and more naturally creative than men's. Women have imaginations and men have lies, and if you don't believe me just look at the Readers Letters section of any male porn magazine and ask yourself just how true are the true confessions. The bitter truth is that men are simply more emotionally limited than women. We have qualities a plenty — our ability to lie means that we are usually more reliable keepers of secrets than women, for example — but as a rule few men are capable of using their flagrant dishonesty for anything other than pure deception for its own sake.

Men's parents do not help, of course. Part of the reason why men lie is that until recently this was exactly what they were brought up to do. It all starts off with the cruel notion — itself a terrible lie — that brave boys don't cry, and it ends up years later with the kind of macho chest-beating dishonest crap which brutalises the emotional lives of most men, and of the unfortunate women who are doomed to be close to them. Men are *supposed* to lie, damn it. To admit to fear, vulnerability, loneliness, failure, is still, despite the advent of the so called New Man, impossible for most men. To admit to anything other than perfection is somehow to admit to not really being a man. To tell the truth is to castrate yourself, and heaven knows, very few men are going to do that if they can help it.

The fact that Irish men have so much political, economic and social power is another reason why they lie. Let's face it, running the banks, the government, the police, industry, the army, the media and just about everything else is simply not conducive to telling the truth. It is all very hard work, after all, keeping women out of power and in their place. It is bloody difficult to do if you're going to make problems for yourself by telling *the truth* all the time.

Needless to say this is all very silly, because the one thing you can safely say about women is that they *always* know when men are lying. It may not strike them immediately, but give them time and they will tumble it. I don't know *how* they do this, but they do. Women have a built-in bullshit detector. It is as intrinsic a part of being a woman as having a womb. Perhaps Mother Nature has conditioned women to develop this phenomenal skill at recognising every single measly trick in the feeble male arsenal. Perhaps it is just practice, or shared experience. I don't know. But by the time women get to be thirty they can actually predict the lies their men are going to tell, sometimes hours or days before they do so. There are women I know who actually have evenings out together to compare their men's lies. So there is no point at all in lying to a woman. A lie, to be a genuine lie, must at least have a fighting chance of success. And lying to a woman is like trying to make water run uphill. As a short term thing you may think you will get away with it. But sooner or later, you will fail.

Irish men need to be liberated from this terrible burden they have to lie. We are trapped, wounded souls, condemned to dishonesty by our very maleness. You women should all feel very sorry for us. You should help us to liberate ourselves. You should forgive us and support us, because we're all so very nice really. And if you believe *that* for even one second, I used to go out with Madonna, actually, until I dumped her for crashing my Jag.

Part IV: After the Fall: My Ankle and Me

In County Monaghan, near the little town of Newbliss, there is a wonderful place called Annaghmakerrig. Annaghmakerrig is a large and comfortable country house which was bequeathed as a workplace to the artists and writers of Ireland by its former owner, the late and very great Sir Tyrone Guthrie. The deal is that Irish artists may apply to come and stay for a period of up to three months while working on a creative project. If accepted, they are fed, watered, kept warm and given a room or studio in which to work. When they leave they are asked to pay a contribution of about half what it costs to keep them there.

In 1991 I was living in London, but in the Summer of that year I came over to Annaghmakerrig, to try to get started on a novel. Things were going very well. I loved the silence of the place during the day, and the companionship at night, the long laughing walks down to the nearest pub, The Black Kesh.

One Sunday morning during my stay a Swedish photographer arrived at Annaghmakerrig. She wanted to take my photograph for the back of the Swedish edition of one of my books. It was a lovely sunny morning, and the house was full of writers and painters, all working and talking. I took the Swedish photographer around and introduced her to everybody. The feeling in the house was relaxed. After a time, somebody suggested a soccer match.

We trooped out to the lawn, writers and artists all, and somebody found a football. Now, I should explain that this lawn was raised some six or eight feet above the car park, a sharp slope at the edge leading down to the gravel below. We broke into teams anyway, athletic wordsmiths versus namby pamby visual artists. The game began. I really was enjoying myself, I must say, all fifteen solid stone of me leaping about with the alacrity of a young gazelle. Until disaster struck. Following a deflected power header from a normally quite reticent young poet, I lunged for the ball, skidded over the turf arms flailing at the air, and crashed to the ground.

I distinctly remember hearing the bone crack in my ankle. There was no other physical sensation at all for several seconds. Then I started to feel hot and nauseous and incredibly thirsty. The light faded and shimmered. Everything around me went bright and then dark. The pain began.

I had never in my life experienced pain like this. It seemed to shoot up and down my leg, up and down my spinal cord. It seemed to grab hold of my heart and squeeze hard. It was agony. I roared. I cried. I swore and cussed and profaned.

I was carried into the conservatory by a promising young screenwriter, a composer of atonal sonatas and a muscular experimental novelist. An enthusiastic debate then ensued among the gathered artists about what might be the matter with me. The more conceptual painters seemed to feel it was a sprain, the sculptors said it was a mere bruise, but the novelists — Irish novelists are very frequently given to melodrama — said it was probably a severe compound fracture which would require major surgery. The discussion became quite heated. It was only with considerable effort that I managed to persuade one neo-realist — a part-time acupuncturist — from going to get her needles and inserting them briskly into one of my power points.

My ankle was now the size of a small watermelon. I lay on the glasshouse floor moaning and whimpering, while the artists dithered and fussed and the Swedish photographer kept circling like a deranged vulture, snapping at me with her Leica.

"I *like* eet," the Swedish photographer kept saying. "Yays, I like eet. It breeng out the pain in your hawrt. Eet ees eemportant for the arteest to have pain, no?" I will not repeat now what I said to her, but take it from me, Dublin-Stockholm relations have been a little strained since.

The novelist Colm Tóibín drove me to a hospital, all the time chanting a poignant line from a Sam Shepard play — "Give my son back his leg! Give my son back his leg!" When we arrived, my limb was encased in plaster up to the knee. They did their best to patch me up. Unfortunately, their best was not really good enough.

Colm drove me back to Annaghmakerrig, where I was treated with great kindness by Bernard and Mary Loughlin, who run the centre, and by all the artists also. But I was not happy at all. My leg was agonizingly painful. And some days after the break, I noticed that my toes were turning a rather spectacular shade of deep purple. The painters kept looking at it and wondering aloud just how much red you would have to mix with just how much blue to come up with a colour quite like that. I decided that I had had enough of the countryside.

I cadged a lift back to Dublin from the painter Mick O'Dea and limped along to what had been my local hospital before I had moved to London. The young doctor took one brief look at the X-rays of my battered limb and shook his head dolefully. "There's three things beginning with F that you won't be able to do for a while," he said. "Two of them are fighting and foxtrotting. And I'll leave the third to your imagination."

He explained that they would have to put me to sleep and break my ankle again in order to mend it properly. I was astounded. I had never been in hospital before in my life. I rang my friends from my bed in the ward and told them the news, with the lip-trembling tone of one who has just been diagnosed as suffering from cancer. I really did make a meal of it.

As if things were not bad enough already, there was another severe shock in store. The anaesthetist turned out to be the very first girl I had ever gone out with. I had not seen her since the night of our big argument at the fifth year school dance. She was married with a baby now, she told me, as she snapped on her rubber gloves, told me to roll over on my stomach and discreetly raised the hem of my paper hospital gown.

"You ever get married yourself?" she asked.

"No," I replied.

"Oh," she smirked, "*what* a pity."

Let me tell you, it is a very disconcerting experience to crane your neck and watch the first person you ever broke it off with fill up a syringe with potentially lethal chemicals and smilingly prepare to insert in into your buttock. I don't think I will ever forget the pure terror of those moments.

When I woke up after the operation my father was there. He helped me into a wheelchair, pushed me out to his car and brought me home to his house. Thus, after six years of living away from home in England, I found myself suddenly back in my parents' house in Dublin again, where I would remain for almost three months. It was strange. I could not move around much, even on crutches. I had to let my family do things for me. They had to help me bathe and prepare food, and at first I found this completely depressing. It really did get me down. I hated being so weak. But one afternoon my stepmother Viola said an extraordinary thing. She told me she thought that this new reliance on other people would not make me weak, but that it would make me strong. She said that it would make me a better person. She was right too.

Before the fall, I had been pretty self-sufficient. I had been full of shit, actually. Maleness, to me, was all about not needing anyone, ever. It was about being solitary, in charge of your own life, in control of your fate. But as my then sixteen-year-old brother Eoin cleaned the spaces between my left toes with a Johnson's cotton bud every day, never once complaining or shirking his task, I came to realise pretty quickly that the notion of personal control was a peculiar and unreliable male myth. Allowing my father or stepmother to make me the occasional cup of coffee proved as therapeutic for me as any amount of expensive analysis.

Viola fixed up a room for me to work in. She bought me a thick pair of padded cycling gloves so that I could manage the crutches more easily. When my father came home from work at night, he would help me out into his car and we would go for long drives in the countryside together, sometimes talking, but other times just silently enjoying each other's company, in the way we had not had the chance to do for many years. It was a lovely Summer in Ireland that year, and I still think about those long warm nights, the glow of the evening sunlight on the fields, and the feeling between us in the car as we drove around the lanes and backroads of County Wicklow.

In the months after that fateful football match, I finished the first draft of my novel. But I also learned to lighten up, to be a little more relaxed and a little more dependent. I learned that what is difficult about love for many of us Irish men is not giving it, but being prepared to take it. Feeling secure enough to admit to vulnerability and weakness. Breaking my ankle that Sunday morning in County Monaghan helped me to do that. I sometimes think it was probably the best thing that ever happened to me. It helped me swallow my pride. It made me more human. It taught me a lot about what love really is, and what being a man really is. And it taught me that the human heart, like the human ankle, is ultimately a pretty resilient body part.

Chapter Eight
The Write Stuff: Irish Writers And Writing

Part I: Return To Sender

One of the interesting things about being a professional writer is that you get into a lot of trouble for the things you write, some of which you don't really mean, or if you do, you change your mind by the time they appear in print. But you *do* mean other things, and when you get it in the neck for them, it drives you half way to distraction and drink. For instance, I got a letter recently attacking me for something I had written in the London *Independent*. I had argued that part of the problem with the North of Ireland was that many southerners felt it was foreign to them. My correspondent got his boxers in an awful twist about this. "The war in the North" he informed me, from the vantage point of his address in Hackney, "is Ireland's central drama." Well, tell it to the one in five Irish people who don't have a job. Or to the frightened and lonely women who are forced across the Irish sea to have the terminations of pregnancy to which they are so clearly morally entitled. "The war" is not Ireland's central drama. Ireland's central drama is — and always has been — the conflict between private life and public fantasy.

"Apart from the novels of Ronan Bennet," my attacker fumed, "there is no modern Irish writing about heroism, idealism and sacrifice." Nothing against Ronan Bennet, but this is all absolutely astonishing! Has he read Evelyn Conlon's stories, or Dermot Bolger's *The Journey Home*, or Paul Durcan's *Daddy, Daddy* or Eugene Mc Cabe's *Death and Nightingales*? These Irish books deal movingly with notions of heroism and sacrifice. The heroism of those who do not have the luxury of pontificating about "Irish unity" — whatever those words might mean — because they are struggling to be human in a society that has brutalised them. You don't have to set novels in the H Block to say important things about political loss. Thankfully, most young Irish writers have learnt this.

I don't have a problem being a writer and having a political view. I don't even have a problem with the labels. I would call myself a democratic socialist, and even a republican too, if that's OK with the Hackney branch of the Troops Out campaign. I believe most republicans in the North are decent people, as are most loyalists. But the idea that a united Ireland, or a United Kingdom, is worth killing or dying for is simply a lie. It has stunted the development of radical politics in Ireland, and been used to repress generations of working people. When I write about the North, that's what I write about. That's my political view.

In that context, it is significant that in the work of the younger Northern writers like Robert McLiam Wilson and Glen Patterson there are none of the Boys-Own posturings my correspondent admires so much. In their work, we just don't see the armies of macho men who trample the pages of so many of the execrable earlier novels about the North. Perhaps we in Ireland have at last grown tired of being told what to say. That brand of vicious censorship which sought to silence our writers in the fifties did not work. This new brand of right-on censorship will not work now. You cannot tell writers what to write about. When you do, you debase language. And when you debase language, you defile the very democracy we all say we want so much.

My correspondent informed me of the huge amount of "political literature" in the third world. The third world country I know best is Nicaragua, having spent time there, and having published a novel set there. In revolutionary Nicaragua, everyone was a poet. My correspondent would have loved it. Lots of political literature, oodles of the same kind of sloganising garbage churned out by the bright talents of 1930's Britain, as poet after poet trooped over to Spain to take a pot shot at Franco's fascists, pen a few sonnets, and mosey on back to Oxford before the new term began. Nicaraguan poets wrote political poetry and most of it, though deeply felt, was terrible.

But out of the mish-mash of propaganda, five or six stunning voices emerged. I'm thinking of writers like Claribel Allegria. Although she participated bravely in the anti-imperial Sandinista revolution, she did not write turgid epics about the evil yankees and the glorious proletariat. She wrote delicate love poems that will still be read when all the "politically engaged" stuff about tanks and tractors has been forgotten. Maybe that, in the end, was her ultimate victory over tyranny. And maybe this new concentration on the dignity of individual lives is what is so powerful — and so profoundly political — in the work of the new Irish writers whom my correspondent so roundly chastises.

He should have a lash at writing a novel about the North himself. I won't tell him what to put in it. But I'm damn sure he won't tell me what to put in mine. He's welcome to his heroism, and I sincerely hope it helps him to construct good sentences. In the meantime, the rest of us have to get on with the oddly tricky business of writing about real, complicated, and unheroic lives.

These letters you get, honest to God now, they'd make you wonder about people. It's odd, really. I have never written a letter to a newspaper in my life, let alone written privately to a journalist. Yet, for a while, every single brain-damaged imbecile in Ireland seemed to develop a thing about the column I was writing for a Sunday newspaper, and they seemed to want me to know about it. Like, hey, I care. If there is a support group for raving idiots somewhere in the midlands — and I feel absolutely sure that, oh, no, never mind... they obviously used to photocopy this column every week and pass it out to the gibbering faithful at their meetings. And the thing is, they were wasting their time. If I gave one single solitary pick of the nose about what these people thought about anything I would have set up a charitable foundation for them so that they could all have new straightjackets. But I really didn't. There is absolutely no point in sending abusive letters to Irish writers these days. It only encourages them, in fact.

Jonathan Swift's will left money to the city of Dublin to set up the first refuge for lunatics there. He added, in a pithy codicil, that if he'd had enough spondulix, he would have left enough money for a twenty foot wall to be erected around the entire island. All I can say is that very often when I got a letter forwarded to me by *The Sunday Tribune*, Jonathan Swift would come into my mind.

For instance, there was a man up in Letterkenny who wrote to me at least once a month. When I say *wrote*, now, I am using the term is its broadest possible sense, such was the hieroglyphical sprawl that dribbled forth from his feeble bic. The man was clearly a drooling troglodyte of some kind. The letters were always written on these bits of white cardboard like the bits of white cardboard that you get in packets of tights. I don't know whether he bought a lot of tights, this guy, but, hey, I'm a liberal; what he did in his private life ain't no concern of mine. (I'd recommend Pretty Polly, actually). But there were pages of the most unbelievable abuse in this poor eejit's letters to me. He must have put so much effort into it, the sad little git. This man questioned my parentage, "if any," as he once put it. He berated my politics — I have apparently swung between active Provo membership and West-Britonism of the most Woganesque kind in his ruined imagination. He seemed convinced that I was a sexual deviant of a particularly rampant and overactive nature, which, in fact, I found oddly flattering. But he really wanted to insult me, for some reason, this dribblingly delirious little Donegal dickhead. Next time I find myself in Letterkenny, I'm going to come and find him, so he can insult me to my face. That's if they unfasten his chains and remove his gag for long enough, of course.

And there was an amusing old witch down in West Cork who is clearly in need of severe treatment, if not euthanasia. She wrote me regular letters which always began with the wry words "Dear Arse-Bollocks." Now, how one can be both dear and arse, not to mention, dear and arse *and* bollocks, simultaneously, would be a matter of speculation to some people, particularly to students of biology and to contortionists also, I imagine, but not to me. I showed her letters to every single person I met. They usually laughed so much that they had to go to the toilet for quite some time. I wish her well, this twisted and lobotomized virago. She provided me with no end of entertainment.

I have been accused by correspondents of being in the CIA, MI5, the masons, and once, bizarrely enough given the unbridled paganism of my column, the Knights of Columbanus. I once got a letter from a reader in Mayo who said "you are the ugliest person in the whole world. You have a face that would stop a clock." Another came from a social leper of some kind in Athenry, saying

"you and your brood of bastard children are all dead by Tuesday."
Well, my brood of bastard children all seem to be doing fine so far,
or so the orphanage informs me. Another from a reader in Sligo,
saying "you are a curse and you will die roaring with your legs in
the air." Well, all I can say to that is, you never know your luck. We
are a very literary nation, right enough. Roddy Doyle and John
Banville better watch out. There's an awful lot of talent out there,
just waiting to be discovered.

Part II: Barrytown International:
The World of Roddy Doyle

Roddy Doyle is not just one of the most important Irish writers of his generation. He is a publishing phenomenon. In addition to winning the highly prestigious and upmarket *Booker Prize* in 1993, his books also sell in the kind of amounts usually reserved for mass market pulp fiction, the Jeffrey Archers and Barbara Taylor Bradfords of this world. *The Barrytown Trilogy*, containing *The Commitments*, *The Van* and *The Snapper*, has rarely been out of the bestseller list since it was published. *Paddy Clarke Ha Ha Ha* has now sold two hundred thousand copies in hardback. An insider at his publishing company told me recently, "we've stopped selling it to human beings now. They've all bought it. We're going to have to try selling it to the sheep."

But to judge from the snobbish, elitist and class-obsessed garbage that gets written about him from time to time, certain literary journalists and members of the Dublin chattering classes are a little uncomfortable with Roddy Doyle. What seems to get them down is not just his stunning and unprecedented commercial success, but the critical acclaim he has simultaneously received. A bestseller who can be briskly dismissed as utterly lacking in literary merit is safe enough to tolerate. But a bestseller who wins *The Booker Prize*, by writing a book about a working class family on the northside of Dublin, is an odd and dangerous creature. Indeed, in the pages of some of our newspapers, it often seems that Roddy Doyle himself is being reviewed, and not the books that he writes. Like the North, or divorce, or the beef tribunal, Roddy Doyle has become something on which people are expected to have a position.

Doyle's more intelligent detractors at least put up an argument. They say his work is clichéd and full of stereotypes. They say it's childish, moronic, sentimental, too full of dialogue, that it's mawkish and leans too heavily on a certain outmoded "gas" approach to Dublin life. They say — with some force — that if it had been written by an English writer, Doyle's work would be accused of being racist.

143

But the point is, it isn't written by an English writer. And surely Roddy Doyle is as entitled as any other Irish novelist to expose what he sees as the country's shortcomings in his own way, and on his own terms. Anyone who has ever carefully read his work can see that he is a consummate and very skilled literary stylist. The work may look easy and, of course, it reads easily also. But anyone who writes knows one thing above all others: the easier it is to read, the harder it was to write.

It's important to understand that Doyle's literary relationship to his own Irishness is a complex one. From time to time, particulary in the English newspapers, the juiciness of his dialogue has been compared to that of Joyce's characters. But it's not a very useful comparison. In some important ways Doyle is much more firmly in the tradition of the English comic novel. He has more in common with PG Wodehouse and Dickens than he does with Flann O'Brien or Brendan Behan, for example. Like these great English comic geniuses, he takes stock characters — stereotypes, if you like — and subverts the readers' expectations of them, playing with them in ways which are often extremely subtle. If he resembles any Irish writer it is Sean O'Casey, and even then, it must be noted that O'Casey, like Oscar Wilde, was greatly influenced by English traditions of the music hall and Victorian melodrama. In recent years, O'Casey's work has been brilliantly re-interpreted by younger directors, who have dug carefully into the text to unearth the suffering and pain buried beneath the laughs. Future generations of readers will do this with Roddy Doyle also. Time and again in his work, what looks at first glance like cliché is exactly the opposite of that.

The history of Irish writing in the twentieth century has been predominately a history of rural Ireland. Some of our most interesting contemporary prose writers, John McGahern, Colm Toibin, Evelyn Conlon, Patrick McCabe, Eugene McCabe, have documented the nuances of the small town with precision and truth. But like Dermot Bolger, Roddy Doyle celebrates another Ireland just as profoundly at odds with its own mythology; an Ireland of the suburbs, which has really been absent from the pages of Irish fiction for too long.

If Doyle's success implies something about the richness of the new Irish fiction, it says a lot more about the poverty of contemporary British writing. It was interesting and informative to note that last year's *Booker* shortlist was dominated by writers who were not themselves British. The most important winners and shortlisted writers in recent years — Salman Rushdie, Timothy Mo, Ben Okri, Kashuo Ishiguru, Rohinton Mistry — have not been British by birth. The English critic Auberon Waugh has recently attacked the *Booker* with characteristic vigour and equally characteristic absurdity, arguing that it's not worth having if it keeps getting won by foreigners. It's a little like abolishing cricket because the English are so bad it. Perhaps Waugh should have a think about why all these foreign Johnnies keep strolling away with the loot. Perhaps he should realise that the English novel is in a critical, perhaps terminal, state of decline.

Ultimately, the debate between the best of the new Irish fiction and the writing being done in England is an aesthetic debate, but it has a political and moral dimension also. It has to do with a communal notion of what art is actually for, and the role that art can play in the life of the society in which it is produced. "Fundamental accuracy of description," wrote Ezra Pound, "is the one sole morality of writing." Naming the world, he meant, describing it with faith and precision and affection, the way Roddy Doyle does so brilliantly, and in that process changing the world. Surely this is the real purpose of art, to change the world. But if you want to change the world, the first thing you do is change the way people see it. We really do need to do that in Ireland, and few writers in recent years have helped us to do it as much as Roddy Doyle has.

Samuel Beckett once remarked that Irish writers had been "buggered into existence by the English army and the Roman church." Times change, of course, and the targets change too, but the great thing about being an Irish writer is that there's always something to write *against*. There's always a windmill to tilt at. The only thing that all Irish writers have in common is a spirit of iconoclasm. In the work of some of our important writers it is more pronounced — Evelyn Conlon, for instance — but it is almost always there, in my view. It is certainly there in the work of Roddy

Doyle. He writes with passion about people who are dispossessed. It simply would not have occurred to an English novelist to write about working class characters in the joyful and magical way he does. In post-colonial England, it seems there is nothing for a white middle-class novelist to write against, and novelists in England do tend to be white and middle class. The recent controversial anthology of Best Young British novelists was a dismal and dreary collection. Even the ravages of the Thatcherite state have not yet produced a single novel which will be read in fifty years time.

We have had a snowstorm of breathtakingly dull English novels set on university campuses, written by university lecturers, and usually about university lecturers trying to write novels. We have had legions of Hampstead adultery novels, about bonking in the suburbs and downing chardonnay in Tuscany villas. We have had an odd kind of retro-drama of English culture, as writers retreat into a miserable invented version of a cosy Victorian past which never existed in the first place. Outbreaks of nostalgia are always a sign that a culture is in pretty big trouble, and in Britain now, nostalgia is the national sport. And we have had the worst of all things, the English "novel of ideas," wherein the desires and aspirations and sufferings of real characters have been replaced by a crassly undergraduate spirit of so-called formal experimentation. Martin Amis wrote a skilfully executed but deeply shocking book called *Time's Arrow* about the holocaust, where time went backwards. The best writer of his generation reduced to gimmicks and gameshow trickery, in the face of the most appalling event of the twentieth century. It was a telling moment in the history of British culture.

Roddy Doyle, and the best of his Irish contemporaries, realise one important thing. Readers want stories. Postmodernism is dead, consigned to the museum of academia where it belongs. It's one of the reasons why American cinema, for example, has always been so strong. Stories about ordinary people tend to be appreciated by ordinary people, and, oddly enough, stories about tweed-jacketed sociology lecturers and their laconic therapists tend to be appreciated by nobody at all. The same is true for novels. People want to read stories which inform their lives, which bring news from the world of the writer to the world that the rest of us inhabit.

Readers want to know what it is like to be someone else for a moment, so that they know in some profound sense what it is like to be themselves. This is the miraculous power of fiction, the power which Keats called the sympathetic imagination. Even the most linguistically and formally gifted writer in Ireland, John Banville, confessed recently — and it did seem like a confession — that his books were full of stories. They are too. That's one of his many and great strengths.

Behind the laughter, Roddy Doyle's work is deeply iconoclastic. There is a passionately moral dimension to the world he creates, and a great skill involved in that creation. Few Irish writers write better about childhood, for instance. He captures the speech patterns of youth brilliantly, the weird logic of the incessant questions, the non-sequiturs and semi-understood obscenities. The emotional landscape of his work is broadening all the time. For a whole generation of younger readers, Barrytown has become a real and vibrant place, full of stories which inform and amuse and provoke.

Doyle has steadily improved as a writer. Each of his books is better than the last. *Paddy Clarke Ha Ha Ha* contains many brilliant passages of fresh, evocative description. The book is very funny too, of course. The dialogue is sharper, more disciplined.

But there is a darkness in Doyle's world also, which existed long before his controversial and disturbing television play *Family* ever hit the screens. The most powerful scene in the film of *The Commitments* happened while the song "At The Dark End of the Street" was playing, and that was appropriate. Doyle is very good at what's going on in the dark end of the street. Anybody who has survived an unhappy marriage will recognise the terror in Paddy Clarke's conversations with his siblings. Like the great English comic writers who are his aesthetic ancestors, Roddy Doyle has become an archaeologist of the deepest places of the heart. He knows that there is a very thin line between laughter and tears. And he realises, in the wry and truthful words of Samuel Beckett, that there's nothing quite as funny as human suffering.

Part III: James Joyce and the Irish Tourist Industry: Reflections on an Invented Tradition

Ireland is an idea with many histories. Even the phrase "Irish history" is fraught with deconstructionist possibilities. What do we mean by the words "Ireland" and "Irish"? And what do we mean by history? The retrospectively linear narrative that leads neatly to national independence, or the more accurate if unwieldy chaos of revisionism that suggests we still do not know quite what we are? Irish history. What inclusions and, more importantly, what exclusions, does the phrase imply? Historically, geographically, socially, what *is* Ireland?

And when James Joyce wrote that Irish history was a nightmare from which he was trying to escape, what did he mean? Which history? Which Ireland? What kind of escape? Is exile a matter of physical location or mental indifference? Is it something else? And what, if anything, do young Irish writers feel about the answers to these questions now? Nothing, I suspect. I suspect Irish writers have other things on their minds. But anyway, let us stay with James Joyce for a while.

I remember books by James Joyce being in the house when I was a child. I remember searching my parents bookshelves for something vaguely pornographic or at least erotic, and instead finding a copy of *Ulysses*, with its galleys loose, and its battered black paperback cover half torn off, and its yellowed dog-eared pages faintly redolent of mould and dust.

I can remember the appearance of the book, and the way the word "James" was exactly the same size as the word "Joyce" on the ripped front cover. The words of that name loomed out at you, large and white and bold. The book felt heavy and substantial. It was as thick as the bible, and, like the bible, it seemed to radiate an almost religious energy.

My family lived quite near the Joyce Tower in Sandycove, that stately plump monument to Stephen Dedalus, Buck Mulligan and poor old Haines, the fearful Oxford Englishman. I passed by the tower every day for fourteen years, on my way to and from school.

I always thought of it as James Joyce's tower. I never realised until I was a young teenager that the tower had been built by a conquering imperial force, and thus had other histories also.

One day when I was seven or eight I was sitting on the number 8 bus, coming home from school, and the bus happened to stop beside the Joyce tower. There was an old man sitting beside me. He looked at the tower and suddenly a terrible anger seemed to infect him. He started to rant and rave. The old man told me that James Joyce was nothing but a dirty little pup who had never done a decent day's work in his life, a dirty little gurrier who had run Ireland down for money; these were the actual words he used. James Joyce had "run Ireland down for money," the old man said, "and he had told dirty lies about Irish history."

I was astounded. I asked the old man what it was exactly that James Joyce had said about Ireland, and Irish history. I wondered what you could possibly say about Ireland to deserve such abuse, and where James Joyce had got this money, and how much money was involved exactly, and just what had he spent it on.

I remember thinking about this. I tried hard to imagine what it could possibly have been that Joyce had said about Ireland. At night I used to look at his book for answers, but I couldn't understand a single word of it. Nevertheless, I was captivated by the idea of James Joyce. I could nearly see him, all alone, up in his tower like a demented scientist in a horror film, brewing a thick soup of curses and betrayals, this gurrier who had told lies about Irish history and run Ireland down for money. And I decided that when I grew up, if the opportunity ever came my way to never do a day's work, and run Ireland down for money, I would seize it with both hands and never let it go. It seemed like a fine way for a person to spend his time.

Years passed. I first read his books in college. I was lucky, in that I had people to explain them to me. The analogy with the bible was often to come into my mind again, for it was clear that you could make James Joyce say whatever you wanted him to say. He was like an academic version of a ventriloquist's dummy. Depending on whose hand was up him on which day, what he had to say would change substantially. To the people who taught me history he was one thing, and to those who taught me Anglo-Irish literature — whatever that is — he was quite another. I enjoyed the books, I suppose, although I have to say that when I started to write fiction myself, the fact of Joyce's existence — or Wilde's or Yeats' or Synge's for that matter — never bothered me much.

So where has he gone now, the strange little man who took over the historical conqueror's tower and made it his own? Where might we look for the ghost of James Joyce? Has he not now become a player in the very Irish history from which he tried to flee?

That version of Irish history known as the Irish literary tradition seems to me to have much more to do with tourism than art. Here is an extract from a recent book, *Anatomy of a Changing State*, by the former Fine Gael minister for education, Ms Gemma Hussey.

The capital city is not the flagship of national tourism, as it is in so many European countries. A chaotic traffic problem and an inadequate public transport system add to the difficulties for the tourist. The failure to capitalize on the worldwide appreciation of James Joyce...and other Dublin writers is exemplified in the disappearance of 7 Eccles Street, the home of Joyce's Bloom.

It is a fascinatingly revealing comment. In this form of discourse, Irish literary history has suddenly become acceptably Irish again. It is not something to be condemned any more. Neither is it to be discussed, or studied, or even just read and enjoyed. It is something to be "capitalized." It is a source of profit and employment and national revenue. It is almost a natural resource which we have been lucky enough to dig up by accident. It is the literary historical version of off shore gas. Learning how to tap it more efficiently, and package it more effectively, and present it more attractively to tourists, is analogous to building better roads and providing more late night busses. Joyce's work — or rather, simply "Joyce" himself, for there is no mention of his work here — has become something which must be preserved, like the house of Leopold Bloom, like the idea of an Irish history which the Fine Gael party believes we may all share. Poor Joyce must be saved from "disappearance." It would only be a short step for Ms Hussey to suggest Albert Reynolds flying over to Zurich in the new government jet, digging Joyce up, having him stuffed and mounted and placed in a museum in Temple Bar.

Perhaps he could even be resuscitated, brought back to life, so he could play for the Republic of Ireland in the next World Cup, where even in his current state he would be at least as mobile as several of the more superannuated of big Jack's jolly green giants. It is certainly an almost Joycean irony that Ms Hussey, who participated in a government which wanted to tax children's shoes, expresses such a powerful desire to preserve an inner city building on the basis that it was once inhabited by a fictional character. If only the people who lived in the Sherriff Street flats were fictional too. Then life, unlike art and Irish history, would be so much more simple.

We pride ourselves on this predominant version of our literary tradition, yet no other country would do this to its writers. Does London capitalize on Dickens? How does Paris capitalize on Proust? How is the local economy of Florence improved by the happy fact that Dante once lived there? In other countries, writers are read. In Ireland, they are celebrated. They are turned into characters in a popular historical narrative, or gift-wrapped cultural products. Like local cheeses or Aran sweaters, we think it's great that we have them, although we'd never dream of consuming them ourselves.

Irish history is full of ghosts. Tone, O'Connell, Connolly, all appear in Irish ballads as ghosts. Joyce's favourite song about Irish history, "The Croppy Boy," is narrated by a man who has been betrayed and then executed. When Yeats wrote about Parnell, he addressed him as a gentle shade, not as a far from gentle politician. We name our streets and our railway stations after these ghosts. Heuston Station, Cathal Brugha Barracks, Pearse Street, Connolly Station. Part of the problem with Ireland is that everything is named after someone. In Dublin, there is a railway station called Sydney Parade, and for many years, I thought Sydney Parade was one of the leaders of the 1916 Rising.

The literary subsection of our history is similarly obsessed with ghosts. In Ulysses, Stephen Dedalus sets out to prove that Hamlet is the ghost of his own father. But in our popular culture, Joyce has become his own ghost. This is a version of Joyce and Irish history which has absolutely nothing to do with anything Joyce wrote. It is the Joyce of the biscuit-tin cover and the Southside Dublin coffee-table. It is a nostalgic world of sepia prints and parasols and period costumes, where the Guinness is cheap, the poor are happily eloquent, the rich are comic and O'Connell Street is still Sackville Street, full of charming little trams rather than disco-bars and burger joints.

The invention of this tradition has been deftly handled. As Doctor Declan Kiberd has argued, the fact that except for Yeats all of the most important Irish writers of the last hundred and fifty years have been revolutionary socialists has been forgotten by those who teach history in our schools. Wilde, Shaw, O'Casey, Synge, Joyce, Behan have been surgically removed from their contexts. The main result of the tradition is that our country is now run by people who do not read novels, but who can tell you how many Nobel prizes Irish writers have won.

I lived in England for nearly seven years. The literary tradition is quite useful there, for defending yourself against the more crude stereotypes of Irish history. But it merely inverts the stereotype. We tell people that Ireland is "the country of Joyce and Yeats and Beckett," when it is just as much the country of SPUC, Padraig Flynn and Daniel O'Donnell. The tradition has become a weapon in an odd kind of cultural revolution. It is a form of national self-assurance. We four million people who share this tiny sod of turf called Ireland cannot actually live in peace with our histories, but somehow that's alright, because we're so literary after all. In London, the tradition even haunted our jokes. An Irish labourer goes for a job on a building site in Kilburn. The cockney foreman asks if he knows the difference between a girder and a joist. Yes, the labourer says. Goethe wrote *Faust* but Joyce wrote *Finnegans Wake*.

History was a nightmare from which he was trying to awake. The first time I read that, I didn't understand what Joyce meant. It read like something that had been translated from some foreign language. How could Irish history be so important that anyone would try and escape from it?

Colm Tóibín, who seems to keep turning up in this book, spoke in a recent interview about something that had happened in his home town of Enniscorthy. There was a square in the town where

Cromwell had butchered people, he said, but he had discovered that there was no independent evidence that this event, so central to the town's psychic history, had ever actually happened. The story reminded me of something in my own past.

As I believe I have mentioned to you already, I was brought up in Glenageary in the suburbs of Southside Dublin. The road we lived in had been a field, until 1963, the year I was born, the year my parents bought a new house there. Glenageary was a place that had no history. For years after my parents bought the house, Glenageary did not even appear on maps of Dublin. It was a place that did not exist in history. It was a place that first appeared in 1963, like myself, and like sexual intercourse in the Philip Larkin poem, and The Beatles' first LP. It was a place where you went to reinvent yourself and your future, by reinventing your past.

Glenageary was full of Dublin working class people who, like my own parents, had made good in Sean Lemass's Ireland and become middle class. And it was full of country people who had migrated to Dublin to find work, then turned their backs on the land. The only echo of a rural past was in the names they gave their houses. Mountain View, Glenside, River View. These people were living lives which were very far from the ideal which Yeats and de Valera had so incongruously shared. The maidens were not dancing at the crossroads. They were watching The Rolling Stones on the latest colour TV set. And if they were not exactly fumbling in the greasy till, they were certainly fumbling in the latest Zanussi washing machine from time to time. Glenageary was *Gleann na gCaorach* in Irish, the glen of the sheep, but the only sheep around when I was a child were the ones wrapped in clingfilm and deposited in the brand new freezers which hummed their hymns in every double garage.

Having BBC was very important in Glenageary. Having the odd pseudo-English accent that Southside Dubliners develop was very important. The connections with personal or national history were tenuous indeed. Of course we had our token suburban gaeilgeoirí family, who knitted things and insisted on ordering articles in Irish in the local shops, and who tended to shout "*bualadh bos*" at you for no apparent reason. But generally, as children, we had no interest in anything even remotely gaelic, except, perhaps, early Horslips records. We did not understand a single word of Peig Sayers, but we knew the words of "*An Dearg Doom*" off by heart.

Glenageary was full of people reinventing themselves by reinventing their notions of Irish history, and forming themselves around new notions of Irishness. This is what suburbia was for. You didn't have to go into exile any more to escape from the nightmare of Irish history. The good times were here. This was the new Ireland. Joyce was wrong to say that the shortest way to Tara was via Holyhead. The shortest way to Tara was now via Glenageary, and history was as dead as doornails.

I went to the school that Eamon de Valera had attended. It was a middle class school. It was the kind of school where we brought in tins of fruit for the poor — or, as they were called, "those who are less fortunate than us" — at Christmas. We weren't taught history there. We were not taught, for instance, about how these people had become poor, and how luck had had very little to do with it, and how they would remain poor, because of an economic system which required them not to be rich. I mean, we had a class called "history," but I don't know what we were taught in it, apart from the colouring in of maps. There was a copy of the 1916 proclamation in every classrooom, with its appeal to the dead generations and its call to armed revolt against England. But we were taught in that school that the troubles in the North had been caused by criminals and delinquents and crazy psychopaths. The North was some weird foreign place that had nothing to do with us, or our parents, or our beautiful options. When I tell people that we were never taught the Irish national anthem in my school, the school that educated Eamon de Valera, they don't believe me, but it's true, we weren't. I still don't know the words now. (If you hear a high-pitched whirring sound at this stage, it is poor old Eamon de Valera, spinning around in his grave.)

But history persists. Down the road from where we lived in Glenageary was a field, through which a rudimentary path led to Sallynoggin church. It was said by some of the neighbours that there had been a mass rock there in the olden days, and that Cromwell had butchered a number of priests in this field, and that the field was haunted by the ghosts of these martyred monks.

My parents always told me not to believe this. They said all that kind of talk belonged in the past, and I went along with that. Until one night, I saw a ghost. I was coming home on a winter's night, and suddenly, about two hundred yards in front of me, I clearly saw a man walking slowly along in a monk's cowl, his head bent low, his hands folded in his sleeves. He was moving very slowly and white light was radiating from his body. I wasn't scared. I was excited. I turned the corner and the ghostly priest was gone.

For a while I was a local celebrity. I was the boy who saw the ghost. This was back in the days when Glenageary didn't have as many celebrities as it happily does now.

In later years I learnt that the story about the mass rock was completely false. There had been no mass rock, no ancient path, no Cromwellian slaughter. If Cromwell had ever been to Glenageary, he had had the good sense to put his head down and keep going. The history of the place had been invented. But I had still seen the ghost, and it was utterly real to me.

Freud said that the Irish were the only race who could not be psychoanalysed, because they were too much given to fantasy. And certainly, in Ireland, things which are not there are often much more important than things which are. Joyce's work reverberates with this knowledge. It is full of phantoms, apparitions, people who are not there any more. It is full of ghosts. Many of the most important characters in his work are dead. Parnell in *The Portrait of the Artist*, and "Ivy Day In The Committee Room." Young Rudy Bloom and old Paddy Dignam in *Ulysses*. Poor Georgina Burns and Michael Fury in "The Dead." And the spectre of Stephen's heart-scalded mother, so much more scary in death than she ever was in life.

Similarly, the ghost of Joyce is much more terrifying than anything he actually did, or wrote. I read *Ulysses* again recently and I mentioned this to a young Irish novelist I know. "Oh really," he said. "Is it any good?"

It was a joke, I think. But it was an interesting question too. Is *Ulysses* any good? It's important, yes. It's a milestone, a turning point in twentieth century fiction. But is it any good?

The problem for those of us who write "Irish" fiction is that Joyce is so frequently described in superlatives. The greatest, the deepest, the most obsessive, the craziest, the funniest. He is always there, the line goes, always peeking over your shoulder, the monolithic spectacular superstar Joyce who tore up the rulebook and wrote the novel out of existence. But the notion that young Irish writers are lying awake in their beds worrying about James Joyce or Irish history is simply untrue. Young Irish writers are busy telling stories, writing sentences, busy with the grim and unglamorous work of writing fiction which says something to readers about their lives. When they are not doing this, they are worried about their German publishing rights, and who is making the movie of their first novel, and will the tax free scheme for artists remain in place even under a Progressive Democrat government. For a young writer now, James Joyce is probably the biggest irrelevance in a history that is best ignored.

He left UCD, announcing that he was going off on the mail boat to forge the uncreated conscience of his race. It must have raised quite a laugh in the student bar at the time. Certainly, these days, if there is one single young Irish writer who thinks that he or she is forging uncreated historical consciences then I haven't met them, and I'm really not sure I'd want to.

Who can honestly say that if they met the snobbish, arrogant, prematurely aged Stephen Dedalus of *The Portrait of the Artist* they would have had any fun with him? Who can say that *Ulysses* does not contain long excruciating sections of unadulterated tedium? And as for his last book, "I've even read *Finnegans Wake*," says a character in an Aidan Mathews short story, "although, admittedly, that was for charity."

Modern Irish writers want to forget about Irish history. But Joyce tried to get vengeance on it, "Oh Ireland, my first and only love," he raged, "where Christ and Caesar are hand in glove." But modern Ireland has got its own back. Joyce is not a writer any more. He is a celebrity, a fitting subject for witty anecdotes and gas stories on chatshows. He appears on our postcards, on our stamps, on our banknotes, on T-shirts usually sold in the duty-free sections of Irish airports. The last thing you will see, as you emigrate from an Irish airport, is a poster of James Joyce. He appears everywhere, but not, interestingly, on the leaving certificate English course, never mind the history curriculum. He is celebrated in summer schools and quoted by our political leaders, which latter phenomenon is almost always an accurate signifier of a writer whose work is rarely read by the general public any more. There is a statue of him in Saint Stephen's Green, and another one on the campus at UCD, just across from the new coffee bar, which has recently been renamed, in tribute I suppose, "Finnegans Break." There are Joyce key rings and boxer shorts and shaving mugs. Dublin pubs and restaurants and hotels are called after his characters. You will always know a really lousy Dublin pub, in fact, because it will be called after somebody in Ulysses, and have a faded poster of Georgian Doors sellotaped to the wall behind the bar.

So I feel sorry for James Joyce. When his friend Samuel Beckett wished the terrible curse of an honoured name on his enemies, he had a point. Joyce is respectable now. He is safer than de Valera ever was. He is beyond criticism. The extraordinary young visionary has become the grand old man of modern Irish writing. Or to borrow another memorable phrase from Ms Gemma Hussey's masterwork, he is "the colossus of letters straddling the international consciousness of Irish culture." He is the old father, the old artificer. I think he would have felt highly ambivalent about this. Was there ever a writer whose work resounded so poignantly with rage against the father, on the one hand, and a pure desperate yearning to be fathered, on the other?

I suppose this is how Irish writers are doomed to see him, and the historical meta-narrative he railed against, and thus became so linked to. We want them both to be there, and we simultaneously want them both to go away. We want to reject them, but as Joyce said himself, you can't reject anything you haven't first been seduced by. For despite their influence, and the love they inspire, parents are tricky creatures, especially literary parents. They fuck you up, wrote Philip Larkin. And nobody can fuck up a young writer the way James Joyce can.

Think of those gloomy and desolate Dubliners. Those long sentences groaning with the weight of adjectives and obscurities. "The heaventree of stars hung with nightblue moonfruit." A line so emotionally evocative yet substantively meaningless that it could have been written by Bono.

If Joyce is Our Father, then hallowed be his name. But his books should be read more, and his face should be taken off the money. Joyce was an anarchist and a rebel, an artist who swore the oath of the devil against the Irish past, I will not serve. We should not make him serve Ireland now, either its banjaxed tourist industry or its smug invented history of itself as a paradise of literary production. Neither, I think, should we serve that past ourselves, when modern Ireland is crying out loud to be celebrated, imagined and changed.

Part IV: The Modern Irish Writer and England

The problems of being a young Irish writer these days are exacerbated by the fact that we all have English publishers, and thus, have to deal with the English nation on a regular basis.

I had cause to ponder this recently when I went to an upmarket bunfight at the Arts Club in Picadilly. It was the first time in ages that I'd worn a suit and tie, and I must say, the suit felt thoroughly rented. The unwitting star of this book, the seemingly ubiquitous Colm Tóibín, was receiving the Encore prize for his very fine novel, *The Heather Blazing*, and I'd gone along to clap his back and skull a bit of free champers and indulge in a bit of *caint, craic agus ruaile buaile*.

Colm made a funny speech about Ireland and England. He told us about a row he'd once had with a publisher who had omitted the *fadas* from the word Tóibín on the cover of one of his books. He had pointed out to this publisher — an enthusiastic English left-wing activist — that being Irish wasn't actually optional these days, that we had fought for seven hundred bloody years for the right to have *fadas* over our names if we damn well pleased. But he added that such sensitivities seemed, oddly enough, to become suddenly less pointed when the English had just handed one a cheque for £7500 sterling. He did very well, and everyone laughed, and the party seemed to loosen up.

Anyway, when the speech was over I was flitting around chewing the fat — and I must say, there was plenty of fat there to chew -when all of a sudden this tall sharp-faced woman lurched over and started talking to me as though addressing a public meeting. Her name was Arabella or Trixibella or Bicycle Bella. One of those names anyway. Let us just say, the broad was not from Ballymagash. She smelt like a copy of "Cosmopolitan," and it became apparent with some speed that she was either very seriously brain damaged or quite the worse for drink.

"Blecks," the woman hissed at me. "Sorry?" I said.

"Bloody wogs," she said. "They kidnapped him."

"God, did they?" I whispered anxiously, believing myself to be in the presence of a lunatic, or a fascist, or both.

"Yes they bladdy well did," she said. "They came around to my hise and bladdy well kidnapped him while I was ite. Bastards!"

The woman was so upset that I thought she was talking about her husband, but it turned out she was actually talking about her dog. A party of afro-Carribean youths had apparently kidnapped said dog — a pedigree of some kind — and had sent her a tersely worded ransom note next day, to the effect that she'd better cough up with five hundred smackers pretty pronto or else poochie would be pushing up the daisies.

She had coughed up the spondulix, and the mutt had duly been delivered back to her, understandably shaken by its ordeal, but seemingly unharmed. All had seemed to be hunky dorey, but then, suddenly, the poor dog had been taken ill. And then, tragically, it had died. A week to the day after she had forked out the five hundred to ensure its safe return, it had just dropped down dead.

"Stiff as a bladdy board," she said. "Bastards."

"Perhaps," I mused, "the strain had been too much for it?"

"Mmm," she nodded. "Perhaps that was it, yes. He was a very sensitive creature. I believe he just gave up on life, you know."

"Really?" I said. "Do dogs do that?"

She shook her head dolefully. "He never liked blecks," she said, "I'd cut their bladdy balls off with a machete if I could. And do you know, I *loved* that dog."

"Did you?" I said. "*Did* you?"

She turned to me and clutched at my lapel. "I loved that dog," she said, "more than bladdy life itself."

There were a lot of novelists at the party the other night, all talking about the plots of their forthcoming books. But nothing I heard was more captivating than the story of this woman and her ill-fated canine. Yet, it struck me that if you put the above conversation into a novel, people would not believe it. Which is a shame really, because every word of it is true. It's sad. Perhaps Mark Twain was right, after all, when he said "it's no wonder the truth is stranger than fiction, because fiction, after all, has to make sense."

But all Irish writers dealing with England have to contend with the lines between truth and fiction — or between truth and bizarre fantasy at any rate — tending to get suddenly blurred from time to time. Let me tell you a story about a young Irish novelist I know, who was in the offices of his London publishers earlier this year. He had a novel coming out, this fellow, and he had been invited in to have a chinwag with the heads of the sales and marketing departments. They wanted to discuss their ideas for the promotion of his book.

Thus, clad in the Sunday best and scrubbed to within an inch of his life, this wide-eyed Irish novelist found himself sitting in his publishers' office, feeling very excited as copies of the press adverts and posters for his novel were handed around. Everything looked wonderful. A lot of work had been put into this. Roddy Doyle move over, he thought. The bigtime, here we come.

Then, suddenly, his eye fell upon an item on the typed agenda which he had been given. "MURPHY'S STOUT PROMOTION," it said. Curious, he asked what this meant. The head of sales explained that he'd had an absolutely brilliant idea. See, this young novelist WAS Irish, after all, and, hey, we all know what the Irish are famous for. So, naturally, it had occurred to the head of sales, that, you know, it would be a really good lark to ask a drinks company — Murphy's in this case — to sponsor the publication of the book. He was IRISH, this young novelist, so, like, booze was the obvious thing. Spiffing fun, eh? It's the kind of really imaginative idea for which, I imagine, this head of sales gets paid a considerable salary.

My friend was taken aback, for a number of reasons. In all his years living in London, he had rarely been subjected to so crass an example of racist stereotyping. An Irish author, so we'll get Murphy's involved! (Nothing at all against Murphy's, of course, who, I should add, had not actually been approached about this dumb idea.) But it's beyond belief, is it not? Thankfully the fine black novelist Ben Okri is not published by this particular company. Doubtless, if he was, they would want to give away a free coconut with every copy of the paperback.

Another reason my friend was upset was that his novel is about a family which has been almost completely destroyed by alcohol abuse. Thus, he felt that sponsorship by a drinks company might been just a teensy weensie bit inappropriate. And he felt that the head of sales could not have actually read his book, or he would have realised how cringe-making his suggestion was.

He tried, our young Irish novelist, in his shocked state, to register his feelings about this squalid little example of ignorant racism. But things were about to get worse. The twilight zone was about to be entered. The head of sales of this major London publishing house looked at my pal and said, "erm, sorry, do you mind if I ask you something? Are you Catholic or Protestant? Because that has a lot to do with it in Ireland, doesn't it? What you drink I mean? Catholics drink Guinness, don't they, and Protestants drink Murphys? Or is it the other way around? I can't remember. But it's true though, isn't it? You can tell whether an Irishman is Protestant or Catholic by the kind of beer he drinks, HA, HA, HA, HA, HA?"

He made his way home, this author, feeling hurt and angry. He tried to control his feelings, to convince himself that he was over-reacting. The English were not racist, he told himself; some of his closest friends were English. It was only on the tube that he had another glance at the press advertisement for his book. And there, in the small print, was a reference to the author tour arranged by the publishers. There would be a nationwide tour, it said, of "Ireland and mainland Britain."

I wanted to tell you this small story, because I think it shows something important. While our political leaders try to negotiate peace — and the best of luck to them — down in the grassroots, there are ignorances so profound and caricatures so powerful that they are beyond the talk of politicians. Appalling stereotypes exist on both sides, yes. We are not saints of tolerance in Ireland, by any means. But Britain is still, sadly, one of the most racist societies in Western Europe. And the Irish are still the people the English understand least. And we're just not sure, me and my very good friend, if they will ever really forgive us for the unspeakable sin of not wanting to be like them.

Part V: On a Dark Desert Highway: The Role of the Publicity Tour in Modern Irish Fiction.

I had a novel published in the Spring of 1994. It was called "Desperadoes." With hindsight, the name may have been a mistake. Two and a half years of telling people the title of this new book, only to have them go "Oh really, you're an Eagles fan, yeah? I always liked that 'Hotel California' myself. On a dark desert highway, coo-hool wind in ma hair. Groovy, that."

You have slaved away for years crafting this noble, intelligent and perceptive tome, only to have it sullied by comparison with a tawdry so-called "song" by Southern California's answer to The Osmond Brothers. You have spent all that time virtually alone, writing. But now, suddenly, you have to go public. Now, you have to talk about it. Now, you have to do an author tour.

You arrive in the first town. Your publishers have mistakenly put you up in a sensationally expensive hotel, thinking you were somebody else. It is the kind of hotel where they knock on the door at eleven o'clock at night and come in to turn down the bedsheets. You are not used to this. The kind of hotel you usually stay in, they knock on the door at eleven o'clock at night and shout "time's up, Mac."

But you begin to feel good about yourself. Hey, you're a real author now. You've made it. You strut around the enormous bathroom like a black polonecked peacock, opening and sniffing the miniature plastic bottles of hair tonic, shoe polish and hand-cream. You sniff so hard that you begin to hallucinate. The room pulses and vibrates in the manner of early Led Zeppelin videos, or the beginnings of flashbacks in Australian soap operas. But you're feeling cocky. All that hard work was worth it. You should really go home right now, while you're still feeling good. But you don't. You make the mistake of turning up to do your reading.

Nothing in life brings you back to reality like arriving at a bookshop in a rainy Northern English town to find the pallid and overworked staff trying to spread out and look like a crowd.

If you are very lucky, there will be about thirty people at a reading. Perhaps ten will have come to hear you read, and, miracle of miracles, to buy your book. But ten of the others will have come to shuffle up to you before the reading begins and explain frankly how they read your last book and thought it a smouldering mound of dogshite, how they are all writing much more interesting books themselves, and how, in point of fact, they would not buy your new book even if somebody put a kalashnikov to their nether regions and threatened to leave them singing soprano. Of the remaining punters, four will be distant cousins who live in this God-forsaken locality, begrudgingly press-ganged into turning up by their parents, who have threatened to disinherit them otherwise. You will not have seen them since you were seven, when you gave one of them a severe Chinese burn for saying your mother had a moustache. There will be two postgraduate English literature students from the local university down at the back, loudly swopping epigrams from the complete works of Michel Foucault. And there will be at least one amiable schizophrenic who has wandered in for the free glass of *Liebfraumilch* and a tepid sausage roll.

You stand about for a few minutes feeling nervous. You attempt small-talk with the manager and his underpaid staff. If you are Irish, as I am, the small-talk will invariably be about how well Roddy Doyle is doing. "Oh yeah," the manager will laugh, "we had Roddy here last May and they were hanging out of the rafters. We turned three hundred people away." You sweat like a sodden sponge. You swig from a bottle of warm Harp. You light up a cigarette, forgetting that you're in a bookshop, so you're not allowed to smoke. You stub your cigarette out in an empty beer bottle. Moments later, you forget that you have done this, and you take a big reassuring slug from the beer bottle. You chunder all over the cash register.

Nobody has a tissue. So you absent-mindedly rip pages out of big thick books like The Bible or *A Suitable Boy*, by Vickram Seth. When the mop-up is finished, the manager sighs and says you would have got a much better crowd if it wasn't for The Match, or The Weather, or The Time Of Year, of The Fact That Brookside Is On Tonight. What he really means is that you would have got a much better crowd if you were Roddy Doyle. You feel people's eyes glaring at you, and then glaring at the life size poster of you which has been sellotaped to the wall behind the wonky lectern where you are going to read. In the photo you are slim, smiling, relaxed, groomed and then thoroughly airbrushed just to be on the safe side. In real life, you are overweight, tired, tense, messy, grinning like a botched brain surgery case. You cut yourself shaving earlier, so a crimson hunk of toilet paper is dangling from your double chin. You couldn't get the trouser press in your room to work, so your chinos look like you recently had sex without taking them off. The manager introduces you. "Joe will be reading from his new novel, *Desperadoes*." Then he grins, broadly. "Hope all the Eagles fans are in tonight." You stand up and begin to read.

The till bleeps and jingles all the way through your reading. All the jokes on which you worked so hard fall utterly flat. As if to compensate for this, people laugh at the tender moments with such ferocity that you fear they will rupture themselves. Then, just as you get to the particularly poignant bit about granny dying with the cute little puppy the orphan gave her in her arms, the schizophrenic stands up, drops his trousers, starts going on about being followed by the government and begins to masturbate vigorously. Glancing up, you notice that the manager is gnawing his lip now. His own lip, that is. Not the schizophrenic's lip.

You finish the reading and sit down to a torrential trickle of applause. Then, the worst part. The manager says there is time for a few questions. Total silence. "Come on," he urges, "don't be shy." Coughs. Nervous titters. One solitary piercing fart from your second cousin. Silence again. If you cracked your knuckles, the resulting sound would seem like a burst of rifle fire.

Back in the hotel you eat all the peanuts in the minibar. This makes you unbelievably thirsty, so you start drinking. You fall into a coma and wake up at dawn on the bathroom floor, singing "Drop Kick Me Jesus Through the Goalposts of Life," with the plastic bottle of body lotion in your mouth and the disposable shower cap on your head. The hotel manager is knocking on the door, wondering what the commotion is about. You invite him in for a drink. He is cross. He tells you he would like you to check out. You don't understand. You grab him by the lapels. You can check out any time you like, you tell him, but, woah, you can never leave.

Chapter Nine
Conversations on a Homecoming

Part I: Fly me to the Moon

When I came back to live in Ireland in 1993, I started writing a lot of journalism. One of the most interesting things about doing this is that you often find yourself interviewing people. It's a strange and uneasy relationship, where you can ask the most extraordinary questions of people you've never met before and expect honest — or, at least, half-honest — answers. Most of the time you are struck by how boring or tedious or pretentious famous people are. But sometimes you come away feeling glad you met the subject. You get to know what makes them tick, or why they bother working when they're so rich, or maybe you don't, maybe they just fill you with a fleeting sense of the sheer joy they derive from doing whatever it is they do. Since I started writing journalism that's happened to me more than my fair share. So I thought you might like to know about it.

Let's begin with the world of politics. Now, I don't know about you, but when the next election comes I intend to give my number one vote early and often to the Natural Law Party. God, they're a fine party. Recently I spoke to the Dublin candidate and party leader, a pleasant fellow called Mr John Burns. I must say, I found his approach to realpolitik arresting. "We're not fighting the election in any way," he clarified, "we don't actually believe in organised party politics." (In that case, I almost suggested, he should join the Progressive Democrats.) "We see all the other politicians as our colleagues," he said, which will cheer them up no end, I feel sure. The main policy of his own party is "to reduce the level of incoherence in collective consciousness," to share with the Irish electorate "the tradition of Vedic science as interpreted by Maharishi Mahesh Yogi" and to harness "the infinite creativity and organising power of the universal natural law." Phew. Forget the beef tribunal report, try getting *that* through a tricky cabinet meeting.

167

I was fascinated by all of this, but I pointed out that I was disappointed not to have had one single doorstep visit from an NLP candidate or supporter. "Well, one of our policies is not to canvass," he said, "we feel people should be free to make up their own minds." So how does the NLP spread the message? "We do smiling and driving," he said. "We drive around town and smile at people. And we go to DART stations. We feel elections should be a time of national celebration."

Mr Burns concedes that his electoral chances may be somewhat limited. But should the NLP ever receive the mandate it so richly deserves, he feels that Ireland would best be run "by a group of experts in yogic flying," (a form of spiritual activity during which the devotee lifts off the ground and hovers in mid-air). When the NLP ascends to power, he and his colleagues will be responsible for setting up this group. Thanks be to Krishna he is not in the Labour party, otherwise, no doubt, he would be appointing one of his relations as chief flyer to the Taoiseach's Department. But how big should this group be? I wondered.

"About seven thousand," he replied, "ideally."

And how would they all be recruited?

"Well, look at the numbers involved in administration at the moment," he said, "you have the police, the army." So would the Garda Siochana be re-trained as yogic flyers? "Not necessarily, but we'd take anyone who wanted to get involved." Myself, for instance? "Sure." And Albert Reynolds? (who, in my book, has the considerable advantage of already spending a good portion of his time up in the clouds.) Mr Burns pondered, just for a moment, before giving the thumbs up to the idea of an airborne Albert.

Mr Burns himself has been levitating "since 1978", sometimes putting a pretty considerable distance between his arse and his axminster. "Two feet is nothing much", he sniffed. I was pretty thunderstruck by this, but he said yogic flying was actually seen as "almost trivial" in the party. "Almost all of us do yogic flying," he said, "although some of us go up but we don't stay up." Interestingly, Mr Burns recommends the lotus position, because in any other, he alleges, "it is impossible to give yourself a good thrust." I really was impressed by now, but Mr Burns was modesty personified. "When you've been doing yogic flying twice a day for sixteen years it all gets a bit mundane," he said. I can tell you, Mr Burns should live my life.

It is easy to scoff, yes, but Mr Burns is utterly serious about his views. And perhaps there is something to this yogic flying business. I mean, it is often said that pigs might fly, so what not ambitious backbenchers? Certainly, it all gives a new meaning to the phrase "parachute candidate." And I, for one, do not mind confessing to the fervent wish that the entire Fine Gael front bench would flap in ducklike formation, by yogic means or otherwise, out of the Dáil, up over Saint Stephen's Green, and into the bloody stratosphere.

"We want to create a heaven on earth," Mr Burns concluded, "a new world, and a new Ireland." What a guy! Of course, it was only when I put down the phone that something occurred to me. This new yogic Ireland? Just how much would your average Palestinian millionaire with a keen interest in dogfood have to shell out in order to get himself a couple of passports to it?

Part II: Nice Day For a White Wedding:
Billy Idol in California

The Russian taxi driver asks me where I'm going, and I tell him I'm going to interview Billy Idol, and honestly, the limo swerves, brakes squealing, and my life flashes before me on Pallisades Drive, just outside Los Angeles, California. "Jesus," he says, "Billy fuckin' Idol? Jesus! Wait till my kid hears about this. My kid got all his records. Every fuckin' one. *Fuck.*"

We are on our way to a place called the Aha Spa, a new age and holistic "healing centre" much patronised by his supreme Idolness. It has been suggested that we meet here for the interview, because it has, as they say in this parish, a "good vibe." Stepping out of the taxi, the air is hot and very dry. You can feel it through the soles of your shoes. I'm early, so I hang around, light a cigarette and attempt to "chill." A woman with a poodle glares at me. I swear to God, the poodle does too.

"That's like, *rully* bad for you," the woman says. "Smoking gives you cancer."

"I have it already," I tell her. "There's very little time left."

"Oh Jeez Louise," she says, "Oh God, rully?"

I shrug. "Three months," I tell her. "Four, if I'm lucky."

She says "God" a few more times, then leaves. Very suddenly, Billy Idol appears from round a corner, comes strolling along the path, with his PR person, a fellow journalist and the manager of the Aha Spa. We shake hands, me and Billy, and he says "awight?" in a half Californian, half Sarf-East London drawl. I prepare myself for an onslaught of ribald rock 'n' roll jokes, but he begins to chat amiably about the cleanliness of the air in these parts, how it's better than it is in the city, how the LA smog is getting worse every year, and how even London has smog now. Sheesh, the man really does seem to know a lot about air. His PR woman points out that Billy has a huge lipstick kiss on his left cheek, and he wipes it away with the back of his hand, looking rather shy, as if he's been caught out in something. He sits down at a wooden log table with the other journalist and they order a bottle of mineral water. They will be an hour, I am told.

So I go for a walk, and I read over my notes. The air smells of bougainvillaea and suntan lotion and the heat seems to suck the oxygen out of your lungs. Born William Michael Broad, in Wales, thirty eight years ago. Lived in suburban Bromley with Mum and Dad. Mum calls him "Will." Dad sells tools. Granddad bought him a Ringo Starr drum kit at age eight, little Will bitten by rock and roll bug. Grows up a bit. Gets fat. Gets glasses. Gets "O" Levels. Doesn't get laid. Other kids hate him in school. Becomes punk, age fifteen. Gets laid. Has first fuck to "Mony Mony" by Tommy James and the Shirrells. Later has hit with same song. Owes quite a lot to Tommy James? Leaves school for Sussex University. Starts English degree. Changes name to Billy Idol. Leaves after six months to be in punk band, Generation X. Generation X awful and embarrassing. Everybody leaves. Billy not taken seriously by other punks because he likes rock and roll and comes from Bromley. Ironic really, because if ever there was a middle class culture it was punk, and if ever there was a double-garage band, surely it was The Clash? Billy comes to America. "Hangs out" in New York. Big hit in the clubs. Kiss's manager takes him on. Big hit all over. Has kid with former Hot Gossip dancer, Perry Lister. Moves to LA. Says hello to the big time. Says goodbye to Perry, who moves out. Now he's into aromatherapy and cyberpunk. Big surprise.

I think about this Billy Idol, and what to ask him. See, the thing is, I've never been a real fan exactly. I mean, yeah, I thought "White Wedding" was a cracker, and yeah, "Mony Mony" is good for getting a party going. But Billy Idol? I mean to say, he ain't exactly Elvis, is he? Costello *or* Presley. This is the man whom Johnny Rotten once dubbed "the Perry Como of punk," but actually, it should have been Tommy Cooper. Billy Idol has always seemed the most *English* of pop stars. He loves dressing up, posing, sneering at the camera, saying naughty things, dropping his drawers in public, having a *larf*. He's a seaside postcard with a peroxide haircut. There's something charmingly old-fashioned about his brand of entertainment. In another life, Billy Idol would have been the ringmaster of a very odd circus, the owner of a freakshow, or the guy in an East End music hall who used polysyllabic adjectives to introduce the clapping seal act.

And cyberpunk? What will I ask him about cyberpunk? I've been reading up on it, all about internets, and cyberspace and virtual reality, but what do you actually ask someone about all that trainspotter shit? It's for sad people in hush puppies isn't it, cyberpunk? All wittering on to each other on their little modems and sprocket oscillators, all squeezing their pustules and calling each other "Scarlet Devil" and "Masked Avenger." A Tony Hancock sketch, "The Radio Ham" comes into my mind. "I have lots of friends...all over the world they are, everywhere...none around here, mind you." I feel uptight. I turn a corner and there is a poster advertising "GREAT HOLIDAYS FOR *YOUR* PET." And I walk on, pondering the wise words of my Russian taxi driver. "Los Angeles," he said, "is full of fuckin' morons."

It is now two thirty in the afternoon and I am flat on my back in the Aha Spa, feeling tense, in a reclining chair with a woman called Jeannine standing over me, holding a set of headphones and grinning. Jeannine, it has just occurred to me, looks very like one of The Mamas and Papas, but I can't remember which one. What's about to happen next is something Billy's PR woman has told me Billy does quite often, so I feel I should try it out.

Now, I don't know about you, but flat on my back, legs akimbo, is not a position I am comfortable adopting, unless it is with somebody with whom I've been to the pictures at least twice. Still, I stare up Jeannine through my spread-eagled legs and I must admit that she looks oddly attractive from this vantage point. She steps forward and puts the headphones on me. Then she brandishes a sort of plastic blindfold, into which a matrix of tiny lightbulbs has been screwed. She beams with the intensity of a medieval martyr, and puts the blind over my eyes.

"Now Joe," she says, "you're gonna find this, like rully mellowing. It's an internal experience. OK?"

"OK, Jeannine," I say.

"Let's geddit *on*," she laughs. "Ha ha ha," I chortle, dutifully, and she leaves the room, a whiff of lemon-scented perfume hanging in the air.

Suddenly, I am alone and feeling practically malarial with nervousness. The chair makes a soft humming sound and begins to vibrate. My sphincter becomes prehensile with anxiety. A click in the headphones is followed by a soft sibilance, and a tape of New Age keyboard music begins to play, you know the kind of thing, heavy on the echo pedal, all minor seventh chords, the occasional plangent "whoo-whoo, yeah-oh" pretty far back in the mix. Billy Idol likes *this*?!! Well, it's pretty damn far from "Anarchy in the UK," I can tell you. It is the kind of music you hear in Californian lifts and North London wine bars, *om lala om a borshsha lanamaracha om*, the words all sound like the names of small and particularly vicious statelets of the former Yugoslavia. The chair begins to rock on two axes, slowly at first, then building up speed. The lights begin to flash in my eyes. Billy fucking Idol, the man who penned "Rebel Yell," is into this stuff?! I try to remember what Jeannine said about this being a mellowing experience, although, in fact, I am getting an extraordinary headache and I feel like spewing up my hash browns.

Half an hour later, and I have spent several minutes staggering around in the blinding sunshine, gathering together what are left of my thoughts. When I come back into the Aha Spa, his Billness is sitting in my chair, wearing mirror shades, grey shorts and a black T shirt with the word "cyberpunk" emblazoned in a circular logo. His hair is spiky, so full of peroxide that you feel he would spontaneously combust if you lit a match in his presence. His left eyebrow is raised. His chin leans against his right fist. His facial expression is reminiscent of a Roman emperor in a bad Hollywood movie, who is about to say, in a languid drawl, "that slave on the left, he amuses me, put him to death." He is looking rather well these days, tanned, relaxed, extremely healthy, rich; his fingernails gleam as though they've recently been subjected to the attentions of a particularly enthusiastic manicurist. In short, he looks a million miles away from the scrawny carbuncular punk who stares out grimacing and drooling from the early publicity shots.

Now, Billy's "people" have instructed me to read the novel *Neuromancer* by William Gibson, in preparation for this interview. This book, they have told me, has been a major influence on Billy's new album. Thus, I have spent many long hours trudging through Gibson's turgid prose, and it's not the kind of book I like at all. It's full of people with metal limbs, taking designer drugs, having sex with girls who have nipples like peach stones, and using words like "mycrotoxin" and "bleebebarbb" and "zargathon." I ask him about the book, what he felt when he met William Gibson.

"Great," he says, "we got on well."

I ask him what he liked about the book.

He liked the spirit of it, he tells me. He liked the feel of it. "Hmmm," I say. Rather suddenly, he pounds on the armrest. "This is where we're going, and we're farking well going *NOW*."

"Yes," I say.

I ask him if he identifies with the central character, Chase, and he raises his eyebrows and says yeah, he does, "don't you?"

Sidestepping quickly, I point out that the social milieu Gibson portrays is pretty dull and bleak, and that there's no pop music in it. I ask what Billy Idol would do in a world like this? He shrugs. "I'd be Chase," he says.

I'm feeling nervous now; I feel the sweat trickling down my spine. This doesn't seem to be going at all well, and I get the distinct feeling he doesn't actually want to talk about this naff bloody book at all. Still, I press on. I ask him a spectacularly undergraduate question next. Chase, I point out, is jokingly called "artiste" by one of the other characters. Does he think that Gibson is proposing that his hero is, in fact, a metaphor for the contemporary artist, in the sense that he must adapt and change in order to survive in a hostile world? Billy snuffles with laughter. He peers at me like I've just puked up on his chinos. "You could be right," he grins.

Tittering anxiously, I decide to abandon the Neuromancer strategy, and to ask him, instead, about music. And something odd happens then. Things improve. He perks up. And before my very eyes, Little Willie Broad becomes Billy farkin' Idol.

He thumps the chair again. "It takes you out of your own farking world. I mean, all music. It means you don't have to be anything you don't want to be. It takes you on a journey, and there's no limits. With Beethoven, it was like, the farking countryside isn't just that, you know, it's God, you know what I mean?"

Written down, it reads a bit like an outtake from Spinal Tap, I know, but listening to it is genuinely affecting. He talks about music with a naivety that is quite touching. He waves his arms and gesticulates and raises his voice when he talks about rock and roll, and he speaks intensely and the veins in his neck begin to throb, and it's like overhearing the enthusiasm of a fifteen year old in his best mate's garage band.

He tells me all about his new album, *Cyberpunk*. It was produced by Robin Hancock, who has worked with Madonna, and recorded in ten months, using a computer-controlled mobile studio which Billy set up in his house. It's kind of a concept album, all about cyberpunk and virtual reality, and he's very proud of it, and he thinks it's the best thing he's done.

I ask him if he can remember the first time he heard the word "cyberpunk" and he tells me that it was two years ago, just after his motorbike accident. He was flat on his back in the Mount Sinai hospital in downtown LA, his leg strapped into an electronic muscle stimulator, when a journalist called Legs McNeill came to interview him. It was just after his album *Charmed Life* came out, and McNeill had the audacity to suggest that Billy had abandoned his gob-in-your-eye punk roots.

"I told him I farkin' hadn't," Billy says, "and anyway, he sees this thing on my leg, and he goes, that's very cyberpunk."

I ask to see his scar and he points to his shin. The abrasion is a revolting oval mass of salmon-pink tissue, maybe six inches long. It looks like a satellite photo of a distant and spectacularly unfriendly planet.

I read him a quote from a 1988 interview. "The point of riding bikes is to get to the other end of the journey. If you crash and fall off, you're an arsehole." He laughs, and visibly relaxes. "Yeah," he goes, "I did say that, didn't I?"

The laugh takes you completely by surprise. *Hoo hoo hoo*, it goes, like Santa Claus on speed. "*Hoo hoo hooargh.*" There was always a guy in James Bond movies, a dusky villain with an unspeakably evil laugh, who went "but pliss, not so fast Meester Bond, now it ees time for yeux to die, *hoo hoo hoo.*" Next Bond movie, they should cast Billy Idol, just to do the laugh.

He asks where I'm from, and I tell him Dublin. His face lights up. We're getting on well now. He tells me that his Mum is from Cork, and that his Irish roots have become very important to him. His Irish uncles and aunts were all musicians, he says, one of them played the piano and sang, and another was a great saxophone player. He recalls gigging in Dublin last year, coming on stage in a sequined Republic of Ireland football shirt, with EIRE in gold on the back. "They went absolutely farking crazy," he laughs. "I like to think there's a bit of the old Irish" — he pauses, headbutts the air, clenches his fist — "a bit of all that, you know, in what I do."

I ask how fatherhood has affected him. "A lot," he says, "you have a kid, and you have an investment in the future." His son, Willem Wolfe Broad — the second name is in honour of Wolfe Tone — is now five years old, and I enquire whether Junior has expressed any interest in an air-punching, lip-sneering, rock and roll career.

"Well, he has a nice little voice," Billy says. "That's the difference. He might be in trouble there. I mean, I can't sing, and he *can*. But it's whatever makes him happy."

And he tells me how he was asked to give out a gong at the recent MTV awards, and how, in true rock and roll fashion, upon leaving the stage he "went like this" — raises thumb to nose, sticks out tongue, wiggles fingers — into the camera, and how, when he came home, young Willem opened the front door and performed a similar gesture at his Dad. He laughs loudly as he tells the story. He seems to get a real kick out of talking about his son.

California has been very good to Billy Idol. He came to America at a time when he freely admits his career was at a low. "I mean, yeah, I'd done some really stupid embarrassing things." But one night he was in an LA club when his song "Dancing With Myself" came on, and everyone started to pogo wildly, and he realised that if it wasn't exactly home, it was a place he could sure as Hell get used to. "I made the best of being here in every way I could," he says, "and I turned my music around, so now it has a bit of direction."

He's right about that. The new album seems crafted and layered, the songs complex, some of them genuinely disturbing. It features, for instance, a brave and rivetting cover version of the Lou Reed classic, "Heroin," technofied and sampled, and based around another borrowing, the line from the Patti Smith album, "Horses," which is chanted over and over again in Billy's strangely appropriate growl. "Jesus died for somebody's sins, but not mine."

I ask him about this song, and about his own past relationship with heroin. Now, Billy Idol doesn't like to be serious. There's nothing he likes better than having a larf, and being every inch the wacky rock and roll prankster, but when you get him talking about his drug-ravaged past, there is real pain in his voice and you kind of suspect it was no joke, and we're suddenly back to Will Broad again. The heroin user, he says, shaking his head, "is the loneliest person in the world." I ask him to elaborate. "I thought I was going to die," he says, trying to smile, "I mean, the only thing that got me off of it was music, in the end. Because I had another life, that wasn't just taking drugs." He has stopped taking heroin now, but admits, candidly, that he "will always be a drug addict." There's silence between us for a moment, and then, suddenly, the boyish grin returns as though he's putting on a mask, and he attempts brightness once again. "Heroin," he tells me, is a particular favourite of his mum's. "She's going around the place singing it to everyone. She called me up when I sent them a tape of the album, and she said, we think it's lovely Billy, but how are your sinuses, are they any better now?" Mrs Broad sounds like a truly remarkable woman.

I ask him if he's like his father, and he mishears me. "Oh, he's really great," he says. "I love him." "No," I say, "Are you *like* him?" And he nods. "Oh, am I like him? Well, you know, it's funny, you get older and you see the similarities. We didn't get on when I was younger. But then one day comes and you just realise it's all so much bullshit."

The first single, "Shock to the System," is another strong track. "That song was originally about Galileo," Billy explains. "It was like, the pope refused to say that Galileo was right, and I mean, that was the biggest shock to the system ever. And I just wanted to say, you're *fucked*, arsehole, *hoo hoo hoo*."

The album, and the six different versions of the video for "Shock to the System," contain a pretty hefty dose of anti-Christian imagery. I enquire about the nature of Billy's religious beliefs and they are, shall we say, unorthodox.

"I mean, Tolstoy wrote about it, didn't he? In his early works? He said like, if we were all fucking Christians then how could a bishop ever bless a war? I just think those people are *arseholes*."

With a sudden whirr, the chair in which the pert Idol buttocks are parked — the chair, indeed, in which my own posterior was so thoroughly vibrated not an hour ago — begins its rocking motion once again. And it's oddly disturbing, for some reason, trying to conduct an interview with a person who is suddenly swaying before you. It's a bit like trying to chat someone up when you're very drunk. But we press on regardless.

I put to the now undulating muso the irony that he christened himself Billy Idol as a tongue-in-cheek punk joke, and that now he really is an idol, in America anyway, that he's actually become the object of his own satire. "*Hoo, hoo*, yeah," he sniggers, "well it's better than Bill Broad, innit? I mean, Bill Broad sounds like some farking skinhead, dunnit? I suppose it is ironic, but I could never figure out why nobody else came up with Idol. It's so farking ridiculous. It's great." And he laughs again. *Hoo hoo hoo*.

And he still misses England, he says. "I miss, you know, the weather in April and May." I ask him how he thinks he's perceived on this side of the pond and he grins behind the mirror shades, carefully considering his answer. When it doesn't come, I put it to him that the English sometimes tend to celebrate failure rather than success and he grins. "Yeah," he says, whispering now, "but you know what?" For the first time in our conversation, the top lip curls up into the famous Idol sneer. "What?" I say, "Tell me?" He leans forward. "*FARK* them," he snarls, then explodes into laughter.

"I used to think it was great," he sniggers, "nobody in England would recognise me. I used to love that. Nobody gave a shit about me."

As tactfully as possible, I suggest that popstars in general are not known for their not wanting anyone to give a shit about them, and that what he has just told me is not actually true.

He glares at me, then laughs again. "Yeah," he chuckles. "Yeah, you're right."

And an odd thing happens to me, then. See, the thing is, Billy Idol really does laugh a lot. And there's a line in a short story I read recently about people who laugh a lot. (The story is by Aidan Mathews). "To be honest, I almost wish he didn't laugh quite so much. It's usually a sign of profound personal unhappiness. Cheerfulness is a quiet condition; glee, on the other hand, is only desperation on a good day." This line comes hammering into my mind, right there, in the Aha Spa. It's the weirdest thing. So I ask Billy Idol if he's happy now, and he stares into the middle distance, looking a little surprised to be asked something like that, and he keeps smirking, and pretending to double-take. "Well, I have my demons," he shrugs, "like everybody else, but basically I suppose so, yeah."

"Like what?" I ask. "Your demons? What are they?"

He takes a long swig from his bottle of Evian and wipes his lips with the back of his hand. He doesn't seem to want to talk too much about his demons. So I ask him if he's ever had therapy. The tone of his voice suddenly becomes more serious. He begins to choose his words with care and deliberation.

"I saw a psychiatrist once," he says, "well, I was forced to see one really."

I enquire why, and he peers at me. I know he was sent to see a psychiatrist by a California judge, when he pleaded guilty to a drunken assault on a female fan, and I'm wandering if he's going to tell me.

"Well, it was the lowest point in my career," he says, "no, scratch that, it was actually the lowest point in my life." He pauses, then goes through the whole story, honestly and without excuse, about the fan, and about how he hit her, when he was drunk.

I ask if the therapy taught him anything about himself that he didn't already know and he scratches his scarred shin and beams. "Only that I don't need a psychiatrist," he says. The Billy Idol mask is on again. That's as close as I'm going to get.

The PR woman comes in and asks if I want another five minutes. "Yeah," Billy says, "that's OK. Another five minutes." I look through my notes, but I can't find anything else I want to know about. So I ask what he'd be doing if he hadn't made it in rock and roll. "I'd be dead," he says, flatly. And I ask him if he likes being a star and having to think about his image.

"Well, I'm the LV now," he shrugs, disingenuously, "I mean, I'm the lead vocalist. In Gen X, I started off being the guitarist. But I ended up doing the job nobody else was prepared to do." He runs his fingers through his hair, snuffles with laughter, shakes his head. "And you know, sometimes, I think I'm still doing it."

This is how he likes to be seen. Billy Idol, punk-at-heart and reluctant star. It's a line he's very good at pushing, and as you say goodbye and shake hands again, you almost believe him, because he's so generally likeable. But later that night, a message comes to the hotel that the photoshoot which has been planned for the next day, and which involves twelve people being driven two and a half hours into the desert, has been cancelled suddenly, at a cost of thousands of dollars, because Billy Idol, the new-age punk rocker who doesn't give a toss about his image, is "unhappy with his stylist." A telling moment.

Well, we've all come a long way from the Spirit of '76. The stench of sweat and stale beer is now the heady perfume of pine and suntan oil, and the glare of the Marquee lights is the California sun, and Billy Idol is no shambling punk any more, if he ever was one to begin with. He's still tough, of course, and he says he won't compromise, just the way all the other old punks used to say that, before they ended up advertising jeans on the telly. Still, with Idol, at least you get the feeling he understands fully the compromises he's making, which is something. Which is oddly endearing, in fact. That's the thing about Billy Idol. He's the least reluctant celeb you're ever likely to meet. He just *loves* it all. It's brilliantly refreshing, and it makes you forgive a lot. There's no moaning about lack of privacy, no whining about artistic integrity, no pontificating about angst or the rainforest or Buddhism. He's every teenage kid who ever strummed a tennis racket in a mirror and dreamed about being a star. Except now he's actually doing it, which is actually very appealing. The clown prince of rock and roll, still sneering, still surviving, still punching the air and doing the job that nobody else is prepared to do, but only by accident of course. Only by accident. He never wanted it. No way. Just worked out like that. And hey, if you believe that for even one little minute, I got some *rully* prime swampland in Florida for sale.

Part III: Mixed Motives:
An honest chat with Terry Waite

The burly figure of Terry Waite comes loping across the front square of Trinity Hall College, Cambridge, in a smartly-cut blue suit. He glances up at the drizzling sky and wrinkles his nose in disapproval, then beams and shakes hands with a firm grip, as though greeting an old friend. It might be nice to talk in his room, he says, the room where he wrote his book.

Waite is an Honourary Fellow of this college, a modest-looking place which nestles in a side-street among the ornate Victorian facades of the famous university town. He spends most of his time in Cambridge now, lives here all week, returns to his family home in London only at weekends.

His six-foot-seven frame seems vast in the small room. There is a single bed, a desk. There are two simple chairs. There are metal bars in the window. The sparseness, and the bars, make the room disquietingly reminiscent of a prison cell. "Why I came here was almost to recreate the experience of solitude. When I came to this college, when they offered me a fellowship, I said I'd like a small place where I could just recreate that."

For the past year, since his book *Taken on Trust* came out, Terry Waite has not had too much solitude. He has been touring Britain doing signings and interviews, explaining to the public how a policeman's son rose from humble beginnings to become the Archbishop of Canterbury's envoy, how he began to work for human rights, how his reputation as a liberator of hostages eventually came to be tarnished by his association with Colonel Oliver North, how he walked into the clutches of Hezbollah militants in January 1987, and how he then spent seventeen hundred and sixty three days and nights in captivity, during which time he was savagely beaten, chained, blindfolded and repeatedly threatened with shooting. His shy eyes have stared out from television screens, tabloid pages and Sunday supplements alike, as his every private humiliation has been gradually made public. Doesn't he find it painful, reliving such experiences?

"Well, it's a balance," he says. "On the one hand an enormous number of people have turned up. I've been quite overwhelmed by the warmth. It's a nice opportunity for me to say thank you to the amazing amount of people who were personally touched by this. That's one thing." He pauses. "There *are* times when it is a bit difficult, but I don't dwell on that."

The book contains three inter-linked narratives, a memoir of his childhood, an account of his career, and a description of his captivity. Did he write them separately and edit them together later?

"No," he smiles, "I wrote it all as it appears." He chuckles as he reaches out and unlocks his briefcase. "You'll be the only journalist to see the manuscript. There it is. Look!" The briefcase contains perhaps fifteen foolscap notebooks, the pages completely covered in miniature spidery handwriting. "No-one else has seen this except the editor."

He is very proud of his book, and defensive about the mixed reviews it has received. "It's not an apology or a political document," he says. "It's written from the perspective of being in a prison cell, taking the reader into that experience. And then taking them further into the thought processes of the mind. One critic said my family figured as mere shadows in the book. And he's right, but he doesn't get the right reason for that. When you are in solitary you become so introverted that you can't bear to have too much emotion. You try and bring people back into your life from the past, but it's too painful."

While Waite's book lacks the immediacy of Brian Keenan's *An Evil Cradling*, it is strong on the eerily altered state of mental reality which develops during extended solitary confinement. A line from TS Eliot seems to hover over the pages; "time past and time future, perhaps are contained in time present."

"Very much so," he agrees. "I almost quoted that in the book. What I thought was, how strange to be here. I am learning to live for the moment. And in that moment the unconscious is filled with the past. And in some ways your concept of lineal time simply changes. You are not able to discern between day and night. It makes your concept of time an even bigger mystery. It's something I'd like to write more about."

Something else the British press would like Terry Waite to write more about is Colonel Oliver North, his intelligence contact at the National Security Council during the Reagan years, the man who encouraged him to go and meet the kidnappers, while simultaneously and secretly negotiating the sale of weapons to their controllers in Iran. Waite claims to have only discovered North's arms-dealing escapades following media exposure at the end of 1986, after which he made his ill-fated trip back to Beirut. But has he fully revealed the extent of his relationship with North?

"Well, I've described it as it was, as I knew it. There *are* elements I have forgotten, certain events. But what has happened subsequently is that commentators in the press have made judgements based on hindsight. Total nonsense. I *did* only first know about it when it came to my attention, as I describe in the book. That's how it was. There's no deception."

When it is suggested that his willingness to stroll into a situation of deadly danger following the North revelations was naïve and surprising, he folds his arms and seems to tense up.

"People *may* find that surprising. I think they have real difficulty puzzling it out, and therefore they give a very superficial interpretation to it. Some have said, you know, self-publicity. Well, what good is publicity if I get a bullet in my head? It's such an empty argument. There is a principle here. Having been compromised so badly by America, I couldn't walk away from the hostages."

But why not? Why not simply let somebody else with an untainted public image take over the negotiations?

"Because I was the only person who had face to face contact with the kidnappers. Even North has said that. And there was a moral decision. If the church picks up the case of people, it doesn't let them down when the going gets bad. I wouldn't do that."

Outside, a small group of tourists drifts slowly past the window, peering in from the path as though admiring some exotic creature in a zoo. They nudge each other in excited recognition, but Waite doesn't seem to notice them.

What was his attitude towards Hezbollah before his capture? He must have had a great trust to put himself so freely into the hands of a criminal organisation which had bombed embassies, gunned down opponents and tortured hostages?

"No, I don't have a *great* trust. I have a trust. I've always believed when dealing with terrorist organisations — which I've done all my life — that one of the dangers is that they do attract paranoid psychopathic people into their ranks. But terrorism is not the root problem. Terrorism stems from situations of long-standing injustice. Where that isn't dealt with, terrorism comes up as a symptom of a deeper disorder. I don't condone terrorism, but I understand why it happens."

So does this understanding extend to his captors? Can he understand why they kidnapped him?

"I'm still puzzling it out," he sighs. "I think there are a number of reasons about which I'm not sure. I think one reason is that if I'd had any success in Kuwait (where he was trying to secure the release of Father Lawrence Jenco and other American hostages) it would have taken some of the power away from Iran. I think the Iranians wanted me out of the way. And they wanted to know what I knew (about North)."

He feels that the kidnappers themselves were uncertain about the reasons for his capture. "Hezbollah never declared that they had me," he says, "which is interesting. I think had Brian Keenan not got my name out, and had I died in captivity, they would never have claimed responsibility for taking me."

He speaks fondly of the Irish former hostage.

"People assume, wrongly, that we were locked up together, but we never were. He was just in the next room. But I've met him since, and I *like* him." He laughs softly. "You know, when he was released, Brian said he had heard me crying out in the night, but I don't think that's true, unless it was in my sleep. Brian had to make up this story because if he had revealed how he knew where I was — which was by us all tapping messages on the walls of our cells — he would have jeopardised those hostages who were left. He made up a story which enabled him to tell my family and the world that I was alive. I owe an enormous debt of gratitude to Brian. He may well have been instrumental in saving my life."

For a man who has repeatedly put himself on the line to rescue others, Waite has had an uneasy relationship with the press of late. It has been alleged that his fellow captives did not like him, that they doubted his motivations, resented his publicity-seeking. "You could no more stop Terry calling a press conference than stop water running downhill," jibed his former cellmate Terry Anderson. (Waite laughs with uproarious good-humour when reminded of this.) In his book, he writes self-critically about the strain of being locked up twenty four hours a day with three other men. He admits to "wearying" of them, to arguing, to insensitivity and to losing his temper. But he says he spent many hours praying, analyzing his failings and his true reasons for wanting to release the hostages.

"In that situation of extremity where you are alone with nothing but who you are, you have to face up to the light of truth. Truth shines with a penetrating insight into all your motives. So when you make your self-analysis you think yes, when I was a child there *was* a craving for acceptance. And there still is. I've never believed that there is any such thing as a pure altruistic motive. All motives are mixed. If someone says they have an altruistic motive, I question that. Because *I* don't. But to fall into the hands of the living God is to fall into the searchlight of truth, the judgement of truth."

Didn't he ever doubt the existence of his living God?

"It wasn't ever a question of losing faith," he insists. "It was a realisation that faith doesn't bring any false protections. There's so much nonsense preached about the Christian faith. All you have to do is pray and you'll be safe, what nonsense. There has to be a differentiation between faith and magic. All you can do is look at the life of Christ and maintain faith in the most extreme circumstances. But you'll always have to wrestle."

Asked if he has read Beirut-veteran journalist Robert Fisk's recent review of his book in *The Irish Times*, Waite laughs. "Is it bad?" He sits with the tips of his fingers touching while an extract is read to him by this reporter. In the extract, Fisk, a close friend of Terry Anderson, openly accuses Waite of being a self-publicist, an adventurer, a name-dropper who suffers from an overwhelming desire to be pitied. Waite looks immediately astounded and upset by these accusations.

"Well, I wonder if he's saying more about himself than he's saying about me. I have acknowledged in the book that I am a human being. And what he's saying is, this man is not a saint, he's a human being. Exactly what *I* would say. Certainly, I went all out for publicity for the cause of the hostages. If he interprets that as self-publicity, then all I can say is that there is an element of ego in all publicity. Of course there is."

Fisk also asserts that Waite, whom he met on several occasions, was self-important, arrogant and "hooked..by the world of high-speed car chases."

Waite shakes his head. "*No*. Nonsense. I really do think that is nonsense. I don't think that's true at all. I don't see, when I struggle to examine my own motives, how he, who has a fairly superficial knowledge of me — you don't actually get to know someone intimately by meeting them two or three times as a journalist, when I was in fact cautious with him — he can't make a snap judgment about my motives. He knows *nothing* about me."

But why does he think these accusations have been made?

"Well, he has said in a very *very* inadequate article in *The* [London] *Independent* that I "fantasised" about the release of the hostages. And because of that rather extraordinary comment about fantasising, I tend to say, I'm uncertain, Robert, about some of your judgements. Yes. You are right when you say I am flawed. You are right, I am. But you are *not* right when you try to tell me what my motives are."

Waite is so flustered and upset that he seems to be utterly unable to concentrate on the next question. His eyes dart nervously around the room and he keeps shaking his head. Apart from his family, and freedom itself, does he recall what he missed most about being in captivity?

"Books," he says, absent-mindedly. "Or extraordinarily simple things. The sky. Or just to feel the wind. Very simple things."

The reply is unusually brief. He seems preoccupied, still smarting from Fisk's attack, incapable of fully engaging with the ongoing conversation. As the next question comes, he interrupts. "Can I ask you?" he says. "What does he say about the *book*?"

When told that Fisk clearly doesn't like it much, he looks even more disconcerted. He glances out the window, pursing his lips hard. Does such criticism hurt very deeply?

After a moment, he sighs and waves his hand in a gesture of dismissal. But there is a genuinely wounded expression in his eyes. "I've had so much of it during the last year. I mean, you get beaten by the Hezbollah, then beaten by your so-called friends. You constantly get taken on trust, by Oliver North or by Robert Fisk, and at the end of the day, all you say is what really matters is those who really know me. I wouldn't pretend it doesn't hurt, because I do look for acceptance. I think *most* people do. Having said that, it doesn't really matter."

But, clearly, it does matter. The subsequent attempted question — about the generally high regard in which he is held by the British public — leads him, yet again, back to his critics, this time with real anger in his voice.

"Yes. I can only go by the recent response which is extraordinarily positive. Which makes me say, what are these so-called long term Beirut hands, Fisk, the others, what are they *really* saying? What are they *really* saying? What is their *real* agenda? I do actually believe that they're saying more about themselves than they're saying about me, to be honest. *Why* does their animus get so stirred up in relationship to me? There's something stirred up and disturbed there. That's my answer."

It's not actually an answer to the question asked, but he cannot seem to focus on any new topic. He bows his head and laughs suddenly. He wants to change the subject. He is coming to Ireland to promote his book, he says, and he is looking forward to it. He and his wife have fond memories of holidays spent in the Ards peninsula and the Mourne mountains. And during his captivity, half-remembered fragments of Joyce's work were a consolation.

"I think people in Ireland will understand this book," he says. "There is a great political sense in Ireland. But there is that other sense also, of intellectual and emotional feeling."

On the subject of Ireland, and as a frequent negotiator with illegal organisations, does he think the British government should engage in talks with the IRA? He nods slowly, appearing to mull over his response.

"All I know is that what ought to be done by those with responsibility — if I can put it like that — is this: I think that when you look at the history of Ireland as an island, as well as looking at the development of the two sections of Ireland, it is a tragedy. It proves what I was saying earlier, that these conflicts arise out of long centuries of injustice. Nobody can look at the history of Ireland with any kind of compassion without being driven to desperation and almost driven to tears by it. The Irish people have always been so oppressed. It's a terrible history. And it's been terrible for both sides."

The young woman responsible for organising publicity for his publishing company suddenly enters the room and remains standing by the door with her coat on. Our time is up, but he continues to speak.

"Somebody has to address the damage (in Ireland) and say it's time for an initiative. And you can only do that by engaging in a long-term process of healing and talking. I don't think you could — or should — ever force a political solution on people. You must create structures for dialogue, political structures for dialogue. If you don't create those structures, you will never bridge the divide..."

The publicist glances at her watch and reminds him that he's due at his next book-signing event in less than fifteen minutes. He peers up at her and attempts a grin. "Our friend Fisk," he says, "he's done a pretty savage review in Ireland."

She smiles, says it doesn't matter, tells him not to worry, that it's time to go now. But Terry Waite does look worried, as he turns around and sighs deeply, and begins to stare out again through the iron bars of his window.

Part IV: The same as it ever was:
In London with David Byrne

David Byrne is peering through the fifteenth story window of his West End hotel. The rooftop panorama of London is magnificent, but his expression is curious rather than joyful. He has a thin face of almost impossible vulnerability, long black hair greying at the roots and tied in a ponytail, large brown eyes which stare at you nervously when you ask him if he likes the view and then dart shyly away while he thinks up an answer. He moves constantly while he thinks; his fingers twine and twist, his head nods up and down, he purses his lips and blinks repeatedly and grits his teeth. You can almost hear the cogs grinding in his brain. "It's a good view," he says, finally. "I guess it's so good I may find it a little hard to concentrate on anything else."

For the generation now in its early thirties, that is to say, the generation whose mother thought it was a little too young to get itself a mohican haircut and stay out all night at punk rock concerts, David Byrne was a hero who inspired almost religious devotion. The band Talking Heads, which he founded in New York in 1975, and with whom he made ten albums before they split in December 1991, completely reinvented American pop music, revitalising an exhausted and self-parodying genre with subtlety, humour and intelligence. Part of his appeal was that Byrne was always an outsider even within the admiring world of punk and New Wave. His songs were crafted and perceptive. While The Sex Pistols gobbed at interviewers and leered into cameras, Byrne dressed like a member of The Beach Boys — short back and sides, neatly ironed slacks and preppy V-neck jumpers rather than bondage trousers, nasal piercings or swastika T-shirts. In interviews he was notoriously reticent. Onstage, in outlandish performances which he claimed were influenced by Kabuki theatre and Southern baptist preaching, he danced, wrote the film critic Pauline Kael, "like a black man's parody of how a clean-cut white man moves." On albums like *Remain in Light, More Songs About Buildings And*

Food, and *The Name of This Band is Talking Heads*, Byrne and his group relentlessly explored the moral and emotional topography of a world turned upside down.

Jonathan Demme's 1983 film of Talking Heads in concert *Stop Making Sense* transformed the underworld cult band into huge international superstars. Their music started to be played everywhere, on juke boxes, on mainstream radio, in pubs. Never again would yuppies be able to sit in wine bars without hearing the arresting lyric "I'm a psycho killer, *qu' est que c' est*, you better run, run, run, run, run, run, run away," barked out in Byrne's high-pitched and menacing whoop. To his critics, he often seemed self-consciously quirky, impenetrably idiosyncratic, several sandwiches short of a picnic, if not sometimes downright certifiable. To the people who bought the records, he was a stand-up comedian, a musical genius and a secular prophet, all rolled into one scrawny and hyperactive body.

The morning I meet up with him in London is the morning after he has begun his 1994 world tour in Wolverhampton. I point out that Wolverhampton, although no doubt a very fine place, is not usually thought of as a wild and crazy rock and roll town. "I guess we wanted to test out the new equipment," he quips, "see if it worked OK. Show off our new songs, our new clothes, you know. Our new haircuts. Everything new we have."

I tell him a story I once heard from a music business insider, offered as a telling signifier of Byrne's waspish uptightness. Byrne, I was discreetly informed, rarely loses his temper. But when he does, he storms around his apartment raving and ranting like a maniac, finds something that is already broken, and breaks that. He throws back his head and laughs. "Oh no, that's too practical. Way too practical for me. It's a good story though. Politically correct anger, huh?"

In the years since the Talking Heads split, Byrne says he has "become a lot more normal." He is happily married to the designer and actress Adelle Lutz, with whom he has a daughter, and he has been working hard on a number of projects so various in scope that when he appeared on the cover of *Time* magazine two years ago he was dubbed "Rock's Renaissance Man." He co-wrote, directed and starred in the critically acclaimed feature film *True Stories* and produced a number of travel documentaries. He has also written film music, (winning an Oscar for his score for Bertolucci's *The Last Emperor*) and set up his own independent label, Luaka Bop, to record and distribute music from Asia, Africa and South America. Such cross cultural enthusiasms have rubbed off on him, and Byrne's first two riotously celebratory solo albums, *Rei Momo* and *Uh-Oh* were recorded with a sixteen piece Latin dance band and a host of international talents, including Celia Cruz, the queen of Cuban salsa.

His latest album is a radical departure. Backed once again by a blindingly talented but skilfully understated four-piece rock band, the songs on *David Byrne* are spare, forceful and much more emotionally direct than anything he has done in the past. The record feels "more like a new beginning," he says, than an inexorably logical step in a career which he once described as "one long improvisation."

"That's why I felt justified naming the record by just putting my name on it. It feels like my first record in some ways. The big Latin band was a lot of fun but this is very flexible now. We can learn a song really quickly, or rework an old song without too many problems."

The tone of the new songs is strikingly intimate and confessional. (In "Angels," for example, he sings, "I can barely touch my own self/How could I touch someone else?/I'm just an advertisement/ For a version of myself.") The "I" character of the narrator seems to be much more identifiably David Byrne than the various wacky personas he has employed to proclaim his ironic worldview in his previous work.

"That's true," he says. "All records are unreal, in that recording is not a totally natural process. But there is an attempt for this record to describe some real emotional experiences almost in the way that a country and western record does. Like Patsy Cline for instance. I love her records. The production sometimes is really spare. There's very little there. There's often a spare quality which I find very moving."

The first song he wrote for the album was "Buck Naked," a delicate and almost prayerful fable of death and vulnerability, inspired by personal tragedy. (Give me your heart/I'll give you mine first/give me your time/I'll give you my trust/And we're buck naked now/We ain't got no clothes/we're bare assed for sure/in the eyes of the Lord.)

"I wrote that song when my wife's sister (the New York model, Tina Chow) was dying of Aids," he explains. "She was on her deathbed, and I wrote the song for my little four-year-old daughter, partly just to see what kind of music she would like, but also I suppose to explain to her and to explain to myself what was happening (to Tina). I started out just playing it to the little one, you know. But then I realised that this song showed me I could do songs like that."

And did his daughter like the song? "Yeah. She liked it because the word 'naked' was in the title," he laughs.

Other songs on the new album, such as "Crash," "Sad Song" and "You and Eye," are similarly poignant. (I met my love at a funeral/ I'm so tired of goodbyes and burials/of friends I have known/some I just met/standing around/it's hard to forget — now isn't it?) This from the man who penned some of the funniest lines in the history of new wave music. ("If you make that decision/they will make that incision," in what must be the only pop song ever written about a father having a sex-change, "Now I'm Your Mom," from *Uh Oh*.) So why the new emphasis on sadness?

"I suppose sadness or melancholy is so rich compared to happiness, which always seems so light and fluffy and shallow to me. It's like a greeting card world full of fluffy animals and smiley faces. Sadness is a lot more dramatic. I'm not talking about depression, that kind of sadness where you have to be hospitalised, you can't function, you can't rouse yourself out of bed in the morning. But a little bit of sadness is pretty nice, I think. It's good to savour it, not to brush it away. Not to wipe that tear from your eye.. (laughs).. but to squeeze another one out."

He says he was always introspective, even as a child. Born on 14th May 1952 in Dumbarton, Scotland, he moved with his parents to the United States at the age of two. His father was an electronic engineer whose job necessitated uprooting the family and relocating to a new city every few years. "I was happy, you know. I was loved and cared for. But I wasn't terribly social. I wasn't alone or lonely. I had friends, but I was also very happy to spend time alone." The teenage discovery of pop music filled him with a breathless excitement, the echoes of which are still endearingly present when he talks about the memory now.

"I guess I was listening to a little transistor radio one day," he recalls, "I think it might have been 'Mister Tambourine Man', The Byrds' version. And it wasn't even the words. It was almost the sound. Amazing. You have to imagine that. I hadn't really heard any pop music at all before that. I think my Dad might have had some Mozart string quartets or something, to which I didn't pay that much attention. But then this sound came along, and I remember thinking hey, *wow*, what's *that*? That's what *I* wanna do."

Did he want to play rock and roll straight away? "Not really. For a while I was torn between the arts and the sciences. I feel there's an equivalent area in the sciences where creativity is allowed free reign. But after a while it seemed that in the sciences it was a more difficult place to get to, to be able to go in whatever direction your muse told you. It seemed hopeless. It would take years and years to get anywhere, before, you know, you could even have your own set of test tubes. So I thought, forget all that, I'm gonna go to art school."

He attended Rhode Island School of Design and Maryland Institute College of Art, and after his graduation in 1974 moved to New York, where a year later, with Jerry Harrison, and two old college friends Chris Franz and Tina Weymouth, he set up Talking Heads. Looking back, is he proud of the work he did with the band?

"A lot of it I'm proud of. Not all of it. I don't listen to the records very often, although sometimes they intrude on me still. There are some really good songs, but others that don't hold up as well. Just disposable pop songs I guess. That one 'Pulled Up', I find the scheme of that and the words of it kind of embarrassing now. But 'Once In A Lifetime', I think, holds up pretty well. And for this tour I want to learn one song from the last Talking Heads record, 'Cool Water'. It fits the depressing genre pretty well." (laughs)

When the Talking Heads split came, it was not exactly surprising. The band had not played live together for seven years, and had not recorded an album for three. Still, the break up was painful and very public. With uncharacteristic openness, Byrne admitted to the press that the group had been awash with "weird tension and bad feeling...it was unhealthy and ugly." Does he see the other band members now?

"Not very often. They don't live in New York any more. I saw Jerry about two months ago when he was in town to produce an album by Black 47 (a young New York-Irish band), which I'm anxious to hear. We have dinner, you know, lunch sometimes." He drifts into silence.

And Weymouth and Franz? Has he made up with them?

He purses his lips, joins the tips of his fingers. "No, no." He sighs and pauses for perhaps twenty seconds. "No. Jerry and I remain in contact. With the other two, if anything, it's gotten worse." Silence again. When I ask if he feels that they resent him for breaking up the band, he nods, looks genuinely aggrieved and says nothing.

So what are Weymouth and Franz doing now, musically? He shrugs and peers through the window. "I don't know, actually. I really don't know."

He seems uncomfortable thinking about it, still uneasy with the fallout generated by his departure from the weird little new wave club band which he led to international superstardom. But turning his back on that level of fame doesn't seem to bother him at all. "There's not as many people interested in my work now," he says, "but there's still enough people." One last question. What does he feel when he reads about himself? Is he anything like as odd as the press make out? A smile illuminates his anxious face.

"I don't know. I just read a piece that said I was. I think I'm a lot more normal than they say I am, certainly than I used to be. But this person I keep reading about is like the weirdest and strangest guy in the world. It's always flattering to be written about, but it really does seem like at some point you're becoming a projection, that they're projecting onto you what they want you to be. And woe unto you if you disappoint." He laughs softly. "It seems that the broad outlines have been pencilled in already, like a cartoon, and you're meant to stay within those lines."

He peers out at the view again, squinting in the sunlight. He grins and shrugs. "I guess I'm not too good at that," he says.

Part V: A nice job for girls:
A performance by Stephen Berkoff

Interviewing actor, writer and director Stephen Berkoff is like attending one of his plays. He gestures wildly, puts on accents, grimaces, leers, bulges his startling blue eyes, and stabs the air with his finger as he scorns "the present crop of inanely narrow-focusing British writers."

"They wear their consciences on their sleeves, belong to the right club, the thinking liberal man, I'm a raw sensitive human being, green party and left wing, all that cobblers, and in their lives they represent a totally right-wing, fascistic, narcissistic thing that's got nothing at all to do with it.

They're writing out of their own arses, writing a reflection of their own ugly faces".

Berkoff, the fifty six year-old son of a London factory manager, likes to portray himself as the subversive *béte noir* of British theatre, the eternally proletarian angry young man. He says he is "a dissident," "an explorer" and "a radical," although actually his work has been performed in the National Theatre and the highly commercial West End, and as *The Guardian* has said of him recently "he is not so much a rottweiler as a showbizz pussycat with an impressive snarl." He came to Dublin in the Summer of 1994 to perform his show *One Man* at the Gate.

"I like Dublin. It's got an exotic environment. It's a more loving sensual city (than London). The Irish have taken to me because they've got their antennae highly tuned to my kind of language and imagery. Which the English don't. Years of class in England have prevented the natural organic surfacing of the poet. If you a have a class system, it tends to act like a kind of contraceptive. The middle classes are like a big durex preventing any kind of dissemination from taking place."

"England is a nation of tiddlers. Tiddling away in the theatres, doing the same stuff, bourgeois, boring, middle-class, superficial. That's why I always find it refreshing to go to Ireland."

The latest show contains three sections, "Dog," "The Actor," and an adaptation of Edgar Allen Poe's classic story "The Tell-tale Heart." Berkoff describes the overall piece as "a homage to the performing arts," wherein he uses "everything from mime, panto-mime, comedy, satire, expressionistic movement, everything."

"The Tell-Tale Heart is about people who are stripped down, their sensitivities exposed so that they are almost all nerve-endings. I used to feel like this myself. I used to feel that my skin was stripped bare, and I was all nerve-endings. I think maybe it's because I drank too much tea."

Might there have been any other reason, apart from the tea?

"It comes from years of inbreeding. We were Russian immigrants and I can make no secret of the fact that my background had a certain semitic flavour. With small groups you inter-marry. So the group became more and more kvetchy. ("Kvetch" is a Yiddish word meaning a paranoia or irrational worry. It is also the title of a Berkoff play).

"The Actor" is an autobiographical piece, based on the *Marche Sur Place*, a sketch by the great mime artist Marcel Marceau.

"I owe a debt to mime," Berkoff says. "It's one of the purest arts. It is a working-class art, it came from the Comedia del Arte, from the ordinary man who had no props, no sets, no beautiful costumes, just himself."

The third piece, "Dog," is "a cartoon about the thing we most fear in England, the awful manifestation of all our horrors, the British yob. Only here has the yob achieved such a murderous reputation. It's the sickest and kinkiest thing, the yob, it even has its own fashion, its shaved heads, tattoos, Doc Martens, this unified neo-Nazi look."

Acting and directing are hard work, he feels, whereas writing is merely "a hobby," which view might account for the generally sloppy and undisciplined style of his new short story collection "Gross Intrusion." The book features a black man buggering a white man to death, and a man performing fellatio on his father in a sauna. (Berkoff has never seen a psychiatrist, incidentally, "because it's too hard to set up the appointments.")

"Writing is a most exotic hobby. You've got to do a proper job as well. Years ago all the writers had jobs. Shakespeare was a company manager, Kafka an insurance clerk. You've got to get up every day, hard work, sometimes very boring. Writing is not a real man's job. It's like needlework or sewing, a nice job for girls."

Asked about the recent local election victories of the neo-fascist British National Party in the East End of London where he lives, he replies that it "is to be applauded."

"There's always a fear of the stranger amongst the British working class. They are the underdog. The vote itself was a kind of instinctive reaction. They felt they were losing not only their homes, their well-being and their jobs, but losing what they *are*. So therefore their reaction was true. And as a true reaction, it is to be applauded."

"If they corrupt their instincts and say well, you know, it's very nice to have everybody here — if they were to say (affects Cockney accent) *yeah, that's awight love, yeah, you 'ave that flat, love*, and (affects Peter Sellers-style "Pakistani" accent) *Oh, tank-you-velly-much* — if they were to do this, I think they would be vitiating their natural spontaneous reflex action. Therefore, the vote for the BNP was a very healthy response, and a very good response. Because what it does, it wakes up the country."

And what about the widespread public concern about the victory?

"I think people who are alarmed by this don't live in areas where they have to share with fifty per cent blacks or Pakistanis or whatever. People in Kensington aren't going to be outraged, where you don't see a black face. Here it's dominating the whole area."

"For me, all cultural mix is very good. My favourite restaurant is Indian. But you have to think of *them* (white working class people). Maybe I'm a bit more enlightened..I can distance myself...They react with a pure instinct, the same instinct that an animal would react to. You could say that the BNP is the most pure reaction. So in a way it's to be admired."

Does he always want to be the rebel he still claims to be, or is he in fact harbouring a repressed desire to belong to the British theatre establishment?

"If you were on the inside, the kind of people you would have to deal with would so sicken you that you would soon come back out. The dissident is always the explorer. The person who has radical views will always upset the status quo. To be inside would mean that you had become a follower rather than a leader, swamped by the melange of sogginess. So I'm very happy to still strike an attitude."

Chapter Ten
The Road to God knows where

An Irish World Cup Diary.

Wednesday 15 June. 7.20 a.m., Dublin Airport. I am shattered. I only finished my packing at three this morning. Now I am here in the check-in queue, so tired that I would quite cheerfully swop my plane ticket, my hotel voucher and my category A tickets for all three World Cup round one matches for a dark room, clean sheets and half an hour's shut-eye. The queue is enormous. I am surrounded by a group of six or seven middle-aged men wearing Republic of Ireland jerseys, green slacks, green denim jackets, green runners, enormous green sombreros speckled with shamrocks and harps, stars-and-stripes patterened dicky bows. They are carrying tricolour flags and rolled-up banners. One of them is applying green, white and orange makeup to his cheeks, squinting and pulling faces in a small mirror, smouldering fag stuck to his lower lip. "You don't think that's a bit much, do you?" one guys asks, "they're after sayin' on the news the customs fellas wouldn't let you in if you had that stuff on your face." The make-up man turns to him. "Don't be such a bleedin' daisy," he says.

7.40 am: A middle-aged man in an Ireland T-shirt is sitting in the airport bar eating a large greasy breakfast of black pudding, white pudding, beans, sausages, rashers and fried eggs. He is also swigging from a pint of Guinness. I gaze at him for some time, astonished that he could actually consume something like that at this hour of the morning. He catches my eye, raises a forkful of beans to his mouth, winks and swallows. "Keep it country," he says. I take this as an invitation to sit down and talk to him. He is from Mallow, County Cork, and he is going over to the World Cup, and to stay with his brother who lives in Queens. He hasn't seen his brother for seven years. He has a nephew over there who he's never met. "It'll be brilliant," he says. "I'm not that bothered about the football actually, but I just can't wait to see him again."

8.10 am: We get on the plane and take our seats. I watch the fans filing on. There are a lot of men, of course, of all ages, all wearing green shirts, but there are a good few women too, and loads of teenagers and children, some of them quite young. One man swaggers down the aisle with a sleeping toddler in his arms. Father and son are dressed in identical green soccer shirts. A boy of sixteen or so clambers on, wrapped in a tricolour. His mother and father follow him, also wrapped in tricolours. Everyone looks wide-eyed with excitement.

8.30 am: The captain comes on the radio and announces that there's going to be a delay of an hour. "I know you need this news like a moose needs a hatstand," he quips, "but once we get up there, we'll do our best to pedal a bit harder than usual." His name is Terry, he tells us, and we're to feel free to ask him anything we like. For some reason, I am not sure I feel confident being flown across the Atlantic by a man called Terry. Irrational, I know. But there it is.

9.20 am: The plane takes off for the short flight to Shannon. I get chatting to the chap beside me. He, his five year-old son, his father and father-in-law are all going to the World Cup. "It's expensive, but it's the chance of a lifetime," he says, "It's a special memory we'll always have together." We land at Shannon, get off and shuffle into the transit lounge. More delay. The fans converge on the bar. It is very early in the morning but the chanting and singing — "Oooh Ahh Paul McGrath" and "You'll Never Beat the Irish," — has already started. "You"ll certainly never beat the Irish to the feckin' bar," one man says.

11.30 am: All safely back on board, Captain Terry revs up, puts his foot down and soon gets us airborne. There is an almighty cheer as the plane soars into the clear sky. Terry, who is English, comes onto the intercom and expresses the hope that Ireland do well in the World Cup. A new chant begins. "England Aren't In It. England Aren't In It."

12.00 am: I go down the back for a smoke and find myself sitting beside a nine-year old child, my worst nightmare on a long flight. He is very self-confident too, which makes it worse. "I'm going to America," he says. I contemplate telling him that he's on the wrong plane, and that he's actually going to Siberia, but his parents are sitting just across the aisle. "Ireland are cool," he says, "aren't they?" I agree that Ireland are cool. "I have a girlfriend," he says, "and I'm going to marry her when I grow up." I offer heartiest congratulations. "I kiss her," he says, "I kiss her and everything." I say I think he's a bit young to be kissing girls. "I am not," he says, "you put your tongue in their mouths but you don't swop spits." I suddenly realise what I've been doing wrong all these years. Down the back the fans are chanting "Irela-hand, Ire-lahand, Ire-lahand." "Do you kiss girls?" the kid says. I ignore him. "DO YOU KISS GIRLS?" he shrieks. "Not as often as you do," I say. "I bet you do," he sniggers, his little voice gurgling with malevolent pleasure, "can I try on your glasses, fatso?" It is going to be a very long flight.

1.30 pm: Somewhere over Newfoundland. The inflight video is showing highlights from the Republic's qualifying match against Northern Ireland. The Alan McLoughlin goal sends an electric shiver of pleasure up everyone's spine, particularly, no doubt, the spine of the manager of the travel agency which organized today's flight, who owes Alan McLoughlin a very great deal indeed. Every time the score is shown again in slow motion, there is another cheer from the passengers. After the fifth time, the hostesses are cheering too.

2.30pm: We land at Newark Airport and clear customs. The fans are looking more than a little bedraggled after their long day. But they are still singing. "Olé, Olé, Olé, USA, USA, USA." On the hotel bus I get talking to a Dublin solicitor who is here with three other solicitors. I tell him I am a journalist. "You're not to write anything horrible about solicitors," he says. As if I would. (Q: What do you call seven hundred solicitors at the bottom of the sea. A: A bloody good start. Q: How many solicitors does it take to change a lightbulb? A: Are you paying with Visa or American Express? Q: What do solicitors use for contraception? A: Their personalities.)

7pm, The hotel bar. I am having a drink with a group of fans. "Showered, shaved, and sheepshagged," as one of them puts it, they are ready for a good time. The problem of the lack of tickets for the Italy game is being keenly discussed. A huge number of supporters do not have tickets for any of the games. A chap from Galway gives me a phone number he has for a tout. Out of interest, I go to the lobby, ring the number and ask about prices for Ireland versus Italy. "That's the hottest ticket in town, mac," the tout says, "I got four real nice seats together, two thousand bucks." "That would be for the four?" I say. He whimpers with derisive laughter. "What are you, buddy, crazy? That would be each." I put the phone down, canter into the jacks and take my tickets out of my underwear, where they are being kept for safe keeping. Even if I am mugged, I figure, nobody is going to examine the contents of my boxer shorts. I look at my tickets. I touch them. For one moment, I am tempted to sell my tickets for two thousand dollars each, watch the match on the television in my room and write up the piece pretending that I was there. Journalistic ethics get the better of me. And anyway, the television in my room is not working. I fold up my tickets, stuff them down my trousers and go back to the bar. A man from Meath is standing on a chair singing "Boolavogue." When he gets to the line "one more fight for the green again," the roof nearly lifts off with applause.

10.30 pm: The Stephen's Green Pub, Queens. The walls of this friendly bar are plastered with black and white stills of great Irish football games from the last few years. The crowd are young, Irish, working class, sharply dressed. They are out for a good time, spending money like it is going out of fashion. Ireland being in the World Cup here in America is "the best thing that ever happened to me," one guy says, "it's absolute magic." He has been over here working in New York as a furniture remover for eight years, he says, the money is great but the work is hard. "You'd need two hearts sometimes to do it," he says, because the loads he has to lift are so heavy. The crack is mighty in New York, but you'd miss home, Letterkenny, County Donegal. Two lads from Finglas tell me that the trip has cost them so much they won't have another holiday for years. But they don't care. "It'd be great if we do well," one says, "but it's great to be here anyway, Christ, what a place." The jukebox is on loud, playing The Cranberries, U2, Thin Lizzy and The Horslips. Pints of Guinness are passed from the bar, over people's heads, through the crowd. People are dancing around in rings, stamping their feet, holding hands, singing along to the music. One of the Finglas lads fancies a girl who is sitting with her friends on the far side of the room. He keeps smiling at her. She is wearing an Ireland Jersey with the word "KEANE" printed on the back. He says he wonder is she. Keen. She keeps bending forward to talk to her friends, then laughing uproariously before glancing back at him. "Give it a lash," his friend says. He finishes his pint, strolls over, sits down with her and her friends. Half an hour later they are slowdancing to "I Useta Love Her" by The Saw Doctors. A difficult thing to do. His friend turns to me. "Funny old game right enough," he says, and we order Tequila slammers.

2.30 am: As the cab moves across the Queensboro Bridge, the millions of lights in the windows of the Manhattan skyscrapers glimmer and sparkle through the darkness. The sight looks like the most magical thing on earth. "Noo Yawk," the driver says, "everyone thinks it's, hey, like this really romantic place, but actually, there's more weirdos per square inch of New York than anywhere else in the world, buddy, except maybe Russia." The Empire State appears in the distance, shimmering with pale red and blue light. Rain starts to fall on the empty avenue. "Still," the driver sighs, "I suppose ya gotta dream a liddle, and I guess it's a great place for dreamin'. Now that's the funny thing see, about Noo York, cuz sometimes it's so beauootiful, you lose your concentration, see, where ya just drift away in a second, ya know what I'm sayin'?"

"Huh?" I say.

3 am: Slim's All Night Diner, Second Avenue. I am reading tomorrow morning's newspaper. Most Americans know nothing at all about soccer, and there is an article explaining the rules in endearingly simple terms. A tackle is "when one player tries to get the ball from another." A throw-in is "when a player throws the ball into the field of play." The goalkeeper is "the only player who is allowed to use his hands." What exactly the goalkeeper is allowed to use his hands for is not explained. It is now the early hours of the 16th of June, Bloomsday. I remember a story about James Joyce. A young fan once asked if he could shake the hand that wrote "Ulysses." "You can," Joyce said, "but remember, it's done a lot of other things too." If anyone ever asks Packie Bonner to shake the hand that saved the Romanian penalty in Italia 90, I hope he says the same thing.

Thursday 16 June. 10 am: A crowd of badly hungover fans are having breakfast in a diner on Second Avenue. They are clearly finding it difficult to deal with the complexities of American food. One of them asks for a bacon sandwich. The waitress says, "what kinda bread? We got rye, brown, sodabread, white, bagels, black bread, rolls, Italian heros." He says he'll have an Italian hero. This gets quite a response from his pals. By the time they've finished slagging him off, his breakfast has been brought to the table. The plate contains a mound of food, french fries, pickles, various kinds of lettuce. It looks like something out of the Amazon rainforest. He gapes at it, open-mouthed. "Does your one want me to eat this?" he says, "or put shagging Moss Peat on it?"

1pm: The temperature is now almost a hundred degrees, and New York is bathed in a sticky and oppressive humidity. It is hotter here today than it is down in Orlando. It's too hot to walk around much, so the fans are sitting in the air-conditioned hotel lobby, smoking and drinking and talking about Saturday's game. Everyone hopes the weather will cool off, but someone says the forecast doesn't look great. There's no news at all in the papers about the Ireland team, hardly anything about the whole tournament. People are ringing up their friends and relations back in Ireland to get news about the team. Another busload of supporters arrives from the airport. "Jayzsus, I'm dyin'" one of them says, as he drops his cases and takes off his soaking jacket. "If it gets any hotter we'll be carried home in bottles."

8pm: Go out for drinks with a crowd of boisterous Australian Ireland fans who have just arrived at the hotel. Jill from Sydney tells me that the trip cost her and her boyfriend $10,000, but they don't care. (Her boyfriend is already almost comatose with alcohol.) They've been saving for months to come and see Ireland play. The Australians are delighted that England have not qualified. They consume a lot of beer and tell Pom jokes to the Irish supporters they meet. "Where do you hide a pommie's bar of soap?" "Under his facecloth." "What's the difference between a pom and a jumbo jet?" "A jumbo jet stops whining when it lands at Sydney Airport."

2am Friday morning: Go to bed slightly the worse for drink and dream of James Joyce heading in a corner against the Italians.

Friday 17 June. 8 am: Wake up feeling like my brain has turned into spaghetti. Something bit me in the middle of the night. A bloody cockroach no doubt. I have a spot on the end of my nose the size of The Bronx and twice as unpleasant. The bags under my eyes could be packed. I plaster myself with mosquito cream and suntan lotion and go down to breakfast, looking like a turkey that's about to be put into an oven. The Australians are already on the beer. One of them is singing "Pommie dingbats stuck at home, doo-dah, doo-dah." A gang of Ireland fans wander in, wearing giant inflatable green plastic hands and green skiing goggles. The Australians cheer and order beers for everyone. "Hey spotnose," Jill's boyfriend calls, "you wanna lager?" Everyone laughs at the carbuncle on my schnozz. One of the Ozzies says I should dye it green for Jack and the lads, only then, as he points out, "it would look like a flamin' great snot, wouldn't it?" This seems to go down very well indeed. I sit down and order a coffee. The waitress asks if I want milk. "Just a spot," another Antipodean titters. For an instant, I find myself hoping that Ireland get hammered, because I'm not sure I can take more than two weeks of this.

Saturday 18 June. We play Italy. The rest is a bit of a blank.

Sunday 19 June: On the morning after the Italy game I wake up at about seven. I am still wearing my clothes — at least, I think they are my clothes, although they don't seem to fit me too well. My head is pounding like the Kilfenora Ceilidh band on ecstasy. My throat is sore. My mouth feels like Oliver Reed died in it. The sheets, when I roll over, are full of loose change, crumpled beermats and segments of soggy lukewarm pepperoni pizza. I lurch out of the bed, crawl across the shag pile like some sort of semi-comatose and inebriated slug and gaze at myself in the mirror. The sight which greets me is pretty scary.

My eyes are pink as a teddyboy's socks. My lips and teeth are stained black from Guinness. My skin is light green in hue. I look like an alien out of one of the more convincing episodes of Star Trek. I try my best to hose and heave my ruined mug into some kind of order, but I have the distinct and uneasy feeling that today is going to be a bad hair day. Someone spilled a pint over my head last night, I can't remember why or where. All I can remember is this big thick

English plankbrain in a 5th Avenue bar, getting on my nerves. I think I remember saying he was so bleeding stupid he thought a quarterback was some kind of refund deal. And all I can remember then is being in an all night diner with people from Kerry and trying to dry my hair on the Books section of the early city edition of the *Sunday New York Times*. This strategy obviously did not work. My hair is now so dishevelled that I look like Carlos Valderamma in National Health Service spectacles.

I stagger out of my room and into the lift, still wearing the clothes I sat through the match in, went out afterwards in, got plastered in and slept in. I smell like a putrefying yak. Every time the lift stops, more people get into it. It is an odd sight, an elevator full of people all politely coughing and examining their fingernails and softly whistling "Olé, Olé, Olé" and trying desperately not to inhale through their nostrils. On the fourth floor, two of the Australian Irish fans get in, grinning pleasantly. Jim is wearing no shirt, no socks, no shoes, and a pair of shorts so tight that you can almost read the dates on the coins in his pockets. Debs is wearing not so much a bikini as several pieces of deftly arranged green dental floss. Don't you just love Australia? After only a moment, Jim turns around, holding his nose between his index finger and his thumb. "Aw, blow me backwards," he groans, "what crawled up someone's bum and died, mates?" This does a little to break the tension.

Down in the lobby, the scene is like something from the last days of the Weimar Republic. There are empty bottles, pyramids of cans, overflowing ashtrays, upturned potplants, and there are Irish fans sprawled everywhere, looking so banjaxed and bedraggled that I cannot figure out whether they have only just scuttled out of the scratcher this minute, or whether they have been up all night. A man with a pair of underpants on his face is lying under the grand piano. He is rolled up in a tricolour flag, so that he looks for all the world like some class of Hibernian mummy. It is a sight to gladden the heart of Patrick Pearse. A young couple are wrapped around each other on the bar sofa, open-mouthed, both snoring like motorbikes. A trio of middle aged men are sitting on the floor, playing cards for dollar bills. One of them suddenly staggers to his feet, punches the air and bellows, "Come on Lads, Let's Go, You'll Never Beat the

Irish. You'll Nev..." There is silence, punctuated only by a solitary piercing fart and a few weary mutters of "ah, shut your feckin gob, you great eejit."

I cannot find the woman from the travel agency. I sleepwalk back up to my room and sit on the bed, wondering how it is possible to feel this woeful and still be alive. I light a cigarette and count the coins in my sheets. There's almost enough for a tequila sunrise. I cheer up. I extract a piece of the pizza from under my pillow and eat it. I ring down to the lobby. They manage to find the tour guide. I remind her that I will be staying in New York for an extra day, and joining up with the tour tomorrow in Orlando. I sleep. I wake up ten hours later, finish the pizza, sleep again. We beat them one nil, I ponder as I munch. How sweet are the spoils of victory.

Monday 20 June. New York: I wake up feeling a lot better. The minibus arrives at the hotel to take me to the airport. "Are you JFK?" I ask the driver. "What, I look like the back of my brainbox is blown away?" he quips. I am the only passenger on the trip. The driver, Duane, tells jokes all the way. "These two bags of sick walk into a bar, see, and they order a beer, and then one of them says to the other one, gee, I'm feelin real sentimental, cos I was brought up around here. Ya geddit, buddy? Brought up, see? They're, like, bags of sick, OK? HAHAHAHAHA." He has a laugh like a machine gun.

We arrive at JFK and I get on the plane. I get talking to a very nice Mexican woman who is coming to Orlando to meet her boyfriend for the Ireland match. She is a translator of foreign films and tv programmes for the Mexican market. Her favourite show is the BBC's *Only Fools and Horses*, she tells me, although it is very difficult to translate. "For eentstance, in Spanish," she says, "we have no synonym for plonker."

We land at Orlando airport and I ask the taxi driver to take me to the hotel into which I have been booked by my travel agent. This is the Howard Johnson Plaza Hotel on International Drive. The taxi driver explains that he cannot do this, as the Howard Johnson Plaza Hotel on International Drive has actually been demolished a month ago and is now a very nice parking lot.

I consider my position. Here I am in Orlando, a town where I know nobody at all, without a hotel to stay in, having lost the four hundred odd (very odd) fans I am here to write about, and thus, in point of fact, having lost all reason for being here in a professional capacity. I can feel my duty to *Sunday Tribune* readers being severely compromised. I can also feel a very promising expense account about to go up in smoke. Hmmm.

In a dazzling flash of Pilgeresque bravery under fire, I get a taxi to another hotel, check if they have air-conditioning and minibars and then, with no thought at all for my own personal safety, book in. By a stroke of the most pure unexpurgated luck, this turns out to be the hotel where most of my group of fans are staying. There are tearful reunions. I never thought I would end up having tearful reunions with men called Hatcho, Bullso, Whacko, Bowso, Scazzo and Mazzo, but, hey, it's a guys thing. It occurs to me, as I say hello again to Liffo, Meerto, Leppo and Bongo that the Irish team have more fans whose names end in "o" than the Italians and Mexicans put together. I consider trying to come up with a name ending in "o" for myself. Under pressure, "Potato" is the best I can do. If I were Dan Quayle, I console myself, I could not even do that much.

I retire early, leaving the lads merrily emptying the bar. I am overjoyed to discover that there is a karaoke lounge directly beneath my bedroom. The fans are loudly singing hit songs and inserting the word "Ireland" into them at every opportunity. The recent Whitney Huston smash thus becomes:

And Eye-ee-eye-eer-land wheel always love yew

Ireland, Ireland

Wheel always love yew

Ireland, Irela-ha-hand.

As the night wears on, the songs become even more thought-provoking. "Why, Why, Why, Delilah" becomes "Why, Why, Why, Schillachi." "Sexual Healin'" mutates into "Sexual Ronnie Whelan," and then, rather effectively, into "Sexual Terry Phelan." The high point of the evening, for me, is when my dear sister Sinead's poignant lament "Nothing Compares 2 U" is sublimely reinterpreted as "Nothing Compares 2 Phil Babb."

After several hours of this, I fall into a fitful and flickering slumber. I wake up gibbering at some unearthly hour, with a roaring noise in my ear and no idea where in the name of God I am. After a moment or two I become aware that the roaring noise is actually the undeniable — if at this stage tediously unoriginal — sentiment, "One Packie Bonner, There's Only One Packie Bonner, One Packie Bonner, There's Only One Packie Bonner, One..." being sung in the corridor outside.

This full-blooded testimony to the quite phenomenal singularity of Mrs Bonner's baby boy continues unabated for some time. Then, suddenly, from somewhere down the corridor, an unmerciful screech splits the air."IF YOUZE DON"T SHUT YIZZER FOOKIN BEAKS I'LL COME OUT THERE AND I'LL DANCE THE WHOLE FOOKIN LORRA YEZ INTO THE BLEEDIN' CARPET, YIZ SHOWER OF FOOKIN BOLLIXES".

Astonishingly, this seems to work. There is silence, then muffled goodnights, whispered adieux and one softly hissed "I suppose a ride'd be owa the question, Lippo, wha?"

Tuesday 21 June, afternoon: A colleague, David Modell from the *London Independent* magazine, who has been travelling with the same group of fans as myself manages to find me. I am glad to see him. It is rather nice to talk to someone whose name does not end in "o," although I do find myself beginning to refer to him from now on as either Davo or Moddo.

He tells me what happened to the fans on Sunday. Having been delayed for five hours at the hotel, they were bussed out to JFK, then delayed for six more hours with no food and precious little drink before getting on a flight that landed at the wrong airport. "It got a bit ugly," Davo says. "Security had to be called in."

Tuesday night: Davo and myself go for what is called in vulgar circles a good nosebag in a posh French restaurant in downtown Orlando — posh, in America, meaning the waiters don't tell you their names — and then on to an Irish Bar on Church Street, where we skull pints, talk to the fans and listen to hopeless Irish American singers doing toe-curling impressions of Christy Moore. One of the singers says he'd like to dedicate this next song to The Cranberries, "who had to go away to be recognized." I reflect on the fact that my only problem with The Cranberries is that they haven't actually gone far enough away, in my book.

Wednesday 22 June: I am getting World Cup Fever. I do not mean excitement, I mean getting sick. I am coughing and sneezing, my eyes are watering. This is being caused by my wandering about downtown Orlando in ninety degree heat for hours, sweating like a sow in a sauna, and then going into a shop or bar where the air-conditioning would freeze the bejapers off a brass monkey. I go to the chemist and buy as many medicaments as I legally can. The chemist tells me the Irish fans have been stocking up on suntan lotion, a little too late. She has seen several cases of sunstroke already. One balding man had "the top of his poor head plumb near burned offa him." She feels the Irish don't understand just how dangerous the sun can be. "If you're gonna do somethin' useful," she says, "you tell those fellers to get a hat if don't wanna make scrambled eggs outa their brains."

Wednesday afternoon: in a daring Kate Adie-like raid on the outdoor heated swimming pool, I run into an Irish supporter called Brian O'Byrne, who has been running into a lot of people lately. Mr O'Byrne is one of the two Irish fans who cantered gleefully onto the pitch following the Italy-Ireland game, only to be so enthusiastically welcomed by the fun-loving and generous-spirited goose-steppers of the New Jersey Combined Police and Rugby Tackle Department. It turns out that Mr O'Byrne is a successful young actor who is currently appearing on Broadway, and although I must confess that I can often see a compelling argument for successful young actors being placed in handcuffs and then vigorously beaten, (preferably in front of a large crowd) in his case I must say, I would have made an exception. He is a very nice mannerly fellow, who, as he puts it, "just got a bit carried away by the fun." Sadly, as we all saw, he also got carried away by the revolting rozzers and was later charged with the wonderful offence, "tumultuous behaviour for no apparent reason." That's the bit that annoys him. "It was one-nil," he gasps, "what do they mean, no apparent reason?"

Anyway, Mr O'Byrne describes to me being concussed and regaining consciousness a few moments later, only to find Jack Charlton standing there in all his glory, interceding with the coppers on his behalf. "I wasn't sure it was Jack at first," he says, "but then

I saw his hair flapping in the breeze, and I mean, nobody has hair that flaps in the breeze the way Jack's does." Poor Mr O'Byrne will certainly remember the Ireland-Italy game.

Some of the other fans have mixed feelings about Mr O'Byrne and his pitch invasion. They tend to shake their heads, sigh dolefully and say that Mr O'Byrne "let Jackie's army down," or that he "gave the wrong impression of Ireland." They usually say this immediately before donning overlarge green goggles, inflating enormous plastic shamrocks, daubing each other with tricolour makeup and marching in formation down to the pub to get absolutely ossified again, all the time talking about how "disciplined" and "ordered" they are. Most of the Irish fans over here are very nice people, a joy to be with. A small minority of them are adult boyscouts, the most almighty effing pains you ever met in your natural life.

Thursday 23 June. Orlando — the name of a city and not the name of an Irish soccer fan — is practically owned by the Disney corporation. Hence today, against my better judgement, I trot along to Disney World's Magic Kingdom with a group of Irish supporters. Now, dear diary, I do not know if you have ever spent much time in the company of a large group of Irish men who are far away from home, in a hot climate, with only a large group of stuffed animals for company, but if you haven't, then take my advice. Don't. Ever. And if you have, why, then you will what a surreal experience it is.

The first bizarre thing about Disneyworld is that each of the car parks is named after one of the seven dwarfs. There is Bashful, Sleepy, Grumpy, Dopey and so on. Thus, when you get on the little commuter train that whisks you into the park, a grown adult has to call out, over the intercom, "now arriving at Happy, all passengers for Happy and Dopey, next stop Grumpy, hold tight now." For some reason, I find this amazingly funny. We amuse ourselves by thinking up new dwarf names, Sleazy, Sarcky, Horny and Crappy being my favourites.

Once in to the park, we decide to go on the boat cruise through "Small World." There is a sign over the entrance to the tunnel. "Welcome to the happiest little cruise in the world," it says. Reading this, I feel like indulging in the almightiest little puke in the world, which phrase, conveniently enough, also describes the six-year old child sitting beside me. He is humming to himself as he trails his little hand in the water. I utter a silent fervent prayer that alligators are native to this part of Florida.

Half way through the tunnel, a party of Mexican fans are sighted in a neighbouring boat. The chant begins straight away. "You'll Never Beat the Irish, You'll Never Beat the Irish." The Mexicans chant back at us, waving their fists and cursing in Spanish. One of them holds out his right hand, pistol fashion, and begins roaring "bangbang, bangbang." While all this is going on, Mickey Mouse, Goofy, Pluto and Snow White are standing on the far bank of the pond, dancing up and down, blowing us kisses, waving their hands in the air, and singing "Hi Ho, Hi Ho, It's off to work we go." The fans join in. "With buckets and spades and hand grenades, hi ho, hi ho, hi ho."

Outside again, our tour guide, Wanda is waiting for us. Wanda is a very nice young woman from Kissimee. "There's some rully good rides here at The Magic Kingdom," she says, to a chorus of snuffles and titters. "We have big rides, small rides, scary rides, happy rides, whatever kind of ride you like you can find here at The Magic Kingdom." One fan is falling about the place now and another — Crocko by name — is laughing his bloody dentures out. Wanda must be wandering what it is she is saying that has all these grown men nearly widdling with laughter. But, true professional that she is, she continues.

"Er...some of the rides have been here for a long time, but other rides are new, and here at Disney we're constantly looking at ways to make rides more exciting." The fans are slapping their thighs and guffawing at this stage. One usually quiet man from Laois is actually honking with laughter, throwing his ponderous head back and honking like a great big white-legged hysterical mallard duck. Honko, I'm going to call him from now on.

"What's so funny?" Wanda says.

"Nothing, Wanda," Honko replies.

"No, c'mon," she says. "Am I like, saying something funny?"

"Not at all Wanda, you're grand, sweetheart. And c'mre, tellus, do you like the odd ride yourself, Wanda?"

"Oh yes, of course."

"And how many rides would you have a day?"

"Oh, I dunno, three or four I guess. Depends how much spare time I get."

Well, at this stage several of the fans have to go and sit down in the shade, or pour water over themselves, so frantic are their cackles. Some are actually sobbing with laughter. Donald Duck wanders over to one of them and begins gently to peck him on the head with his enormous yellow beak. "Go away ye big feathery fairy," the fan says. A hearty chant soon begins, the scheme of which is based on the considerable rhyming potential of the words Donald Duck. What a talent for poetry the Irish have! Seamus Heaney would have been proud.

Things are about to get even worse, however. An enormous structure depicting Mickey Mouse is pointed out on the horizon. Wanda tells us, her voice fairly brimming over with pride, "and guys, you know what, that's the largest self-supporting Mickey in the whole of the United States."

Well, I don't think I have to describe the communal reaction, really. It is as though the entire party has been blasted with laughing gas. Several of the supporters will need medical attention soon.

"Oh, there are other Mickeys," Wanda sniffs, dismissively, "there's a rully big Mickey in California, of course, and there are some rully large Mickeys in some of the other states, and a big old Mickey over there in Eurodisney. But I gotta tell you, we're real proud of our superb superbig Mickey that we got down here in Florida."

The sun is blazing hot now, and the white stone floor seems to be sucking the heat into itself. Tears of laughter are spilling down the faces of my companions. The seven dwarfs saunter past us, pursued by the mad hatter, the wicked witch of the west, the queen of hearts and various assorted fluffy tigers holding hands. The fans are chanting again now. "You'll never beat the Irish. You'll never beat the Irish." If Wanda smiles any harder, her eyebrows will disappear into her hairline. I close my eyes. I try to imagine just how much money you would have to spend on drugs to achieve this weird a feeling.

Friday 24 June. Match day is here at last! This is very good, because Orlando is the most boring place in the world, and if you did not have the football to go to, you'd end up trying to drown yourself in the swimming pool just to kill a bit of time.

The Orlando city authorities have made a bit of a hames of the traffic arrangements. We leave the hotel in a rattling little coach at 9.30 and arrive almost two hours later, sweaty, dejected and part-broiled, at the Citrus Bowl. There, we are invited to shell out thirty bucks for lurid baseball hats, forty or fifty for ghastly souvenir T-shirts that somehow you know you will wash just once before they shrink in your machine to the size of a J cloth.

The roofless stadium is completely exposed to the midday sun, and is incredibly hot. The Mexican fans are a lot more in evidence today than the Italians were at the weekend. The teams troop out into the baking heat, the Mexicans in green, our boys in white. Jorge Campos, the Mexican goalie, is wearing a rather fetching cape-like number in orange, green, yellow and red. He looks like a part time superhero, and, indeed, would not be out of place on one of the rides at Disneyland. "Ye bleedin' Christmas tree, yeh," shouts one of the fans behind me. "You're only a feckin prettyboy." Another one roars "Jorge Campos, the day-glo Dago."

The match starts well for Ireland. Staunton attacks down the left hand side. The Irish fans start humming the theme tune of the Laurel and Hardy films. This, I am told, is because Steve Staunton looks like Stan Laurel, which I really don't think he does. But anyway. In the 25th minute, Irwin is booked for wasting time. "Referee, you're a tosser" screams the Liverpool man behind me to Swiss Mr Roethlisburger, "you're a bleedin' Barclays Banker, you are, you're a shaggin hand shandy merchant, ref." Further imaginative opinions are widely expressed regarding auto-erotic activities chez Roethlisburger. Two minutes later Roy Keane narrowly avoids featuring in the little black book when he gamely puts the studs into one of the Mexicanos. I see a banner on the far side of the pitch. TOMMY COYNE, SHARPER THAN JIMMY HILL'S CHIN.

Just my luck, the man seated to my left turns out to be a statistic fiend. He tells me that Mexico scored 39 goals in their 12 qualifying games, and then he looks at me with a profound stare. "You'll Never Beat the Irish," we sing, "You'll Never Beat the Irish." Four minutes later, Luis Garcia rockets the ball from outside the area past Bonner's outstretched right hand. That shuts us all up, I can tell you.

The half time break is depressing. Everyone around me is quiet. The statistics man takes a mint from his pocket, puts it in his mouth and sucks it. The thermometer on the stadium wall says that the pitch temperature is 110 degrees. Everyone else is losing gallons of body fluid every minute, but Mr. Statistics looks like he has never sweated in his life.

We start the second half positively. Campos comes under severe pressure from Tommy Coyne. Mr. Statistics is at it again. He leans over and breathes a mouthful of mint at me. Ireland have only ever scored 3 World Cup goals in 6 matches, he goes, with the air of a medieval mystic announcing the meaning of life. I wish he would stop talking. Every time he opens his beak Mexico get the ball and nearly score. "Ah, we're finished," he says, leaning back and folding his arms, "I'm telling you, the goose is cooked now, my son. We'd be as well to go on home."

Garcia slithers into a brilliant position and narrowly misses, his shot just curling away from the post. Mr. Statistics seems almost pleased. "What did I say?" he barks at me, "I told you, didn't I? We're washed up." He does have a point, I must say. We are 51 minutes into the game and bloody fortunate not to be 2 goals down.

Shortly after this, Campos is booked for time wasting, which cheers us all up no end. Terrible slurs of a politically incorrect nature are cast on Campos, on Senor Campos senior, on his good lady wife, on all of Campos's female siblings, on the family pet mongrel, and, indeed, on the entire Mexican nation. Suggestions are made as to what a person could most usefully do with a sombrero, and, suffice it to say, they do not involve the Mexican hat dance. Unfortunately, Campos then saves a John Sheridan shot, which puts the mockers on us again.

It is getting even hotter now. Garcia jostles Roy Keane, who turns and growls and looks as though he's just about ready to batter seven shades of guacamole out of him. "Go on Roy," shouts the Liverpool man, "give the little spic a good kicking for himself. Go on Roy, rip his greasy head off."

A halt is called to our fun when, in the 65th minute, disaster strikes. Garcia scores again, this time blasting it in from the edge of the box. "That's it," says Mr Statistics, "I knew that was going to happen, I told you, didn't I?"

Down on the touchline a row seems to be brewing between John Aldridge, who wants to come on, and one of the FIFA officials, who is preventing him from doing so. Aldridge seems to be pushing the official and roaring at him. "Put the shagging boot into him, John" Mr Liverpool roars, "Get stuck in there, son." "That's not the way at all," says Mr Statistics. "Send him home to Dagoland in a coffin," suggests the Liverpool man, "rip his lungs out." Aldridge and McAteer come on, but things are falling apart for Ireland. Phelan gets booked. He and Irwin will both miss the Norway game. "We may as well go home now," sighs Mr Statistics, "there's no point really, not without those two."

Garcia continues to be absolutely tireless, lobbing in shots from all angles, while our players are beginning to look like sponges which have been squeezed too hard. Then, suddenly, in the 83rd minute, Aldridge bullets in a brilliant header, which bounces right on the line before ending up in the back of the net.

"WAAHHAAYYYYYYY" cries the man behind me. "YESSSSSSSS" roar the rest of the crowd. We jump up and down and hug each other, "*YESSSSSSSSSS, YESSSSSSS, YESSSSS.*" "You know?" says Mr Statistics, calmly unwrapping another glacier mint, "that's actually John Aldridge's fourteenth goal for Ireland."

Everyone is standing up and roaring now. For some endearing cultural reason or another, Mr Liverpool is leading a chorus of "Are You Watching, England?" (The answer, presumably, being "yes, and we're enjoying every minute of your crushing defeat, sad Scouse loser.") Even Mr Statistics shuffles to his feet and cries feebly "come on, boys." I say I think it's too late. There's only a few minutes to go; there's no way we can score. "Actually, you're wrong there," says Mr Statistics, "you see, in 7 of the 17 games played so far in USA 94, crucial goals have been scored in the last 5 minutes."

I make up my mind that if he opens his mouth just once more I will kill him myself, with my bare hands, and then happily skip to the electric chair feeling I've accomplished something useful in my life.

The game boils to a frantic climax. Ireland try to press forward, but the players are absolutely shagged out. The Liverpool man is chanting "You'll Never Beat the Irish," which, at this stage, sounds profoundly optimistic. In the last minute, Campos stops a thunderbolt of a shot from bleach-blond Andy Townsend. One minute of injury time. Then two. Mr Roethlisburger looks at his watch, blows his whistle and poops our party, bigtime. We've been hammered. We sink back into our seats, groaning and cursing. "That was quite a lot of injury time, wasn't it?" says Mr Statistics. "Third highest amount in the whole tournament so far actually. Quite remarkable. Anyway, bye then, I'm off. Best to get out early if you want to get a bus, you know, Cheerio." He stands up and leaves his seat and climbs down the big steps towards the exits. Myself and the Liverpool man catch each other's eye. "Tosser," the Liverpool man says. I cannot help but agree.

Saturday 25 June, New York: Here in America, soccer is having some problems. The massive public indifference to the World Cup is pretty astonishing, especially when back home in Ireland the very leaves on the trees are discussing pennos, volleys and Jack Charlton's intriguingly postmodern ads for Shredded Wheat. It is very strange. A survey in last Thursday's New York Times reported that 71 per cent of Americans do not even know that the World Cup finals are being played in their country. In another poll, taken just after the draw for the tournament, soccer turned out to be a mere 67th in terms of national popularity. It came in behind rock-climbing, log-splitting and tractor-pulling, and, indeed, was only marginally more popular than the ideologically suspect sport of "dwarf-throwing." Don't you just love Americans? When asked to explain the rules of soccer, 12 per cent said that it was played with racquets and a noble 6 per cent told pollsters that it was played underwater, which, I suppose, at least gives a new meaning to the phrase "diving tackle." What a wonderful country!

When the World Cup draw was announced in December 1991 I was here in New York, and it received no coverage at all on

American television and hardly any in the newspapers. Since then, things have not improved much. NBC are only broadcasting nine games live (out of a total of 51.) Even pay-per-view cable television is showing only 21 matches. The problem is that FIFA refused to bend to American television's demands that matches be interrupted every four minutes for commercials. Baseball and American football, being long and spectacularly dull games that go on for hours at a time, are extremely advertising-friendly. Indeed, the only good reason for watching baseball on television is that you get to see a lot of really good adverts. (My current favourite is for a little plastic device which humanely traps cockroaches: "Get your family a cockroach motel NOW. They check in, yes, but they never check out!")

Somehow, FIFA said no to the idea of blistering power-headers, blinding runs down the wing and spectacular diving saves being interrupted by the cockroach motel. Other fine ideas for giving soccer a more American flavour included making the goalposts bigger to allow more goals to be scored (I love that one. Let's have goalposts fifty feet wide, for God's sake), getting rid of the offside rule, and making draws illegal. (This last measure would have been achieved by the adding on of an unlimited period of extra time. No doubt, if introduced, it would have meant that many of Ireland's games would have lasted as long as the hundred years war.)

You can walk the streets of New York without seeing any evidence whatsoever that football's greatest and most compelling ritual has kicked off in this country. There is not a poster, a flag or a banner to be seen, nor a chorus of "Olé, Olé, Olé" to be heard unless you actively seek it out and go trawling around the Irish or Italian bars. Last night I asked a New York taxi driver who he intended to support in the World Cup. "Oh, the Rangers," he shrugged, meaning one of New York's ice hockey teams. Another New Yorker I met in the course of my ramblings opined that soccer was "one of those commie European games for faggots and nazis."

All of this is a shame because the United States actually has a proud history in the beautiful game. Consider, for example, that the land of the free actually took part in the very first World Cup, held in Uruguay in 1930, and even reached the semi-finals on that occasion, before being narrowly beaten 6-1 by Argentina. The match is affectionately remembered not for its scoreline, but for an intriguing incident which took place when the referee called a foul against one of the yanks, the team's doctor scuttled onto the turf to give out, tripped, dropped his box of medicinal aids, shattered a bottle of chloroform and was knocked out cold by the ensuing fumes. He ended up being carted off unconscious, thus adding greatly to the general gaiety of the crowd. The poor fellow took months to recover. (He was obviously not a Charlton Athletic supporter, as I am myself. I can tell you, a couple of Saturday afternoons watching those guys, and chloroform poisoning begins to seem almost invigorating.)

Tuesday 28 June, New York: Up very early to get the bus out to Meadowlands for the Norway game. As usual, the coach is full of boisterous fans wearing emerald green boxer shorts, shamrock patterned T-shirts and tricolour face paint, and carrying all kinds of inflatable green objects, from crocodiles to overlarge plastic hands to giant beer bottles. (How good it is to know that somewhere in Ireland a large factory, on a massive IDA grant, is churning out enormous green blow-up alligators.)

This morning, however, one of the fans also has a large rubber inflatable woman in the seat beside him, spray painted green from head to toe. I should point out to morally sensitive readers that the large inflatable woman is not naked or anything. No, she is wearing a star and stripes patterned bra, a tight pair of khaki cycling shorts and a hideous baseball cap with GIVE IT A LASH JACK printed on the front. For some amazing reason or another, the only seat left on the entire coach is beside this guy and his pneumatic companion, so I am forced to squeeze in there, elbowing her in the ribs as I do so. I feel like a right gooseberry.

The chap informs me that he purchased his latex lovebird in one of the sex shops on Time Square the other day, specially for today's game and painted her in his room last night. She cost a hundred dollars, he says, but she was worth every penny. "She's anatomically correct, yeh know," he confides to me, his eyes wide. She certainly doesn't look it to me, I must say, but I have no intention whatsoever of asking for proof. "D'ya like her anyway?" he asks. I answer candidly that whatever about her anatomical correctness she does certainly seem to have more personality than some of the other people I've met on the trip. "She's a petal," he says. "She's a little dote, aren't you love?" She does not reply. "We're a bit shy in front of strangers," he explains.

He takes a pair of large mirrored sunglasses from his breast pocket and slips them on. Slips them on to the doll, I mean, not onto himself. "Now love," he says, "there y'are, sure yeh don't want to be bloinded be the sun." It is nine o'clock in the morning. I am on a bus to New Jersey, and I am sitting beside a man who is having a fond conversation with a giant green inflatable sex toy. Oh, the glamour of journalism. "I'm goneta call her SheeShee," he says, "because she remoinds me of Sile de Valera."

The drive to New Jersey takes less time than it did on the day of the Italy game. The police seem better organised, and the roads leading from Manhattan onto the New Jersey turnpike are clearer. From the outside, the Giants stadium is amazingly beautiful to look at. As we get off the bus, take photographs of each other and briskly inflate anything in a fifty yard radius that can physically be inflated, Eamon Dunphy arrives in the front seat of a large limousine. (The rest of the limousine, I should stress, arrives also.) Like The Giants Stadium, Mr Dunphy too is amazingly beautiful to look at from the outside, so happy and positive and quite absurdly content do I feel this morning. I close my eyes and try to imagine an inflatable Eamon Dunphy. It seems like a good idea. Perhaps when I go home to Ireland I will put a proposal together for the IDA, so that I too can open a factory and manufacture inflatable Eamon Dunphys. There would be one problem, of course, which is that nobody would really want to blow him up themselves. I mean to say, would you? (But you could always use a bicycle pump, I suppose.)

Inside the stadium, everyone is in great form. I find myself sitting in an area which contains neutral observers, as well as Norwegian and Irish fans. Off to my right, I can see Mr Inflatable Woman in the middle of one of the Irish areas, with his companion sitting now topless on his shoulders and jigging up and down, in the manner of drug-ravaged teenage girls in the film of the Woodstock concert. Every once in a while, he makes her wave her hand at the crowd.

They all wave back. He stands up on his seat, wraps her arms around his neck and her thighs around his waist and kisses her full on the lips. Everyone roars. I wonder what this man does for a living back home in Ireland. After some consideration, I decide he is either a senior clerk with the Revenue Commissioners or a recently appointed auxiliary bishop.

The seat beside me is still empty. Beside that, two well dressed middle aged men are studying the match programme and delicately eating ice creams. They are Americans, and they have just come along to have a look at the game. They have heard all about how well the Irish fans are behaved, they tell me, and they've never been to a soccer game before, so they just thought they'd take the day off work and drop along. They are both consultant psychiatrists, as it turns out. This makes me astoundingly nervous, for some reason. They keep peering at me as though what I have just said is very interesting. They keep nodding and saying "really?"

Ten minutes before the game, a prime specimen of the best of Jackie's army comes lurching up the stadium steps, huffing and panting and spewking out of him like a runaway train. He is naked from the waist up. He has thick green concentric circles painted around his nipples, a green nose painted on his torso, and a leering green mouth painted around his navel, which is pierced with a ring so big that even the Pope would find it a bit OTT. As soon as I see him, I just know he is destined for the seat beside me.

I am right. He pushes past the two psychiatrists, dripping sweat all over them, and slides in beside me. "Howya Pal," he nods, "howa they hangin'?" I assure him that I have no complaints. He then does the worst thing that anyone in the world can do. He grasps hold of his nose between his pointing finger and his thumb, and he exhales heavily, several times, thus evacuating the contents of his nostrils all over his hand. He wipes his soiled fingers on his hair and then down the side of his trousers. He burps magnificently, pulls a beer from his bag, snaps open the ring and offers it without a word to one of the psychiatrists beside him.

"Er, no thank you very much," the chivalrous shrink says. The fan offers it to the other one, who also declines.

"What's wrong wit yooze?" he says, "are yez fairies or wha?"

"Just not thirsty," one replies.

He peers astonished at the non-thirsty psychiatrist, as though he has just been let in on the third secret of Fatima. Then he nods, says "fair nuff so" and gazes at me. He opens his mouth and, without taking his eyes off me for even a single second, pours the contents of the can down his throat as though trying to extinguish a fire. He burps again — "Jayzus, the latest release on the Oirland label" — sits back in his seat, scratches his crotch, puts his hands to his mouth and roars "COME ON YE BOYS IN GREE-AN."

Now, it is an odd thing, but being something of a newcomer to the game of two halves I have observed at this World Cup that most fans will not sing on their own. They always wait for somebody else to start the singing, and then they will join in, no bother, and join in at full volume. But they will not start a chant themselves. It is a wonder, in fact, that chants ever get started at all. There must be one guy, I remember thinking at the Mexico game, one guy in this enormous crowd of eighty thousand people, who actually starts off the chant.

Well, I found him. He is sitting beside me now, singing away with gusto. "YILL NEVER BEAT THE OIRISH. YILL NEVER BEAT THE OIRISH." This goes on, I swear to you, for about four minutes, the phrase just being repeated again and again, until eventually, almost out of boredom, it is taken up by the Irish fans in the next section of the stadium. One of the American psychiatrists leans over, his eyebrows raised as though he is about to ask me a question. I prepare myself to assure him that I had a very good relationship with my mother, thank you very much, but actually he just wants to know if Ireland have ever been in the World Cup finals before. My reply is interrupted by your man, now bellowing ferociously, "WE ARE GREEN, WE ARE WHY, WE ARE FOOKY DYNA-MY, NA NA NANA, NA NANA, NA NAHH." He stands up and begins slapping out a rhythm on his ample breasts. The rest of the fans in our section start singing.

He sits down again, looking contented, and realises with a sudden start that there are Norwegian fans sitting in the row in front of us. His eyes take on the enthusiastic light of a disturbed schoolboy who is about to pull the legs off a frog. He starts loudly imitating the Norwegian fans' voices, in the manner of the Swedish chef character from The Muppet Show.

"Hoorgy, goorgy, woorgy, a woooorgy, woooorgy," he titters, in his singsong intonation, sounding more like a frantic Texan evangelist praying in tongues than an excited Norwegian. "Boorgy, voory, woorgywoorgahwoorgy." They ignore him. After a moment or two he gives one of them a playful smack on the back of the head.

"OOORGY, BOORGY?" he says, "A HOORGEE?" They still ignore him. He reaches out, takes a light hold of one of their collars and begins to drip ice cold beer down his back, screaming with maniacal laughter while doing so. At last, one of the Norwegian fans turns around.

"You are a really funny guy," he says. (Devastating irony is obviously very big in Norway.)

"Ooorgy, coorgy, woorgy," replies the pride of Jackie's army.

"You are hilarious guy, really."

"Ah don't be such a dry shite," he says, "OOORGY, OORGY, come on, will yez do it!"

The band troop on to the pitch below. All the way through the Irish national anthem the guy beside me picks his nose, examining what he has found up there as though it might be a precious diamond or a category 1 ticket for the next round. And all the way through the Norwegian national anthem he stands to attention, one arm by his side, one hand clasped to his naked bosom, eyes closed in a gesture of sincere respect, singing loudly "OOORGY BOORGY WOORGY."

The match begins. Two minutes later, Roy Keane is booked. Mr Oorgy Boorgy gets up and screeches something so abusive that you couldn't put it in a family publication, unless the family happened to be the Borgias. From them on, every single time the referee awards a foul against Ireland, this guy has something to say about it. It starts off mildly enough. A murmured "Jayzus Ref, yeh're a shagginwell dope," or a poignantly sighed "Ah, give the ref a pair of sunglasses and a white bleedin stick." The two Americans smile, with the gentle benevolence of those who make a very comfortable living indeed out of dealing with dangerous lunatics.

But after some time, he starts to get more excited. "You filthy little Columbian BOLLIX," he roars, "that was never offside you manky little disgusting dickhead." He has veins in his neck the size of ropes. I wonder if he is going to have a heart attack, and I fervently hope he is. But after a while, I find that, actually, he is quite an interesting commentator on the game. Any time he roars at the referee, it means that Ireland have done something wrong or illegal and have been deservingly punished, and any time he says "yess, ladss, yesss, yesss, put 'em under PRESSURE," it means that we are playing really badly, and that the likelihood of an Irish goal is receding almost as fast as Jackie Charlton's hairline.

"REFF, YOU'RE DEAD". He starts stabbing the air with his finger and jumping up and down, sweat pouring off him in meandering rivulets. "You're dead, Ref, yew are dead, I'm warnin yeh now, I'll see yew outside Pal, and I'll be dug ourra yeh, you poxy little hooer's melt yeh."

Ray Houghton is deftly tackled by a couple of Norwegian defenders. "It takes bleedin two of them all the same," the Pride of Erin cries. "IT TAKES TWO OF YEZ, DOESN'T IT, YEZ FOOKIN VIKING EEJITS." This goes on all the way through the first half, the interval, and the second half. When the rest of the fans are exhausted into relative silence by the heat, your man is still roaring and cursing at full volume. "YEH LITTLE COLUMBIAN COONT YEH, I KNEW YER AUL WAN WELL AND SHE WAS ONEY A BRASSER." Fifteen minutes before the end, the two psychiatrists slip silently away, still grinning like apostles in a renaissance painting. I imagine they must have got invaluable material for a research paper on the therapeutic effects of frontal lobotomy out of the Jack's Army experience.

The game ends in a nil all draw. All around me, fans are trying to calculate where Ireland have come in the group, what the goal difference is, where we will play our next match. Now, I scored an E in inter cert pass mathematics — that's a bad grade, by the way, not an ecstasy tablet, for the benefit of younger readers — so this kind of thing is very difficult for me. Let's see, Ireland beat Italy and Italy beat Mexico and Norway beat...I sit very still, my brain feeling as though smoke is coming out of it. All I hope and pray is that, whatever happens, we don't have to play in Orlando again.

On the bus back to the hotel, I sit beside the chap with the inflatable woman again. Shee-Shee is looking a little less than her best at this stage. Her paint has started to melt in the heat, her breasts are sagging like burst balloons and her head is drooping and flailing as though she is severely the worse for drink. It seems that in the course of the match she has suffered a number of fatal cigarette burns from mischievous fans. Her loyal consort keeps dolefully raising her lithe midriff to his lips and blowing hard, trying to re-inflate her, to no effect. She keeps making a hissing sound and then collapsing again in his lap. "Women," he says.

That night I go out with some Irish friends. The Irish bars on Sixth and Fifty First Street are absolutely crammed full of people. It now seems clear that we will have to play Belgium in bloody Orlando, the only city in the world that would make Las Vegas seem tasteful. I have a lot to drink. When I get back to my hotel it is almost two in the morning. Shee Shee is sitting alone in the lobby, looking by now like she's just gone ten rounds with Mike Tyson. I feel so depressed that I almost sit down and try to buy her a tequila sunrise.

Wednesday 29 June. New York: Get up feeling miserable as the full reality of having to return to Orlando dawns. When I go down to the lobby there are Irish fans everywhere. Most of them will be going back to Ireland today, because their travel packages only covered the first round of the tournament. Some of the diehards have decided to stay, and are borrowing money from those who are leaving. The generosity of the fans to each other is amazing. Twenty dollar bills are being handed around left, right and centre. I have a good gander at the fans who are staying. I notice that the man with the inflatable woman is one of them. She is now in fully deflated state — as, indeed, I am myself — and she is wrapped around his neck like a scarf. I cannot tell you how nauseous this makes me feel.

The fans who are staying are waiting for someone from the travel company to show up. All through this trip there have been problems with the Irish travel agency with whom most of the fans in my hotel have been travelling. They are each paying about two grand each to be here, and, hey, call them old fashioned, but they feel that two grand is a lot of dough, and they deserve to be treated with just a modicum of respect. Through no fault of the very nice tour guides working over here for XXXXX Travel (sorry, can't mention them, because no doubt they'd try to sue), there have been a lot of screw-ups. Granted, the World Cup has presented what I believe are called in the business community "major challenges" to the Irish travel agents, (the main challenge being, how in the name of God will we spend all the money we're making out of this?) but the fans' trip, which should have been the experience of a lifetime, has too often been an unending nightmare of long queues, missing hotel rooms, amazingly long airline delays, shabby and inadequate or non-existent transport, lost luggage and delays in getting their match tickets. XXXXX Travel appear to have send over a mere three people to handle the needs of several thousand people. They have had months and months to get all of this stuff right, but in too many cases they appear not to have done so. The other travel agents have done a decent enough job. And I am sure that there must be hundreds of contented XXXXX travellers. But all I can honestly tell you is that in two and a half full weeks of travelling with the Irish fans, I have yet to meet a single one. Quite the contrary. "I'd never go with XXXXX again," one of the supporters said to me last night, "they couldn't organise a shag in a knocking shop."

I myself have got off relatively lightly. The most serious difficulty I've had to contend with is being stranded alone and friendless in Orlando last week, booked into a hotel which had been demolished a month beforehand. But one XXXXX traveller I spoke to really did know about suffering. His suitcase had been lost twice during the trip, and he had been given a whopping 75 dollars — about fifty quid — to buy two weeks worth of clothes. "I haven't changed me knickers in DAYS," he sighed. Another man had been presented with a 650 dollar hotel bill, for a stay he had payed for in full before leaving Ireland. Many of these fans have extremely imaginative — not to say unprintable — opinions about what should be done with

Mr XXXXXXXXX XXXXXXXXX the owner of XXXXX travel. I don't think he will be getting too many Christmas cards from Irish soccer supporters this year.

I manage to find out where the three XXXXX Travel reps are staying and call all three, leaving messages for them to ring me back as a matter of absolute urgency. About eight hours later, one of them does. I am out. She never calls back. By sheer chance, I bump into one of the reps in the hotel lobby. She was supposed to be here hours ago but did not show up until now. She looks tired, and is walking with a pronounced limp, and is clearly overworked. She says she will call me back later today about getting me a flight to Orlando tomorrow. Guess what? She never does.

Thursday 30 June, New York: Just after eight in the morning I manage to speak to the XXXXX Travel rep again. She sounds very tired, and I do my best to sympathise. She says she thinks she can get me on a flight to Orlando, leaving from Newark at 1 p.m.. She will meet me at my hotel at 10 a.m. and give me all the details.

The sports report on the morning news says we will now have to play Holland, not Belgium. I stroll up Eight Avenue and have breakfast with a couple of fans in a diner. Over scrambled eggs, I read a report on yesterday's game in one of the New York tabloids. "The Irish cheered as though they were at a wake" it says. I read this again, several times, wondering whether it is a misprint, or yet another example of how the Americans have utterly fictionalised our culture. Picture the scene. The mother, played by Mia Farrow, says "Ah son, I've some terrible news altogether for you, your poor father's after dyin'." The son, played by Tom Cruise, replies, "WAHHAYYYYYYYYYYYYYYY, YIPPEEEEE, OH WHAT A BEAUTIFUL MORNING, OH WHAT A BEAUTIFUL DAY."

On the way back to meet the rep I notice that the remaining fans have draped their tricolour flags and banners out the windows of the hotel. Passers-by stop and gaze up at the building, wondering what it going on. Taxi drivers honk their horns. I am suddenly struck by the sheer exemplary determination of these fans to enjoy themselves in the face of grim adversity. I decide to stop feeling sorry for myself. I sit down in the lobby and wait for the rep to show.

Needless to say, she does not turn up at ten. Or ten thirty. Or eleven. Instead, she calls me twice from her hotel to say she will be late. In the end, she calls again to say she won't be turning up at all. She gives me my flight details. Kiwi Air, leaving from Newark in an hour and a half, I really would want to be leaving now, she says.

I explain that I would like my hotel bill for the night before to be charged to XXXXX Travel, as we have agreed, and she suggests that she has not had time to sort this out, so I will have to pay the bill myself. When I have finished choking with crazed laughter, I explain that I have no intention whatsoever of paying this bill. "I have two hundred fans here in front of me to sort out," the rep says, as though dealing efficiently with large numbers of soccer fans would be a very unusual thing for a sports travel agency to do, (which, in the case of XXXXX Travel, it apparently would be).

Out to Newark Airport to collect my ticket for Orlando. The weekend of the fourth of July is coming up, the busiest travel period of the year in America. The traffic is absolutely woeful. Arvo the Armenian taxi driver seems to be obsessed with the fact that the gay olympics have just ended in New York. "They're all fallin in love with each other down there in Greenwich Village," he says, grimly shaking his head, "can you believe it, a guy fallin in love with another guy?" Certainly not if the guy was you, Arvo, I muse, silently.

When we eventually get to Newark Airport, Arvo tells me the fare will be a hefty 45 bucks. He then tries to rip me off by inventing a twenty dollar "Newark Airport Surtax." He wants sixty five greenbacks in all, he explains. I explain to Arvo in polite terms that I don't know how these things play back in Armenia, but I did not come down the fucking river on the last fucking canoe. He insists on my paying this tax. There is a frank exchange of views. I get out of the car and rouse a nearby policeman from his reveries.

Now, New York policemen are very unusual creatures. For a start, they all look far more like robbers than cops, and, indeed, recent widely publicised reports into their colourful activities would confirm that many of them should, in fact, be wearing tights over their faces rather than badges on their chests. Also, they seem to regard dealing with the public as some sort of unpleasant and preposterous imposition. (They should all take up new careers with a certain Irish travel agency, come to think of it.)

Anyway, Officer Monroe sighs deeply and yawns through his nose as I explain my plight. He shakes his massive head, brushes the dandruff off his manly shoulders, shambles over to the waiting taxi and raps on Arvo's window with his wedding ring.

"You breakin' this guy's balls here?" he murmurs.

"No, officer," Arvo replies.

"He sez you breakin his balls."

"He whut?"

"Well, to be fair," I point out, "I didn't actually say that, Officer."

Officer Monroe turns to me. "Thought you sez he was breakin you balls."

"I said he was overcharging me."

Officer Monroe starts examining his fingernails. "Izzy breakin' you balls or not, Pal? Cuz iffen he ain't breakin you balls, hey, I gut woik to do here, y'know what am sayin'?"

A lively debate about the state of my balls, vis-á-vis brokenness, then ensues. Eventually we agree that Arvo's understanding of the American tax system may be in some need of brushing up. I will pay the forty five dollars, and Arvo will go down on his knees and thank God and his Holy Mother and the Blessed Trinity that in the circumstances I am prepared to even do this much.

"Ya betta nut be breakin any more uv ya passenger's balls, Mac," Office Monroe advises.

"I'm not, Officer," Arvo says, "see, he didden unnerstand me. He's a foreigner. He don't speak English so good."

"Cuz any more ballbreakin gets done around here," Officer Monroe explains, and he pauses for what seems an eternity, before plunging into the uncertain and murky depths of a conclusion, "and I mo be doin it."

Officer Monroe strolls back to the wall against which he was so energetically leaning when I rudely awoke him. Arvo slides out of the cab, looking somewhat crestfallen. He opens the trunk and steps back, generously allowing me to remove my own suitcases, which I do. I then very reluctantly open my wallet and pay him what I owe him. He stares at the half-inch thick wad of banknotes as though I've just handed him a fresh dogturd. Then — wait till you hear — the ungrateful little toerag has the nerve to ask me for a gratuity. I can't believe it!

"How about a tip, Mac?" he says to me.

"Why certainly," I smile, "Use a deodorant, Arvo. You'd get to meet more girls."

I trundle my luggage the seeming ten miles through the terminal building, sweating, hyperventilating, (this must be what they call Terminal Illness) and get into line with a huge crowd of Irish fans, feeling like I'm about to have a massive coronary or a complete emotional breakdown. After a twenty minute wait I am called to the counter. The guy behind the counter has the worst bad breath I've ever had the misfortune to inhale. I mean, he's very pleasant and everything, but he really does honk like he ate a broiled skunk sandwich for supper last night. I say I want my ticket, and I want it now.

He tickles the keys on his computer for some moments. Needless to say, the ticket has been booked by a XXXXX Travel employee, so Kiwi Air have never heard of my reservation. The guy actually chortles at the very idea that they have a pre-paid ticket for me. He then tries to call XXXXX travel in Manhattan, but — surprise surprise — none of their representatives is available. I demand to see the guy's superior. He comes over and says there's nothing he can do. So I demand to see *his* superior. He comes out and says there's nothing he can do either. I'm about to ask to see HIS superior, but the queue of angry Irish soccer supporters behind me is getting long and hostile and I feel if I keep demanding to meet people's superiors, I'll go all the way to the top and end up meeting God or something, an eventuality for which, after two weeks at the World Cup, I am not as well prepared as I might be. Rather than meeting God, I end up paying $177 of my own dough for my ticket. This done, I notice that there is a young disabled Irish supporter in a wheelchair behind me, in obvious distress. He has been waiting with a friend for almost an hour, in severe heat, to collect his ticket. It is actually astonishing that people can be treated like this.

The flight is OK. The only truly scary thing about it is the air hostesses' orange foundation. (And before anybody writes in to complain, I know you're not supposed to call them air hostesses any more. I know that! I know they're In Flight Supervisors or something, but hey, how come I'm still just a bloody passenger? If they want to be In Flight Supervisors, fine, but if I have to shell out 177 bucks for something that's already mine I want to be at least a Temporary Airborne Supervisee or some damn thing.)

Three drunken Dutch fans are sitting behind me, belching in harmony and opening bottles of lager with their teeth. There is absolutely no need for them to do this, as the air hostesses — sorry, the Aviation Hospitality Operative Technicians — have bottle openers a-plenty, but boys will be boys, it seems, even in a sexually liberated society such as Holland. I close my eyes and pray hard that one of them will wrench out a ventricular molar, in which case I will be only too happy to offer to do a bit of emergency root canal work with a spanner.

We land at Orlando airport, which somehow amazes me. The way things have been going today, it would not have surprised me to land in the middle of the Gaza strip. The airport bar is full of Irish fans. Having been — I confess it frankly — a little sick of them by last night, this morning I found that somehow I missed them. I don't know why that should be, but it's true. We all have a drink together in the bar, where the TV is showing a repeat of yesterday's utterly epoch-making nil nil draw between Ireland and Norway. We cheer and roar all over again, as though by doing so we can somehow change the outcome of the game.

I would like to stay in the bar with the lads — *oh my God, what's happening to me? I've started to refer to them as "The Lads"?!* — but although I am enjoying myself my nerves are badly at me. I really do feel tense. I have a very negative feeling about today. So I take a spectacularly expensive taxi to my hotel, or, at least, it takes me there, to the Floridian on Republic Drive. It looks alright.

"SETTING THE STYLE FOR GREAT LITTLE HOTELS," the neon sign announces. Maybe this time, just maybe, just once, XXXXX Travel will not have screwed up!

The Floridian Hotel turns out to be owned by a tribe of Florida Indians, or, rather, a tribe of Florida Native Americans, (apologies to all Apache readers) and I am fascinated by this. Just what I need at this moment. A politically correct hotel. When the very pleasant chap behind the counter asks me if I have a reservation I have to restrain myself from saying "yes, but heck, I'm sure it's not as nice as yours."

Naturally enough, the people at the Floridian Hotel, like the people at Kiwi Air, are blissfully unaware of my very existence, and despite my rep's best assurances have no booking at all in my name. I explain that I am travelling with this Irish agency called XXXXX Travel. The chap smiles understandingly. "Ah yes, XXXXX Travel," he says, and he purses his lips and nods with the air of one consoling a good friend on the sudden murder of a close relative. He turns and says something in Spanish to a passing colleague, gently jerking his thumb in my direction. All I can pick out are the words "*XXXXX*," "*Irlanda*" and "*pobre bastardo stupido.*"

His colleague comes over and peers at me in amazement, as though I am Gulliver suddenly arrived in the land of the Lilliputians. I am actually kind of enjoying my new found status now. I am The Guy Who Travelled With XXXXX Travel And Lived To Tell The Tale. His eyes widen. "XXXXX Travel," he sighs, and he makes a whistling sound with his teeth, "*Dios mio.*" I shrug manfully and say aw shucks, it was nothing. He reaches out to firmly clasp my shoulder in a heartfelt gesture of solidarity between oppressed peoples. I reckon I've got a room.

The chaps behind the counter are really very nice indeed. They give me free coffee and a cigarette and they move people around until they do manage to find me a room, but they explain regretfully that I will have to pay for it myself. This is about as surprising as the news that Tuesday follows Monday. I hand over my credit card, which at this stage is beginning to melt into a Salvador Dali-like shape from severe and frequent misuse. The concierge forces a bundle of brochures about Disneyland and Sea World into my quivering hands.

I go up to my very nice room and lie on the soft bed in a crumpled heap, studying the Sea World brochure. Sea World is yet another dismal Orlando theme park, only, unlike Disneyworld, it is full of real animals in tanks rather than fake ones in ridiculous costumes. Still, though. I have a few days to kill before the Holland game, so a trip to Sea World with some of the Irish fans might be interesting. Yup. I might just do that tomorrow. After all, I see in the brochure that Sea World has a special exhibition on just now all about the Bermuda Triangle, which is, of course, just what you would come all the way to Florida to find out about. The Bermuda Triangle!! Where weird and inexplicable and terrifying things happen to the unwary and unsuspecting voyager!! Wow!! Isn't that something?! I just can't wait. Count me in. Though on second thoughts, I feel I don't actually need to pay good money to experience The Bermuda Triangle. Travelling with XXXXX Travel is kind of the same thing.

Sunday July 3, Orlando: Get up early and have a very nice Floridian Hotel breakfast beside the very nice Floridian Hotel swimming pool. (God, journalism is tough sometimes.) The local Sunday paper has an article about an Orlando woman who works for the government in Washington. She is in trouble, because the FBI claim to have found a little dope in her hotel bedroom. (President Clinton denied it was him, apparently.) Later, after I have swum five slow lengths and worked hard on my tan, I trot along to visit Sea World with some of the Irish fans who are staying at my hotel. As soon as we arrive, my good mood evaporates.

Sea World is basically an overgrown aquarium, and if you like seeing dumb scaly helpless animals entertaining dumb scaly helpless Floridians, why then Sea World is the place for you.

We all pay our money and troop in to see the performing dolphins. We are first subjected to a tedious lecture on how incredibly well-trained and intelligent they are. I find all this a bit hard to swallow. If they were that bloody intelligent, in my view, they would be working the West Coast, or Caesar's Palace in Vegas, or, at the very least, appearing in The Gaiety pantomime with Maureen Potter, and not floundering around in a bloody wojus kip like Sea World.

We are then told what terrible creatures fishermen are, because the friends and relations of these poor liddle dolphins are getting caught in the evil anglers' tuna nets every single day of the week. We are all to buy something called "dolphin-friendly tuna," from now on, we are told. A bit bloody selective, isn't it? "C'mre you nice little tuna, till I spread mayonnaise all over you and put you in a sandwich, but dear oh dear, let's be nice to the sodding dolphins." I remind myself to ask for a well-done dolphin steak for dinner tonight.

I watch for a while, absolutely captivated, as the dolphins do really intelligent things, such as head-banging a beachball across a swimming pool and catching gobloads of malodorous mackerel. Wow. Give them a bloody PhD why don't you. Then, some musclebound beachbum in a g-string smooths his way into the pool and does a really stunning trick which involves repeatedly balancing on a dolphin's nose while it streaks up and out of the water with the speed of a thermonuclear missile. The Americans in the audience seem to find this almost religiously inspiring. They are quite hysterical with applause.

The steroid-stuffed prettyboy then puts his arms around the dolphin's neck and allows himself to be dragged around the pool, his gob gurgling in the surf, like a great big unholy gobshite. If the dolphin had any real intelligence it would haul your man down to the bottom and half-drown him, but no. Dolphin and man do a lap of the pool, and yet more totally innocent mackerel get consumed. Again, the applause would burst your eardrums.

What happens next is upsetting. One of the younger female members of our party seems to take a bit of a shine to him — the beachbum, that is, not the dolphin — and she insists we all go over to talk to him after the show. I am, needless to say, very secure and not at all threatened by this. She introduces herself to Guy and asks how he manages to keep himself so fit. Guy blushes and stops trailing his knuckles in the dust and runs his fingers through his mop of blond hair and says aw gosh and gee whillakers and so on, before revealing that he has "isolated his major muscle groups." I am utterly fascinated to hear this. My own muscle groups are so isolated they are practically in solitary confinement. Anyway, Emer from County Cavan seems to be delighted by garrulous Guy and his incredible performing muscle groups, and promptly invites him to join us for lunch. I am horrified by this sudden development, but it seems there is no escape, so I have to comply. It is a very warm day, so I suggest we eat *al fresco*. Guy says no, he would prefer pizza. When I have finished laughing maniacally, I congratulate Emer from County Cavan on managing to get a dose of the hots for the only living creature in Florida who is less intelligent than a dolphin.

After this unspeakably enjoyable victory, Emer and Guy head off for a bite — out of each other no doubt, as well as out of a twelve-inch pizza — and the rest of us all trawl in to have a look at the various sharks and killer whales which have the dreadful misfortune to inhabit this lousy gaff. The great white shark, which ordinarily would take the leg off a donkey and not think twice about it, seems a little intimidated by the Irish fans, and, let us face it, you cannot really blame him. I mean, how would *you* like to be woken up early on a Sunday morning by a large group of perspiring individuals in green shirts, green sombreros and green shorts, all singing "Oooh-Aaaah, Paul McGrath" and reeking of stale Southern Comfort? Well, maybe you *would* like that, maybe I am being presumptuous. But I would not, and, as it turns out, neither would your average shark.

The poor toothsome beastie lies motionless on the bottom of its tank like a surly bored teenager watching the heavy metal half hour on MTV. One fan, observing the scene, claims that this is all a swizz, and that the shark's teeth are not real. I say I didn't know they made false teeth for sharks, but he gamely maintains that they do, and it's a well known fact. He has false teeth himself, as it turns out, and he insists on taking them out to show everybody. "It was our fortieth anniversary recently," he says to me, "and the aul wan, yeh know, the war department, she says to me, Honey, I'd like yeh to nibble on me ear the way yeh used to. Burr I told her no, I won't bleedin bother, be the time I get me dentures in, sure yeh'll be asleep."

We all find this very amusing, but for some reason the shark does not even grin. From time to time it peers anxiously up at us, as we rap on the glass and cry, "come up, yeh bowsie," and "howya Esther Rantzen," and "wouldja smile, yeh dozy aul hoor, yeh." But all this has no effect. It refuses to come up and give us a flash of its molars, whether false or not, so with a final hummed chorus of the theme music from *Jaws* — da NAH, da NAH, daNAH daNAH daNAH — we abandon the great white to its bloodthirsty daydreams of an Irish soccer fan sandwich.

Next stop is the manatee tank. Now, a manatee is not what Peig Sayers called her husband. Rather, a manatee is a large bulky aquarian herbivore, a bit like a swollen walrus, only with cute eyes and inadequate flippers. It moves around pretty slowly and clumsily, and in its more private moments has the depressed and doleful expression of a creature that somehow knows it should really have disappeared from the earth many millennia ago. (You see this pained look on the face of the Reverend Ian Paisley sometimes, particularly when the SDLP do well in elections.)

Yet evolution, which has dealt so ruthlessly with the dodo and the dinosaur, and which is really giving the Duck-Billed Platypus something to ponder when it gets up of a morning, has been inexplicably kind to the manatee. Somehow it has just kept plodding along through the centuries, while all around it much more resilient and handsome creatures have vanished from the football pitch of history as quick as recidivist South American strikers being given red cards and consequent early baths.

One single look at it, and you can see that the manatee was not designed to survive in any environment other than Sea World. It is utterly pitiful. But, unlike the shark, at least it makes an effort when it notices us. It breast-strokes its way awkwardly up to the top of the tank and plummets down again, its dive as graceless and pathetically unconvincing as one of Jurgen Klinsman's. It hauls its bloated carcass back up to have a gander at us — "what's up witcha gorgeous?" one fan says, "jaze, yer the image of the mother-in-law" — then it claps its flippers, bloats its cheeks and releases from its bowels an enormous manatee turd, which ascends all the way up to the top of the tank and floats there for some time before disintegrating. We all clap and whistle. That, after three weeks away from home at the World Cup, is how sad we are. We are applauding incontinent aquatic mammals.

We stare at this ungainly creature for some time, waving our Irish scarves at its window. After a while, it seems to respond to the colour green. I don't know whether it is my imagination, but every time an Irish scarf is brandished, its hapless mug seems to break into an encouraging grin. It keeps coming up and head-butting the window, its great mouth gaping and leering. The manatee is described in my guidebook as "the last beautiful surviving link to our dark prehistoric past." It is thus, I suppose, to the aquarian world what physiotherapist Mick Byrne is to the Irish soccer team. As such, I feel it is worthy of considerable respect. In fact, I like the manatee so much that I intend to ask at the gift shop whether they sell stuffed ones.

Monday 4 July, Orlando: The morning of the Holland game I wake up early. The cold which I have been so vigorously fighting off since the start of the World Cup is now upon me, big time, major league, with fries to go. I am sneezing and coughing and spluttering and trembling and there is enough moisture flowing from my scarlet eyes to fill a good size manatee tank. I am banjaxed, I really am. I clamber from the scratcher, feeling miserable, and I stagger to what the great and good Lord Chesterfield called The Noble Room.

My internal workings are, well, not really working. I will spare sensitive readers the full details. Suffice it to say that I have diarrhoea so bad I feel I could excrete through the eye of a needle at fifty yards.

I wonder what to do about this. I mean, I have a very long and stressful day ahead of me. I decide to get dressed, go down to the pharmacy and buy myself milk of magnesia, vitamin C pills, cough bottle and a good nasal spray. Preferably the kind of nasal spray used by Maradonna. They don't have it, sadly, but they know where I can get it. I am to go to a certain back alley in the bad part of Orlando, find the red door, knock three times, sniff loudly and say, yo dude, "Fat Diego" from Buenos Aires sent me down for half a pound of Colombian nose candy. (I'm not really to do this, if their lawyers are reading. I made that bit up.)

Back at the hotel, I swig down all my medicaments, but I don't feel any better. I feel a little worse, in fact. Ten minutes later, as I don my Opel shirt and my mirrored green sunglasses, I suffer another terrible internal attack and break the hundred yard record in a dash to the jacks. I don't mind telling you that I am pretty worried by now. Lavatory facilities at the Citrus Bowl are not what they might be, and I do not wish to stand in a queue for fifteen minutes and miss an Irish goal. (Poor innocent fool me, I have forgotten that to miss an Irish goal a person would have to stand in a queue for about twelve years.) I ponder my problem for some time. In the end, I decide to just trust in fate and bring along a good stout pair of bicycle clips.

The coach arrives at the hotel to convey us all to the game. We clamber on board, singing "Here We Go, Here We Go, Here We Go" and other such patriotic ditties. On the way down International Drive we pass a busload of Dutch fans, and there are frantic choruses of "Cheerio, Cheerio, Cheerio" and "California Here We Come." One man on our bus opens his window and sings "When it's Spring again, I'll bring again, Eejits from Amsterdam." The Dutch fans stick their trumpets and trombones out their windows and blow them at us. "Eejits from Amsterdam," your man roars again, "we'll wipe the bleedin floor wit yez." What he suggests should be done with the trombones will not bear repetition in a quality newspaper.

Everyone on the coach seems confident of victory. But it may not be as simple as that. When we get to the Citrus Bowl and file in, clutching our inflatable green crocodiles and enormous plastic shamrocks, we see that there are a lot of Dutch fans already in their seats, clutching inflatable orange windmills and enormous plastic tulips and looking strangely smug. They look like they have been there all night, for some reason. For the first time in this World Cup, we Irish supporters will have to contend with a more or less equal number of foreign fans. It is just not fair!

The man sitting in front of me is so fat that the back of his neck looks like a plastic packet of hot dogs. He is wearing an orange football shirt and a large preposterous hat shaped like an Edam cheese with a slice slivered out of it. My God, is he big. He looks like a barrage balloon on legs. The waistline of his trousers is far too low, so that a good half of each of his enormous pendulous buttocks protrudes. You could park a bicycle in the cheeks of his bum. He turns and beams at me, in a strangely unsettling manner. "We will beat you today, yes, Irishman?" he says. "Oh, I don't think so," I grin.

"Yes, yes, yes," he nods, "I think we will beat you today."

"You'll never beat the Irish," I counter, brilliantly.

"Ha," he says, "If you think we do not beat you, then you are a very stupid facker."

"HaHaHa," I simper. He turns around, opens his beer and begins loudly singing something in a strange guttural language which I suppose must be Dutch. Back home in Ireland I am pro-European, pro-Maastricht, the works. Sitting here in the Citrus Bowl behind this circumferentially challenged Netherlander and his globular nether regions I realise with a sudden start that I want to get my hands on the little Dutch boy who put his finger into the dyke in the children's bedtime story and slap the bloody gob off him.

While waiting for the game to start I have a read of the paper. It leads with a story on the murder of Andres Escobar, the Colombian player who scored an own goal and thus knocked his team out of the World Cup. Underneath is a story about an Argentinean man who bet his neighbour that Argentina would win the tournament. This fellow put up his wife — I am not kidding you — as the stake, and when the Argies got knocked out by Romania, he duly handed the missus over to your man next door. Sadly, the good Senora's reaction is not recorded for posterity, but I imagine she must have been pleased enough to hop over the back fence. Let's face it, when your sweetheart has wagered you on a major international sporting event, you have truly lost that lovin feeling.

There is another fascinating story about how much the Irish fans have been drinking in Orlando. A local doctor has written that alcohol abuse might well be a serious social problem in Ireland, which, naturally enough, to me is really a major revelation. I ponder writing Doctor Incredibly Perceptive MD a letter pointing out that alcohol abuse is not so much a serious social problem as the national sport in Ireland, and that if they had World Cups for being scuttered,

Ireland would win hands down. Apparently, he writes, if you have eight beers a day the size of your brain actually shrinks. That's the bad news. The good news is that it makes watching English situation comedies so much more entertaining.

The players troop out to a great roar of applause and the game begins. Right from the start, the Dutch are all over us like a cheap suit. The Irish fans cheer and sing, but somehow we know today is going to be tricky. But at least both sides are playing to win, and this makes the game quite stirring to watch. Then, however, Terry Phelan attempts a pass so clumsy that even Casanova would have found it a bit outrageous. This woeful mistake lets the Dutch get the ball. They express their gratitude by taking it and briskly burying it in the back of the Irish net. The fat fellow in front of me practically ascends body and soul into heaven, so screechingly enthusiastic does he become. Bloody typical. Very unsporting people, the Dutch, I've always said it.

Well, all this is a bit of a downer, as you can imagine. As you sit there in the hundred degree heat, you can't help chewing on the grizzly fact that Ireland have never actually scored more than one goal in a World Cup match. Things go from bad to worse. The Dutch start to take over the game, and soon they are running us ragged. And then that terrible moment comes. It is as though time stands still. Poor dear Packie Bonner, who is very much the hero of the Irish fans, fumbles the ball into his own goal.

Now, I don't know if you have ever heard the sound of a large number of Irish men groaning simultaneously — I mean, I went to a Catholic boarding school, so, you know, I got to hear it almost every night for some years — but take it from me, it is not a pretty sound at all. We are all speechless with shock. Down in the goalmouth, poor Packie looks like he wishes the yellowing patchy grass of the Citrus Bowl would simply open up, swallow him down and spit him out in bubbles. He clenches his fists and hangs his head in pure unadulterated despair.

Well, I think I know how he feels. The likelihood of Ireland scoring two goals against a side like Holland was pretty slim, let's face it, but we have an ice-pop's chance in the bloody Kalahari of knocking in three. It is simply not going to happen. The Irish fans go very quiet. One of them opines — jokingly I must point out — that Packie Bonner is bloody lucky he comes from Ireland and not, like poor old Escobar, from Colombia.

Our hearts go out to Packie. Watching him pace up and down the goalmouth, his face the very picture of horror and misery, is distinctly unpleasant. I cannot help but recall that the last person in Irish sporting history to make such a clanger of a mistake was Dick Spring TD, who, while playing full back for the Irish rugby team some years ago, famously dropped the ball on his own line and allowed Scotland to score, thereby defeating Ireland. (Not only can Dick not pass the buck very effectively, but he can't pass the bloody ball either.) So poor Packie should console himself. We may have been knocked out of the World Cup, but I can see a very bright future indeed for him as Tanaiste.

The game drags dolefully on and ends in bitter despondency and disappointment. Jack and the players are generously applauded at the end, but it's nothing like the unbridled adulation that echoed around the Giants Stadium on the day we beat Italy, or the day we drew with Norway. Even the Mexico game, when we lost, whipped the fans up into a frenzy of appreciation. That's the amazing thing about the Irish fans. They are the only supporters at this World Cup who will tell you — and mean it — that it's not necessarily winning that counts, it's playing the game with a bit of an attitude. But today has knocked the heart out of us. It's not just the fact that we've lost the match that is bugging us, nor even the fact that we're out of the World Cup one whole round earlier than last time. It's the uncomfortable and as yet unspeakable realisation that we were bloody well awful, and we know it.

The bus back to the hotel is very quiet. The fans troop on in silent twos and threes, heads hung low, still wearing their green shirts, their ludicrous hats, still carrying their green inflatable beer bottles and plastic alligators, their faces streaked with green and orange paint. They look as outrageous — even as ridiculous — as ever, but you suddenly see them in a new and revealing light, as they slump into their seats and light cigarettes and sit staring out the windows in total silence. Absolute loyalty crushed is not a pretty picture.

One man gets on with his ten-year old son, who is sobbing bitterly, his hands held up to his eyes. They walk slowly down the back of the bus and sit down together, and the boy sinks his head into his father's chest and puts his arm around him and cries. His father strokes his hair and says nothing. He just gazes straight ahead of himself, gnawing his lip, shaking his head, his own eyes moistening. I catch his eye and he tries to smile. He looks away, out the window, then he looks back at his son. "Sure, it's only a game, soldier," he says, softly, "there'll be another day, don't worry." He ruffles the boy's hair, but the poor kid can't stop crying. He takes his hand and squeezes it. "Ah don't, soldier," he whispers, "don't be upsetting yourself." At this very moment, I can tell you, it is very hard to make jokes.

Church Street, Orlando, 9p.m.: The huge open-air after-match-night party coincides with America's Independence Day. In the packed streets of downtown Orlando there are so many people wearing orange that you would swear it was the twelfth of July in East Belfast and not the fourth in Florida. The defeated Irish fans have cheered up a little and are mingling happily with the victorious Dutch. Up on a stage seemingly made of tied-together beercrates, a hirsute Irish band is playing "The Road To God Knows Where."

We're on the one road
It maybe a long road
And it's the road to God knows where
We're on the one road
It may be a long road
But we're together now, who cares?
North men, south men, comrades all
Dublin, Belfast, Cork and Donegal
We're on the road
Singing along
Singing the soldier's song.

Near me, a crowd of Irish fans are wearing giant orange clogs, and enormous hats in the shape of windmills and tulips. They are dancing around in an unwieldy ring and chanting "You'll Never Beat The Irish," which, in the circumstances, is pretty damn brave.

For a moment, I am moved to suggest that they should actually be chanting "You'll Never Beat the Irish (You'll Thrash The Living Daylights Out Of Them")", but that would be unforgivably cruel and ungenerous.

Down the street, there is a large fairground machine which takes the shape of a circular metal ring about six foot wide mounted on an electronic platform. You pay five dollars to get strapped into this thing and spun around at about fifty miles an hour for five minutes. If you don't gawk your ring up after this experience, you are practically given the freedom of Orlando.

A huge crowd of Irish fans are clamouring around this machine, desperate to have a go. I watch one man I've got to know from the hotel clamber up on the platform and get strapped in. As the circle starts to spin, his friends shout out in encouragement "greasy fried egg," "mowldy banana" and, unimaginatively enough, but perhaps most effective of all, "bag of puke, bag of puke, bagga steamy steamy puke." Others simply make vomiting noises. BHUAAGHHHH, OH JAYZUS, BHUAAAAAARRRGH. They clutch their ample stomachs, roll their eyes and retch. BHUAAWWRGH, UNGH, *UNGHARGHHHHG*. All the time he rotates, a blur of green and white misery, until finally nature takes its course and he spews so copiously that everyone has to run and duck for cover.

I watch as this fellow is efficiently untied — the keeper of the machine keeping him well and truly at arm's length — and released into the dubious custody of his cheering companions, who sponge him down, clap his back and tell him what a fine fellow he is. "Jaze now, ye've balls on yeh the size of church bells," one of them says, which, I think, must be a compliment, although, to me, it sounds distinctly uncomfortable. I wonder what it is about defeat that makes grown adults behave like this.

I fall in with him and his pals and we wander further down the street together, drinking beers and chatting. Everyone is trying hard to have a good time, but you can see in their expressions that actually they're feeling pretty down. "I'd as soon be at home in bed," one man confides, "I'm not in the mood for a party at all." On the corner by Church Street Station, a large scrum of Irish and Dutch supporters are dancing and singing.

> *You put your left leg in*
> *Your left leg out*
> *Your left leg in and you shake it all about*
> *You do the hokey-cokey and you turn around*
> *That's what it's all about.*

As I watch them, a sudden and terrible thought strikes me. Maybe that is what it's all about. Putting your left leg in and your left leg out. *Is* that what it's all about? I mean, you know, you work hard, you pay your taxes, you try to be a good moral person and do the right thing, but maybe it is all a waste of time, because maybe, oh my God, maybe *doing the hokey-cokey, putting your left leg in and your left leg out IS really what it's all about!!*

We stroll on, around the corner of Church Street. A PA system is blasting out songs by Irish bands. "In The Name of Love," by U2 segues into "Here Comes The Night," by Van Morrison. The street is chock full of Irish fans, clustered around the bars on the pavements. A few of them are dancing around, but only half-heartedly. Most of them are just drinking. And then suddenly, a strange thing happens.

The sound of Philip Lynott and Thin Lizzy comes blaring down from the loudspeakers. There is a tumultuous roar of recognition from the Irish fans. They wander from the bars into the middle of the street. They all start to jump up and down and sing along and dance, they clap their hands in the air, first one section of the street, then another section, until in a few moments the whole street is singing, as far as your eye can see, right down to the junction, which must be half a mile away. It's an amazing sight. And the sound! I don't know if you've ever heard "Dancing In the Moonlight" sung by ten thousand Irish soccer fans, but for some reason I cannot really figure out it is unforgettably moving.

> *It's three o'clock in the morning*
> *And I'm on the streets again*
> *I disobeyed another warning*

I shoulda been in by ten
Now I won't get out till Sunday
I'll have to say I stayed with friends
But oh, you know it's a habit worth formin'
If it means to justify the ends
And I'm dancin' in the moonlight
It's got me in it's spotlight, it's alright,
I'm dancin' in the moonlight
On a long hot summer night.

It is a wonderful moment. Somehow, it lifts the whole night. The fans are embracing each other, hugging the Dutch fans, hugging the waitresses, the policemen, hugging the police horses for God's sake and the guys and girls selling beers and ice creams. And singing "Dancing In the Moonlight." The laughing voice of Phil Lynott, reminding us in some weird intangible way that being Irish always has its consolations. So we lost. Big swinging deal. We lost. It's not the end of the world. Everyone is singing together now. "Dancing in the moonlight/It's got me in its spotlight/It's alright." The Irish fan beside me is apoplectic with pleasure. He is singing along with the guitar solos, at the top of his voice. His right hand is strumming his trouser zip and his left is held out parallel to the ground, fingers wriggling spiderlike on invisible frets. His head is shaking from side to side. He takes off his Ireland baseball cap and throws it high into the air. "It's alright," he sings, the veins in his neck throbbing, "dancing in the moonlight, on a long hot summer night!"

I wonder along by myself now, and after a moment or two the crowd sweeps me into a guy I know, an Ireland fan from Derry. He is right in front of me, in a green jersey, and he is wrapped around a young black woman in an orange jersey. Kissing is not quite the word for what they are doing. They look like they are each trying to get a taste of what the other had for breakfast. When he finally comes up for air he peers at her adoringly. "Are you from heaven or what?" he says. "Close," she replies, "Wisconsin." "Dancing In the Moonlight" ends to a roar of applause, and "Linger" by The

Cranberries comes on. The three of us go for a drink, and we bump into more people we know in the pavement bar. The night is warm, and the humid air smells sweet.

You think about these wonderful fans, and what a joy it was to be here with them. Overhead, the fourth of July fireworks suddenly begin to roar into the sky. They spit and fizzle and bang, filling the air with shimmering light and gorgeous colour. The dance music stops and the sound of the American national anthem fills the street. People stand to attention. For a moment, as you sip your drink and munch your hot dog in a rebelliously left-wing manner, you are — you have to admit it — touched by the seductive spirit of American patriotism.

You think about the brave pilgrim fathers, the American constitution, Jefferson and Lincoln, the freedom of the individual, the separation of church and state, the right to free assembly, the desperate immigrants fleeing poverty and persecution to come to the land of the free and the home of the brave and struggle for a better life. You look around, at this great crowd of people, all standing heads bowed, arms by their side, in attitudes of reverent respect. You get a lump in your throat. Then you take another big bite of your hot dog, and you swig your beer, and you think, "feck this anyway for a phoney game of cowboys, I wish they'd bloody put on Phillo again."